NIETZSCHE'S LIFE SENTENCE

Coming to Terms with Eternal Recurrence

D1738771

LAWRENCE J. HATAB

Routledge
Taylor & Francis Group

NEW YORK AND LONDON

Published in 2005 by
Routledge
Taylor & Francis Group
270 Madison Avenue
New York, NY 10016

Published in Great Britain by
Routledge
Taylor & Francis Group
2 Park Square
Milton Park, Abingdon
Oxon OX14 4RN

Printed in the United States of America on acid-free paper
10 9 8 7 6 5 4 3 2 1

International Standard Book Number-10: 0-415-96758-9 (Hardcover) 0-415-96759-7 (Softcover)
International Standard Book Number-13: 978-0-415-96758-7 (Hardcover) 978-0-415-96759-4 (Softcover)

Library of Congress Cataloging-in-Publication Data

Catalog record is available from the Library of Congress

Taylor & Francis Group
is the Academic Division of T&F Informa plc.

Visit the Taylor & Francis Web site at
http://www.taylorandfrancis.com

and the Routledge Web site at
http://www.routledge-ny.com

To the memory of my friend, Tod Clonan,
who danced the night away.

Contents

Foreword

Confessions of a Lifer:
Thus Spoke Hatab

DANIEL CONWAY

> When Dr. Heinrich von Stein once complained very honestly that he
> didn't understand a word of my *Zarathustra*, I told him that this was
> perfectly in order: having understood six sentences from it—that is, to
> have really experienced them—would raise one to a higher level of exist-
> ence than "modern" men could attain.

— Friedrich Nietzsche, *Ecce Homo*

Why Nietzsche was so Anxious

Nietzsche occasionally despaired of attracting readers whom he deemed
worthy of his books. His insights were so exacting, his inspiration so overpowering, his truths so explosive, that mere mortals could hardly help but
miscarry them. In typical fashion, of course, he also raised to dizzying heights
the stakes of readership. His *Zarathustra*, he modestly opined, is "the greatest
present that has ever been made to [humankind] so far" (*EH* P, 4)—
Promethean fire, presumably, was a close second; *The Antichrist* is "the most
independent" book ever produced (*TI* 9, 51); and so on. His authorial prowess
was so magisterial that he helpfully devoted the longest chapter of his "autobiography" to a detailed explanation of why he wrote "such good books" (*EH*
III).

But the unrivaled genius of Nietzsche's "good books" accounts for only half
of what he took to be the problem of his readership. It was also his fate to toil
in an epoch that was stunningly unprepared to receive his effluent wisdom. In
his estimation, his first generation of readers was as ridiculous as his books
were sublime. The hands into which he was obliged to place his precious
teachings would no doubt fumble them, twisting them into cheap platitudes
and, even worse, trendy ideological slogans. As he neared the end of his
productive career, he grew increasingly fearful that he would be mistaken
for his opposite, regarded as yet another moralist or "improver of mankind"
(*EH* P, 2). Alarmed that he might someday be hailed as a "holy man," even
as the "founder of a religion," he launched a noteworthy preemptive strike:
"[I would] sooner even [be] a buffoon.—Perhaps I am a buffoon" (*EH* IV, 1).

One need not leave one's armchair to venture an amateur diagnosis of such anxieties. Nietzsche feared being pronounced "holy" precisely because he (believed he) knew the desperate condition of the likely readers of his books. He was too keen an observer of his times to bequeath his writings without reservation to the indiscriminate and redemption-minded readers of late European modernity. (He stubbornly persisted in writing in German, after all, despite claiming to loathe the Germans as a people dispossessed of their formerly formidable philosophical spirit.) He must have been tempted, like Moses, to destroy his tablets rather than place them into such unworthy, idolatrous hands.

But Nietzsche also knew that there *was* something of the "holy man" in him. He was, admittedly, a "child of his time" (*CW* P), which means that he too shared in the diffuse, post-theistic religiosity that clouded his unhappy epoch. He also knew, or at least suspected, that his residual religiosity would very likely complicate the dissemination of his more radical teachings. He knew, that is, that he would need to cultivate a new breed of *strong* readers, philological warriors who could endure his occasional lapses into religiosity while continuing, undistracted, to receive from him the teachings he was poised to dispense. Such readers surely awaited him in the postmoral future that he so vividly imagined. But what of his *present*, the twilight epoch of late modernity? Were such readers likely to be found in an age that he had expertly diagnosed as irrecuperably decadent?

Although he claimed among his contemporary readers "nothing but first-rate intellects and proven characters, trained in high positions and duties" (*EH* III, 2), this boast is difficult to square with his more typical expressions of contempt for his late modern contemporaries. If such worthies were actually scattered throughout Europe and North America, posted in offices of influence, then his prospects for readership were not nearly so bleak as he preferred to insist. In that event, in fact, he would have been obliged to revisit, and perhaps even to retract, the sweeping jeremiad that he had pronounced on the whole of late modernity.

Nietzsche's post-Zarathustran writings thus stage a full-blown psychological drama: Should he trust his supposedly feeble readers to receive his untimely teachings, guard them from vulgar distortion, and deliver them intact to the rightful audiences of a distant posterity? If so, then how light (or strong) a touch should he apply in his repeated efforts to instruct his readers in the art of appreciating his Dionysian wisdom? Or should he simply trust no one, strategically encrypting his teachings so that only the most Thesean of his readers will penetrate to, and return from, the center of his labyrinthine thought? Is it preferable to be read poorly by many, on the remote chance that someday some wayward disciple will inadvertently bequeath these teachings to those readers for whom they are intended? Or to be read well by so few that his chances of surviving the long *entr'acte* of late modernity are virtually nil?

Such excruciating self-interrogations eventually took the measure of Nietzsche's sanity. Early in 1889, following an explosively productive year of writing and plotting, he fell without return into madness—the result, as legend has it, of inserting himself between a besieged horse and its whip-wielding master. Notes and letters scribbled in early 1889 suggest that in madness he attained the crystalline certainty that his sanity would not abide. As the shroud of madness descended, he presented himself as a resolute lawgiver, as sheltering within his elastic soul "every name in history," and as promising bold political action—including several high-profile assassinations—as favors to his dearest friends.

In light of the drama that filled Nietzsche's final years of sanity, it would be easy enough to misplace the questions of audience and readership that vexed him. Let us then be careful to raise them anew: How should *we* read Nietzsche, especially if we accept in some version his chilling diagnosis of the late modern epoch? While it is easy enough to imagine oneself belonging to those intrepid hermeneuts of "the day after tomorrow"—and who amongst Nietzsche's readers has not surrendered to this all-too-human conceit?—the trickier task is to take seriously his prediction that the twentieth and twenty-first centuries, despite hosting a noisy era of "great politics," would amount to little more than a *Zwischenspiel* in "the Dionysian drama of 'The Destiny of the Soul'" (*GM* P, 7). To do so would be to acknowledge, if not necessarily to affirm, that we are not Nietzsche's ideal readers. As he proudly explains,

> Given this feeling of distance, how could I possibly wish to be read by those "moderns" whom I know! My triumph is precisely the opposite of Schopenhauer's: I say, "*non legor, non legar.*" (*EH* III, 1)

Although Nietzsche is now (and will continue to be) widely read, his putative "triumph" endures. So long as we late moderns remain mired in our desuetude, Nietzsche (or someone on his behalf) may maintain his assertion of superiority over us. Were we the readers he claims to deserve, we would have elevated ourselves by now "to a higher level of existence" (*EH* III, 1) and, presumably, taken up permanent residence beyond good and evil.

Of course, Nietzsche need not be right about us. For that matter, he need be neither sincere nor forthright in characterizing us in such unflattering terms. Whether real or exaggerated, honest or strategic, his preferred terms for engaging with us reveal the irony of his predicament. Although he refuses to affirm us, he has no choice but to rely on us to transmit his precious teachings of affirmation. It is up to *us* to read his books, however poorly, and to recommend them enthusiastically, if ignorantly, to our progeny. For better or worse, we are the monkish intermediaries who must safeguard his books, preserving his teachings until such time as his intended readers arrive to glean their true, full relevance.

One teaching in particular must survive the tumultuous *entr'acte* of late modernity: the idea of *eternal recurrence*. According to the most popular formulations of this idea, we are encouraged to imagine the cosmos as eternally recurring in every detail of every iteration of its every configuration. Doing so will allow us to discern how closely we approach the standard established by those heroic individuals who embrace without revision the eternal recurrence of all that they have been, done, and known. Although Nietzsche's readers dispute the precise implications of the idea of eternal recurrence, they are generally agreed that it is meant to play an indispensable, if unspecified, role in delivering someone—though perhaps not us—to an unconditional *affirmation* of life. Nietzsche himself confirms this interpretation when he identifies the idea of eternal recurrence as the "highest formula of affirmation [*Bejahung*] that is at all attainable" (*EH* III; *Z*, 1). Despite the fact that the cosmos bears no trace of transcendent meaning, moral order, anthropophilic teleology, or metaphysical comfort, we may nevertheless aspire, by dint of the idea of eternal recurrence, to affirm the whole and our humble place within it. Having done so, we may gratefully look back on life, complete with its inevitable disappointments and losses, and shout *da capo*!

Why Hatab Writes Such Good Books

As it turns out, Nietzsche need not have worried about his late modern readers (except insofar as doing so facilitated the expression of his creative genius). Lawrence Hatab has arrived onstage, nearly a full century ahead of schedule, and he has assumed the task of guiding Nietzsche's teaching of affirmation into the steady hands of worthy readers. Hatab is the acclaimed author of several important books and many lapidary essays on Nietzsche, and he has been particularly concerned to defend the elusive teaching of eternal recurrence. Hatab's grateful readers will not be surprised to learn that he has won numerous teaching awards over the course of his distinguished career. His writings reflect the unique ability to transmit difficult philosophical ideas and, having done so, to encourage his readers toward lives informed by philosophical reflection. His prose displays the patient, careful, teacherly manner that Zarathustra and Nietzsche aspired, but never quite managed, to attain.

The secret of Hatab's success, in fact, is fairly simple: he practices what Nietzsche and Zarathustra only preached. Unlike them, Hatab is willing to close the circle of self-reference and own his share in the various failings that they lamented in their contemporaries. He not only accepts Nietzsche's characterization of philosophers as "advocates who resent that name . . . even wily spokesmen for their prejudices" (*BGE* 5), but also turns this insight to his own advantage. Even as we marvel at the clarity of Hatab's prose, the elegance of his arguments, and the reach of his erudition, there is no denying his recourse to intimate revelations, confessional intrusions, and autobiographical anecdotes. He thereby affirms, and in fact discloses to good effect, the deeply personal stake in all philosophizing, including his own.

Readers newly acquainted with Hatab may be surprised by the disarmingly personal intimations that he sprinkles throughout his book. Barely into his introduction, for example, we are returned without warning to the scene of a trauma that continues to grieve him. He later confides that he is "haunted" by the thought of eternal recurrence, "even obsessed by it." So much for an objective, neutral, disinterested philosophical investigation! We soon learn and are often reminded that affirmation is *his* problem, even if it was also Nietzsche's; and that the thought of eternal recurrence is *his* preferred solution, albeit a borrowed one, to the problem of securing existential meaning for one's life. On an even more personal note, Hatab confesses that he finds himself wanting when measured against the eternal recurrence as a standard of affirmation. As courageous as he is in facing up to the ingredient disappointments of life, he is too honest to claim for himself the desired victory. Nothing in Hatab's book is likely to remind us of the interleaf epigraph of *Ecce Homo*, wherein Nietzsche gushes mawkishly about the "perfect day" on which he is able to express—albeit in the reserved form of a rhetorical question—that he is "*grateful to his whole life*." Reading Hatab's book does remind us, however, that Nietzsche honored *Redlichkeit* as "the only virtue left to [the free spirits]" for whom he presumed to speak (*BGE* 227).

We should be careful, however, not to interpret Hatab's forays into the personal realm as just so many tropological adventures, as if he were simply trying on masks and personae for his or our enjoyment. Personal reflections are neither supplementary nor accessory to the kind of philosophy he practices, but integral to it. Hatab is an old-fashioned existentialist, which means that he prizes above all else the pursuit of a passionate, authentic existence grounded in the urgency of honest self-assertion. He consequently brings to bear on Nietzsche's writings an unabashed sensitivity to their deepest sources of personal inspiration. If a philosophical teaching does not reach to the very core of one's being, Nietzsche and Hatab believe, then it is worth very little. This is why Hatab refuses to reduce the idea of eternal recurrence to an entertaining cosmological puzzle or logical conundrum. Just as Hatab came to appreciate this idea as it was communicated to him through the existential pathos it created in Nietzsche and Zarathustra, so he endeavors to communicate this idea by means of the pathos it stirs in him. It is, he believes, a teaching of primarily existential import and should be approached only as such.

It is no accident that Hatab closes his book with an appreciative discussion of laughter; or that he places special emphasis on the self-referential, satyric laughter that Nietzsche believed to be emblematic of the highest human beings. Hatab's comic turn is anything but a digression from his serious study of eternal recurrence. In fact, he persuasively identifies self-directed laughter as the ultimate expression of existential meaning that is consistent with Nietzsche's sketch of a finite, uncaring cosmos. Hatab consequently applauds the laughter of the hero who realizes, belatedly, that his labors are fated to come to naught; of the artist who celebrates the transience and imperfection of his finest creations; and of the psychologist who places his own all-too-human proclivities on display. To laugh at oneself, in short, is to declare one's independence from the need for transcendent, eternal meaning. Self-directed laughter deflects the gravitational pull of one's seriousness and allows one to resist, at least for now, the impulse to retreat to the metaphysical backworld that one has created in one's own needy image.

Those who know Hatab know that he knows whereof he speaks. An affable, gregarious man, Hatab laughs easily, regularly, and often at his own expense. He knows, as Nietzsche and Zarathustra surmised but could not digest, that the enabling seriousness of philosophy is both its glory and its curse. The philosopher cannot help but take himself seriously, even if doing so compromises the eventual relevance of his thinking for life. Hatab has taken to heart Nietzsche's observation that we late moderns need above all else to cultivate and retain a "philosophical sense of humor" (BGE 25). Hence the irreverent title of his book: The idea of eternal recurrence is both the generative source of existential meaning *and* a life sentence for those who are "obsessed" with it. When it comes to reading Nietzsche, Hatab is not merely guilty. He's a lifer, and happily so.

Ecce Homo

Lawrence J. "Larry" Hatab, a U.S. citizen of Lebanese extraction, born in Brooklyn at the great noon of what would come to be known—albeit, fittingly, only in its twilight—as the "Nietzschean" century. Educated at Catholic universities, trained by Jesuits and Augustinians to spread the gospel according to Nietzsche. Dispatched south of the Mason-Dixon line to educate the sons and daughters of the Commonwealth of Virginia, at a university whose name bears proud witness to the state's colonial past. Wed happily but late, as if to affirm *and* dispute Nietzsche's gibe that "a married philosopher belongs," like the basket-bound Socrates of Aristophanic skewer, "*in comedy*" (GM III, 7). Childless, but, like Nietzsche and Zarathustra, responsible for siring thousands of philosophical "children," who lighten the otherwise weary worlds of commerce and industry with their infectious Dionysian laughter.

Lawrence J. "Larry" Hatab. The author of numerous books, essays, and reviews, including a daring treatise on Nietzschean democracy that would be considered a classic of postmodern political theory were it not written so clearly. Nostalgic not only for the heyday of his beloved Dodgers (whose name made sense to him as it never can to those undeserving Californians who don't care anyway), but also for the heady froth of Greek antiquity, whose circulatory myths still inspire his wonder. In this respect, too, he is very much like Nietzsche: one foot comfortably planted in the distant past, the other tapping nervously in an increasingly incomprehensible present.

So many hats (Nietzsche would say *masks*) to wear, and so many more pegs on which to hang them. How to gather these unruly threads of a life and pronounce their adventitious weave a finished garment? How to add up these discontinuous scenes and affirm them as *one* life, *one* person, *one* destiny?

But Hatab has already revealed his answer, his secret. His center holds by virtue of the life sentence pronounced on him by Nietzsche. As it turns out, the good Fathers and Brothers stood no chance in the contest for Hatab's soul. He has become what he is through a lifelong obsession with the idea of eternal recurrence. This is the "one needful thing" that has brought "style" to his "character" (*GS* 290). Responding to the totality of his life and work, I would like to say, *Bravo,* lifer! And, with admiration and all due seriousness, *da capo*!

Daniel Conway
State College, Pennsylvania

Preface

Again with the eternal recurrence? Jokes aside, this text is the "return" of my first book, *Nietzsche and Eternal Recurrence: The Redemption of Time and Becoming* (Lanham, MD: University Press of America, 1978). I herewith return to the notion that first excited my philosophical imagination. When Routledge approached me with the prospect of reviving my study of eternal recurrence (long out of print), I was enthused and gratified, because the editor's pitch reflected my own thoughts: my book had not received much attention, and he thought that my thesis remains distinctive compared with the rest of the literature. I take the role of Nietzsche's advocate, stipulating that he was serious about eternal recurrence, and presuming to show that the doctrine can be defended as central to Nietzsche's philosophy and sustainable in the face of many criticisms and expressions of bemusement, puzzlement, consternation, and frustration typically voiced by readers.

Yet the current work is not simply the "return of the same." It is completely rewritten, and happily so because I cringe when I read the first version. The style is undisciplined and overly pious, I think. My writing has improved and I have outgrown the earnest transformational tone in the first text that marked my approach at the time. I have eliminated most of the historical discussions about time in the thought of Plato, Aristotle, and Augustine. I have also explored in much more detail the way in which a literal reading of eternal recurrence can be defended. Finally, I have addressed (yet not in great detail) the scholarly treatments of eternal recurrence that have appeared in the last twenty-five years, and to which I hope my study can be a worthy contribution (at last).

I want to express my gratitude to a number of people who have aided my efforts in different ways: To all the people at Routledge who made this project possible. To Curtis Brooks and Kathryne Silberman for technical and moral support. To my secretary, Emily Birran, whose command of office operations made it possible for me to write this book while chairing the department. To Alan Schrift, Dan Conway, Christa Davis Acampora, and my colleagues at Old Dominion, for constructive and critical feedback. To my students, who never let me rest easy. And above all, to my wife Chelsy, the best case for living my life over again.

Abbreviations of Nietzsche's Works

Cited numbers refer to text sections, except in the cases of *KSA* and *OTL*. I have occasionally modified published translations.

A   *The Antichrist*, in *The Portable Nietzsche*, ed. and trans. Walter Kaufmann (New York: Viking Press, 1954).

BGE   *Beyond Good and Evil*, in *Basic Writings of Nietzsche*, ed. and trans. Walter Kaufmann, (New York: Random House, 1966).

BT   *The Birth of Tragedy*, in *Basic Writings*.

D   *Daybreak*, trans. R. J. Hollingdale (Cambridge: Cambridge University Press, 1982).

EH   *Ecce Homo*, in *Basic Writings*. The four main chapters will be indicated by roman numerals, with book titles in chapter 3 abbreviated accordingly.

GS   *The Gay Science*, trans. Walter Kaufmann (New York: Random House, 1974).

GM   *On the Genealogy of Morals*, in *Basic Writings*.

HAH   *Human, All Too Human*, trans. R. J. Hollingdale (New York: Cambridge University Press, 1986).

KSA   *Sämtliche Werke: Kritische Studienausgabe*, ed. G. Colli and M. Montinari (Berlin: Walter de Gruyter, 1967).

OTL   *On Truth and Lies in an Extramoral Sense*, in *Philosophy and Truth*, ed. and trans. J. Daniel Breazeale (Atlantic Highlands, NJ: Humanities Press, 1979).

PTAG   *Philosophy in the Tragic Age of the Greeks*, trans. Marianne Cowan (Washington, DC: Regnery Publishing Co., 1962).

TI   *Twilight of the Idols*, in *The Portable Nietzsche*. The chapters will be numbered in sequence by arabic numerals.

WP   *The Will to Power*, trans. Walter Kaufmann and R. J. Hollingdale (New York: Random House, 1967).

WS   *The Wanderer and His Shadow*, Part 2 of *Human, All Too Human*.

Z   *Thus Spoke Zarathustra*, in *The Portable Nietzsche*. The four parts will be indicated by roman numerals, the sections by arabic numerals according to Kaufmann's listing on pages 112–114.

Introduction

This life as you now live it and have lived it, you will have to live once more and innumerable times more; and there will be nothing new in it, but every pain and every joy and every thought and sigh and everything unutterably small or great in your life will have to return to you, all in the same succession and sequence.

— *The Gay Science,* section 341

What is your response to this sentence Nietzsche hands down to us? I find it hard to take. I suppose I could abide repeating many of the good things in my life, but everything? Even high school? I know it's a small thing, but I remember being shaken for weeks after I had accidentally let a friend's puppy out the door on a city street. The little creature pranced around in delight, playing with my frantic attempts to grab him. He darted into the street and was hit squarely by a car. I watched as he twitched, oozed blood, stared at me blankly, and died. My friend ran out to the scene and I fell apart. Even now grief hasn't disappeared when I recall this day. I don't think I want to go through that again.

Why not? There is no mystery about it. Life as we have it gives much that is good and satisfying, yet no one escapes loss, deprivation, failure, suffering, and death. All these things and more come with life too, inevitably. And Nietzsche's sentence likely prompts us to think first of these negative elements in considering a repeat performance. This, too, is for good reason. Who would deny that life as we have it is in the end tragic, that there are essential limits on our aspirations, that destruction and loss are the last word?

Philosophers would describe the tragic abstractly in terms of the finitude of the life world, its intrinsic temporal nature, always subject to forces of becoming, change, variation, conflict, negation, and ruin. Life is tragic in the manner of the self-consuming themes of Greek tragedy. Life both bears and destroys its offspring, and does so in terms of the very life process itself (for example, life forms must feed on other life forms to survive). The tragic is also indicated in the absence of human sovereignty, in the sense of self-mastery, self-determination, and control over the world. We are thrown into life (no self-origination), limited by life (no self-sufficiency), and destroyed by life (no self-constancy or

1

immortality). Indigenous limits on the self are also shown in the nature of time. We cannot control the past because it is irreversible, or the future because it is uncertain, and the present is experienced as this precarious excess eluding our control.

Such a discussion remains unduly abstract, however. The force of Nietzsche's sentence about the repetition of life is found in its personal address, to me and to you, to our lives as we live it in the concrete, with all its details. Here Nietzsche is putting the perennial question of the meaning of life in the most dramatic and acute form imaginable. It poses the meaning question in terms of whether one will say Yes or No to life as actually lived, with no alternative. The potential impact is enormous, it could "change or crush you" (*GS* 341). I confess to having been deeply challenged by this thought of eternal recurrence, even obsessed by it (one reason why I have continued to write about it). I don't think I can measure up to saying Yes, but somehow I think that I should. At least my reaction is in keeping with the personal address essential to the existential import of Nietzsche's powerful idea. Yet Nietzsche was also a philosopher. He saw eternal recurrence and its implications challenging the Western intellectual tradition as well. So eternal recurrence is meant to prompt a response to the following question: What is our existential and intellectual disposition toward natural life as we have it, toward a world ineluctably constituted by time, becoming, and limits?

For Nietzsche, any recoil at the prospect of recurrence suggests a kind of chronophobia, an aversion to time and becoming. And he claims that existential, psychological aversion is the basis for an intellectual chronophobia at the heart of the Western philosophical tradition—which, however, generally expressed its aversion to time on the more impersonal level of the search for truth and foundations of knowledge. Philosophers have long recognized that the sheer flux of temporality gives no stable reference point for knowledge claims, where "knowing" something would call for an explanation secured by methods and principles that are immune to doubt, contingency, and change.

A negative assessment of time and becoming is clearly indicated at the very beginning of Western philosophy, in the thought of Plato. The *Phaedo*, for instance, richly captures both the existential and intellectual challenge of temporality, in terms of the problem of death and limits in life as well as the problem of change and difference with respect to knowledge (*Phaedo*, 65b–67b). The climax of the dialogue is its promise of the soul's immortality and return to a realm of eternal Forms transcending the physical, temporal world. In this way, Plato offered both existential and intellectual relief from the negativity of the life-world by resolving time into eternity and becoming into being.

Aristotle inherited this Platonic paradigm, mainly in the intellectual sphere, by insisting that an eternal, unmoved mover is required so that knowledge and explanation can be securely grounded, which is to say, not subject to the ceaseless dispersal of temporal movement that would ever elude our mental "grasp." Despite Aristotle's criticisms of Plato's transcendent project and despite his careful analysis of temporal movement in the natural world, Aristotle took it for granted that the mind could not accept a world that would tail off into negative states, that could not be traced to some stable, eternal presence.

Medieval philosophy and theology, of course, were based in the Christian faith in God, who exceeds the temporal world as its creator, who is subject to no limits or negative properties, and who promises salvation in a perfect, timeless realm after death and the end of the world. Medieval thinkers all drew sustenance from the texts of Plato and Aristotle, particularly because of a shared preference for the stability of eternal being over temporal becoming. In the Christian perspective, the world can only be justified as a preparation for transcending its earthly conditions.

Modern philosophy, from Descartes to Kant, was in certain respects a reaction against ancient and medieval philosophy, in its rejection of received authority and any philosophical concepts that could not accord with the new science of nature. Yet most modern thinkers maintained a God concept (Descartes, Spinoza, Leibniz, Locke, Berkeley, Kant), generally because of the theological advantage of moral and epistemological foundations, if not the interests of popular faith. As Nietzsche pointed out, even when religious authority was no longer the centerpiece of culture, traces of the Christian God continued to operate in philosophical projects so that anxiety in the face of a groundless world could still be held off in refined ways.

An interesting link between modern and earlier outlooks can be found in the autonomy of the modern rational subject, which exercises its freedom from tradition and common sense by grasping necessary rational principles through its own reflective standpoint. Rational necessity matched earlier resolutions of temporal negativity and contingency, and rational autonomy provided a worldly, secular echo of the old idea of divine self-sufficiency, in the sense of being self-grounded, self-determined, and needing nothing "other" for thought and action. The modern period was characterized by an exhilarating liberation of human reason—in scientific, philosophical, economic, and social movements—to guide its own course and discover foundations that would deliver humanity from doubt, error, and discord. Especially significant was a vibrant practical optimism owing to technological innovations made possible by the new mechanical physics. With a newfound sense of rational certainty and control over nature, modern man can be said to have become its own god, able to solve the mysteries of nature with scientific truth and overcome the dangers and debilitating effects of nature through technological mastery. Not unrelated to this sense of optimism and power was the emergence of various progressive, utopian doctrines that promised "heaven on earth" with respect to overcoming human strife, alienation, deprivation, and subjugation.

The most important representatives of such modern optimism were Hegel and Marx, and yet both were distinctive in incorporating time and becoming into their philosophical projects. Hegel saw time and becoming not as ontological defects, but as the force of a dialectical resolution of opposition, which manifests a progressive development of an integrated, unified Spirit that would overcome the fractured alienation of temporal negation. For Hegel, traditional ideas of a transcendent, divine spirit were simply the initial recognition of a unifying force that would actualize itself in immanent, worldly conditions through the struggle of opposing forces in history that resolves itself in a complex, organic whole. Marx inherited Hegel's sense of dialectical development but rejected its spiritual connotations in favor of fully material conditions. The prospect of communism promised the gradual liberation of all humanity from economic need and social differentiation, completed in a natural collective order of productive relations and capacities that would actualize the essence of humanity as self-sufficient "maker."

It should be clear that Nietzsche's concept of eternal recurrence was directed not simply at personal, existential attitudes toward life. It also fit in with his overall philosophical project of calling the Western tradition to accounts for its chronophobic incapacity to withstand the intrinsic limits to human aspirations evident in natural life. Such incapacity was manifest in both otherworldly forms of transcendence and worldly doctrines of progress. Nietzsche's task was to unmask the presumably positive, optimistic features of Western thought as in fact a consequence of moralistic judgments upon time and becoming, as wishful attempts to surpass or rectify the finite conditions of life. Nietzsche also went so far as to diagnose the supposed "impersonal" status of philosophical systems as in fact a symptom of psychological weakness in the face of life.

An important figure in this story of Nietzsche's philosophical project was Schopenhauer, who was an early influence on Nietzsche and whom Nietzsche greatly admired, particularly for his intellectual honesty. Schopenhauer was an avowed pessimist, who rejected all forms of worldly and otherworldly redemption from finitude as philosophically unjustified. For Schopenhauer, the ultimate nature of reality is Will, an aimless, amorphous force that eludes human knowledge and consumes all its manifestations. In life, suffering and lack are the bottom line. Wisdom, for Schopenhauer, entailed recognizing the ultimate pointlessness of existence and practicing resignation, in a way similar to religious ascetic traditions, but without otherworldly hopes. Schopenhauer's pessimism advocated life-denial and the prospect of annihilation as the only authentic form of "salvation."

Nietzsche came to see Schopenhauer's philosophy as the secret code to the entire Western tradition (see GS 357). First of all, Schopenhauer shared the West's chronophobic assessment of life. Even though he dismissed optimistic projects, his proposal of life-denial showed that he agreed with the tradition's criteria of value, but simply disagreed that such criteria could be realized in any positive form. In other words, pessimism implies that life *should* support human existential and intellectual aspirations but *cannot* support them. Why else turn away from life? At the same time, Nietzsche recognized Schopenhauer's philosophical rigor in deconstructing Western optimism. Schopenhauer was right in that regard. Nietzsche then concluded that Schopenhauer's pessimism was the hidden truth of Western thought, that all the rectification projects in the name of truth, knowledge, salvation, justice, and so on, were in fact esoteric, concealed forms of pessimistic life-denial. Schopenhauer, then, exemplified the Western tradition without all the window dressing. For Nietzsche, every "positive" prospect of resolving temporal finitude was at bottom a form of nihilism, of life-negation.

Nietzsche and Schopenhauer were philosophical brethren in that the core of their thinking was an acute, unflinching concentration on one question: Is existence worth it? Schopenhauer's honest answer was No. Nietzsche's answer was Yes, and he accused Western thought of both evading this stark question and concealing a repressed No. Eternal recurrence was Nietzsche's dramatic way of forcing attention on this primal meaning question and of setting the measure of what an authentic affirmative response to existence would require. Saying Yes to the continual repetition of life would be the antidote to chronophobic alternatives of transcendence, rectification, even nothingness.

It is interesting to note that Schopenhauer specifically indicated his aversion to the repetition of life, saying that "at the end of his life, no man, if he be sincere and at the same time in possession of his faculties, will ever wish to go through it again."[1] Even Kant was reported to have frequently expressed similar sentiments.[2] And Augustine directly argued against Pagan models of eternal repetition in favor of the Christian idea of linear time stretching from a unique creation to salvation after the end of the world. He argued that salvation followed by a repetition of the fall is absurd, and that a "godless" circularity should be corrected by the "straight path" of religious deliverance.[3] Eternal recurrence emerges as a powerful alternative to such ways of thinking. Indeed, its direct impact can even be distinguished from certain attempts in the tradition to justify the actual course of the world as an inevitable consequence of divine nature or necessity (otherwise known as theodicy). For example, Leibniz argued that this is the best possible world, and Spinoza claimed that the world is the way it is necessarily. But Nietzsche does not follow such paths, and eternal recurrence does not stem from considerations of logical/causal necessity or possibility, because such reflective, hypothetical analyses can easily evade the task of direct, concrete affirmation. In short, Nietzsche would not say that this is the best possible world or that this world is a necessary world; rather he would simply advance the stark claim that *this is the world*, period.

In light of this historical background, my aim in this book is to elucidate and defend the philosophical import of eternal recurrence and its central place in Nietzsche's thought. Readers of Nietzsche have usually been perplexed by his avowal of this conception. One should concede, I think, that *what* eternal recurrence describes is actually simple and straightforward: the continual repetition of life in all its details. But *why* a thinker of Nietzsche's caliber would advance such an idea is the interesting question that has prompted a host of interpretations. The literal sense of repetition, however, has generally been seen as problematic, if not false, even by Nietzsche's admirers. Yet my posture in this study begins with a principle of charity stipulating that Nietzsche was dead serious about eternal recurrence and saw it as the climax of his philosophy, particularly with respect to life affirmation. Calling eternal recurrence the "fundamental conception" of *Thus Spoke Zarathustra*, Nietzsche adds that it is the "highest formula of affirmation that is at all attainable" (*EH* III, Z, 1). A notebook passage also refers to eternal recurrence as "the thought of thoughts" (*KSA* 9, 496).

My investigation argues that eternal recurrence should be taken seriously as essential to Nietzsche's thinking and as having a kind of philosophical validity in the light of Nietzsche's critique of the West. Nietzsche's avowal of eternal recurrence can be said to harbor something of a default argument, in that eternal repetition, with respect to concrete life affirmation, was in his view the only effective alternative to other conceivable approaches to the problem of time: (1) the positivistic refusal to engage time as an existential problem; (2) the consolation of an eternal realm beyond the temporal world (Plato and Aristotle); (3) a unique creation and ending of time, with a transformation into eternal salvation (Christian theology); (4) a worldly progressive resolution of the fractured alienation of temporal negativity (Hegel and Marx); (5) a pessimistic ending of time in nothingness (Schopenhauer); and even (6) the idea of eternal novelty (which Nietzsche took to be the cosmological restoration of the old idea of divine freedom). Each of these possibilities can be diagnosed as projects of "evasive diversion," of overt or subliminal recoilings from saying Yes to the concrete conditions of life *as actually lived*. My aim in this study is to articulate how the main currents of Nietzsche's thought can be organized around, and consummated by, eternal recurrence and its concentration on life affirmation. Along these lines, what follows is a brief sketch of what is to come in the text.

Nietzsche's proclamation of the death of God offers an effective entry point to the force of his thinking. God in the West was the ultimate symbol of foundational transcendence. God's demise, however, reaches far beyond religion because a divine reference had been the warrant for all sorts of cultural constructs in moral, political, philosophical, even scientific spheres. With God out of the picture, all corollary constructs dissolve as well. The death of God, therefore, announces the loss of traditional truth principles. With modern secularization, God is no longer the centerpiece of thought, yet we still cling to derivative truths that have lost their pedigree and philosophical legitimacy. With the absence of God we are left with the choice of either a nihilistic collapse of meaning or a revaluation of meaning in different terms according to immediate life conditions. Nietzsche takes the latter option and advances what can be called an existential naturalism: not a reductive naturalism in terms of scientific categories, but an embrace of the finite limit conditions of worldly existence as the new measure of thought.

Nietzsche's conception of will to power embodies this new measure. Traditional philosophy was animated by constructions of binary opposites, with the aim of privileging a positive side over a negative side: being over becoming, eternity over time, constancy over change, good over evil, truth over appearance, and so forth—all providing fixed measures that can resolve negative forces confronting human existence. Nietzsche rejects such oppositional structures in favor of mixed conditions, where each side cannot escape, in fact is structurally related to, the other side. Will to power is Nietzsche's counter-concept to binary thinking because it indicates an "agonistic" force field, where any state is partly constituted by its "contest" with some counterforce, its drive to overcome resistances. So world conditions emerge in a network of *tensions* that cannot be reduced to stable identities. Such an agonistic pluralism also accounts for Nietzsche's proposal of perspectivism to replace traditional standards of uniform and immutable truth.

An important element in this investigation is Nietzsche's early interest in Greek tragedy as a prephilosophical worldview that was not infected by subsequent developments that aimed to transform or reform the life-world. Nietzsche interprets tragedy as a blend of Apollonian and Dionysian forces, of artistic forming powers and ecstatic deforming powers that dissolve boundaries into the underlying torrent of life energies. For Nietzsche, tragedy expressed a correlation of form and formlessness, life and death, creation and destruction, human action and fate, which marked the early Greek capacity to present finite existence on its own terms. But then the advent of Socratic rationalism introduced a recoiling from this "tragic wisdom" in favor of the suspect philosophical constructs that Greek philosophy bequeathed to the West. The discussion of Greek tragedy is significant for two reasons. First, it elucidates important interpretive angles in coming to terms with eternal recurrence. Second, it shows that in Nietzsche's eyes his radical challenge to tradition is in fact not something out of the blue; it taps into concealed resources within the Western tradition itself. It is "radical" in retrieving certain prephilosophical "roots" in tragic drama.

Also central for my analysis is Nietzsche's genealogical critique of Western morality, particularly in the way it diagnoses the psychological basis of chronophobic thought systems. For Nietzsche, genealogy shows that esteemed doctrines are not eternal or based in stable origins; they have a history and emerge in complex contests with counterforces. Moral models of justice, love, and self-control, for instance, are shown to stem from the resentment of slave types against the worldly power of master types. Such moral systems are simply reversals of power rather than a repudiation of power. Historically, for Nietzsche, the master exemplifies life-affirming strength in action, while the slave type exemplifies a reactive, life-denying weakness. Such types also serve as historical precursors for one of Nietzsche's most important distinctions: the creator type (who undermines established conditions in the process of meaning creation) and the herd type (who conforms and defends cultural stability).

The most dramatic element in Nietzsche's account of life-denying dispositions is his portrayal of the ascetic ideal, where an inability to withstand or engage external contests of power directs power internally and conducts a self-consuming battle against natural drives in the name of a presumed spiritual transcendence. Asceticism, of course, has been a powerful force in religious movements, but Nietzsche does not confine his analysis to religion. He claims that the ascetic ideal manifests itself in any avowal of belief that strives to quell or supplant the flux and force of natural life energies, particularly creative energies. Nietzsche goes so far as to say that any conviction in a stable, secured truth—even a belief in scientific truth—is a masked form of the ascetic ideal, which itself is a masked form of nihilistic life-denial. The question of asceticism will climax the sketch of Nietzsche's philosophical vision and bring us to eternal recurrence.

In the light of traditional approaches to the problem of time, which exhibit metaphysical, epistemological, and normative objections to sheer temporal conditions, eternal recurrence can be seen as Nietzsche's formula for the "redemption" of time and becoming. As I have suggested, eternal recurrence, in Nietzsche's view, is the only authentic alternative to other conceivable possibilities with respect to affirming natural life and its temporal flux.

A crucial question in considering eternal recurrence involves the notorious figure of the *Übermensch* introduced in *Thus Spoke Zarathustra*. My argument is that the *Übermensch* serves as the guiding focus for Zarathustra's task of coming to affirm eternal recurrence. The *Übermensch*, in my reading, is less the prospect of some human type or individual, and more an anonymous, structural concept that would render life affirmation possible. The *Übermensch* is nothing superhuman, but rather the overcoming, the getting-over of the human-world duality that in fact has spawned and supported the host of time-negating outlooks meant to preserve and protect *human* interests against a finite, tragic world. The *Übermensch* represents what I will call "world-experience," a decentered experience of the world that is not measured by chronophobic dispositions.

How are we to read Nietzsche's depiction of eternal recurrence? In this study I will concede a point that has become something of a standard view, that Nietzsche probably did not intend eternal recurrence to be taken as an objective, scientific, cosmological fact. None of his published works advanced such a view, the sketches for which can only be found in the *Nachlass*, Nietzsche's unpublished notebooks.[4] Yet we cannot be certain that Nietzsche repudiated such an account or something like it. I concur with a commonly endorsed methodology with respect to the *Nachlass* we should give priority to passages from the notebooks that are not inconsistent with the spirit of published texts. For many, this means that eternal recurrence should not be understood as a claim about world events, but as an expression of an existential task, a test or a means for coming to affirm the conditions of life (which is the spirit of published versions of eternal recurrence in *The Gay Science* and *Zarathustra*). I, too, stress an existential version, but I add something that seems missing in other versions: unless eternal recurrence is taken "literally," its existential effect would be lost; one would always be susceptible to the psychological loophole that repetition "isn't really true." To avoid the possibility of "armchair affirmation," I focus on the *literal* meaning of eternal recurrence, without necessarily endorsing its *factual* meaning. This distinction between the literal and the factual (to be developed in the text) has the following advantages. While not presuming a cosmological interpretation of eternal recurrence, we can better understand why Nietzsche did experiment with an objective, descriptive approach to this notion.[5] In my reading, Nietzsche always regarded eternal recurrence as more than simply a hypothetical thought experiment pertaining only to human psychology; he always took it to express something about life and the world as such. A certain extrapsychological literality would better match the crucial import of eternal recurrence expressed in the published works, and it would also not be utterly inconsistent with cosmological experiments in the notebooks. In sum, my argument is that eternal recurrence should be seen as the only authentic expression of a Nietzschean life affirmation *by force of* its literal meaning. In advancing this argument, I will try to uncover the inadequacies of three typical interpretive approaches to eternal recurrence: (1) those that concede eternal recurrence as some kind of literal claim about the world, but that see such a claim as either false or injurious to other basic elements of Nietzsche's thought; (2) those that redescribe eternal recurrence as a metaphorical or symbolic expression of some insight or philosophical position that has nothing to do with literal repetition (e.g., the nature of time, the moment of action, creativity); and (3) those that construe eternal recurrence as an ethical imperative that can guide action.

In engaging various possible interpretations of eternal recurrence, I side with those who read recurrence as an existential expression of life affirmation, while adding, however, that the literal sense of eternal recurrence must somehow be preserved, if only to register its existential effect. I want to say that life affirmation as such cannot be the *sheer* basis of eternal recurrence, because for Nietzsche, affirmation is a *response* to the idea of repetition that is in some way *given*, indeed that Nietzsche claims came to him as an "inspired" thought (which would be structurally consistent with an *über-menschlich* experience).

In this regard I want to suggest a kind of literality that can be distinguished from "factual" claims by bringing in the literary phenomenon of "suspension of disbelief." I draw on the Greek sense of *mimēsis*, not in the manner of representational copying, but in the psychological sense of audience identification with poetic and dramatic performance (which was the real target of Plato's critique of poetry in the *Republic*). With Nietzsche's frequent references to Dionysian identification in *The Birth of Tragedy*, as well as his ongoing promotion of aesthetic states, I aim to show a way in which eternal recurrence can be taken literally without necessarily committing to a cosmological thesis.

This investigation will have to take on several interpretive problems that have figured in critical responses to eternal recurrence: (1) Does eternal recurrence entail a kind of determinism that not only rules out human freedom, but also Nietzsche's own commitment to creativity? This is an important question, and I will engage it by distinguishing Nietzsche's sense of "necessity" from any kind of causal determinism, and by addressing his perplexing claim that human action is neither free nor unfree. (2) Does eternal recurrence undermine any sense of human selfhood construed as autonomous agency, which would pose problems not only for ethics, but again for Nietzsche's own promotion of creative individuals? I address this question by arguing that one of Nietzsche's prime philosophical targets is the idea of sovereignty, in any of its forms. Here I contest the common assumption that the "sovereign individual" named in *The Genealogy of Morality* is a Nietzschean ideal. A critique of autonomy need not undermine human action, however, because of the central role of agonistics in Nietzsche's texts. For Nietzsche, to be a self, to act in the world, is not self-execution in the strict sense because it cannot be disengaged from the "otherness" of contesting forces that in fact constitute and shape selfhood and action. (3) Does eternal recurrence render moral repugnance and judgment futile or impotent? If I affirm the repetition of everything, how can I object to something I take to be heinous? Again, agonistics must be brought to bear on this crucial question. I argue that affirming everything in Nietzsche's sense is not the same as *approving* everything. If I affirm the repetition of slavery, for example, I also affirm the repetition of my objection to slavery and all other moves against it. The upshot of eternal recurrence is affirming the presence and value of my Other, but *as* other. Nietzsche never saw the affirmation of life as some kind of generalized satisfaction. Differential choices were always paramount in his thinking, and a choice without something "other" to count out is not really a choice at all. (4) Given Nietzsche's perspectivism, how can he defend the "truth" of eternal recurrence in a way that would matter philosophically? Here I will survey the concept of perspectivism in Nietzsche's texts, how it can admit a modest but robust sense of truth, and how an *agonistic* perspectivism could not utterly rule out objections, in fact it would have to welcome them. I hope to show that such a conception of truth need not imply a vacuous relativism.

In the epilogue I explore the role of laughter in Nietzsche's thought, which can open up a fruitful angle on the existentially positive dimension of affirming a life that is intrinsically tragic. The Dionysian roots of both tragedy and comedy in early Greek culture is an important feature of this discussion. In the light of this historical background, I argue that laughter is structurally related to negation, and yet its enjoyment can be seen to complement and supplement tragic negation. A significant focus for this analysis will be the powerful symbolism of the shepherd scene in *Thus Spoke Zarathustra*, where the struggle with eternal recurrence elicits an intense, extraordinary laughter, which Zarathustra even calls "no human laughter" (*Z* III, 2, 2). Such extrahuman laughter again suggests something *über-menschlich*, which could then express in a distinctive way a crucial form of overcoming that is intrinsic to the drama of eternal recurrence: overcoming the "spirit of gravity" (*Z* I, 7). Perhaps this will also help us better understand the surprising mix of two powerful dispositions continually at work in Nietzsche's texts: an unflinching sense of the tragic together with an exuberant spirit of joy.

My intention in this study is to advance an *internal* reading of what eternal recurrence meant to *Nietzsche* in the setting of his texts. I do not claim to rule out or "refute" other interpretations of this fascinating notion, which would be dubious anyway in the atmosphere of Nietzsche's radical hermeneutics (where interpretation goes all the way down). What I do claim is that my reading tries to stay "closer" to the spirit and the letter of Nietzsche's texts. Many other readings are plausible, but they are not, I submit, faithful to the meaning of eternal recurrence as written by Nietzsche. And my interpretation also insists, contrary to most other readings, that eternal recurrence is not simply one theme among others in the texts; its meaning represents the very heart and lifeblood of Nietzsche's philosophy.

1
Nietzsche's Challenge to the Tradition: From Metaphysics to Naturalism

According to Nietzsche, "the fundamental faith of the metaphysicians is *the faith in opposite values*" (*BGE* 2). The Western religious and philosophical tradition has operated by dividing reality into a set of binary opposites, which can be organized under the headings of being and becoming:

being	*becoming*
constancy	change
eternity	time
spirit	nature
mind	body
intelligibility	sensibility
order	strife
reason	passion
good	evil
justice	power
truth	appearance

The motivation behind such divisional thinking is as follows: becoming names the negative, unstable, dynamic conditions of existence that undermine our interest in grasping, controlling, and preserving life (because of the pervasive force of error, mystery, variability, destruction, and death). Being, as *opposite* to becoming, permits the governance or exclusion of negative conditions and the attainment of various forms of stability untainted by their fluid contraries.

Nietzsche wants to challenge such priorities in the tradition, so much so that he is often taken to be simply reversing priorities by extolling sheer becoming and all its correlates. This is not the case, even though Nietzsche will often celebrate negative terms rhetorically to unsettle convictions and open up space for new meanings. In fact, Nietzsche exchanges oppositional exclusion for a sense of *crossing*, where the differing conditions in question are not exclusive of each other, but rather reciprocally related.[1] Nietzsche suggests that "what constitutes the value of these good and revered things is precisely that they are insidiously related, tied to, and involved with these wicked, seemingly opposite things" (*BGE* 2). Rather than fixed contraries, Nietzsche prefers "differences of degree" and "transitions" (*WS* 67). As we will see shortly, Nietzsche rejects the strict delineation of opposite conditions, but not the oppositional *force* between these conditions.[2] He grants that circumstances of struggle breed in opponents a tendency to "imagine" the other side as an "antithesis," for the purpose of exaggerated self-esteem and the courage to fight the "good cause" against deviancy (*WP* 348). Yet this tendency breeds the danger of oppositional exclusion and its implicit denial of becoming's "medial" structure.[3]

In restoring legitimacy to conditions of becoming, Nietzsche advances what I call an *existential naturalism*. The finite, unstable dynamic of earthly existence—and its meaningfulness—becomes the measure of thought, to counter various attempts in philosophy and religion to reform lived experience by way of a rational, spiritual, or moral transcendence that purports to rectify an originally flawed condition (*GS* 109; *TI* 3, 16). In turning to "the basic text of *homo natura*" (*BGE* 230), Nietzsche is not restricting his philosophy to what we would call scientific naturalism, which in many ways locates itself on the "being" side of the ledger. For Nietzsche, nature is more "wild and crazy" than science would allow; it includes forces, instincts, passions, and powers that are not reducible to objective, scientific categories. Retrieving the more primal sense of nature displayed in early Greek culture, Nietzsche insists "the terrible (*schreckliche*) basic text of nature must again be recognized" (*BGE* 230). Nietzsche's naturalism is consonant with scientific naturalism in rejecting "supernatural" beliefs, but the source of these beliefs, for Nietzsche, stems not from a lack or refusal of scientific thinking, but from an aversion to overwhelming and disintegrating forces in nature ("red in tooth and claw") that science too suppresses and wants to overcome. Indeed, Nietzsche identifies nature with chaos, as indicated in his alteration of Spinoza's famous equation: "*chaos sive natura*" (*KSA* 9, 519).[4] At the same time, Nietzsche also rejects a romantic naturalism, which spurns science and calls for a return to an original condition of harmony with nature (*GS* 370). Naturalism, for Nietzsche, amounts to a kind of philosophical methodology, in that natural forces of becoming will be deployed to redescribe and account for all aspects of life, including cultural formations, even the emergence of seemingly antinatural constructions of being. The focus for this deployment can be located in Nietzsche's concept of will to power, to be discussed shortly. First, however, we must locate the historical focus for Nietzsche's naturalistic turn, namely the death of God.

The Death of God

Nietzsche advances the death of God through the figure of a madman (*GS* 125), whose audience is not religious believers, but nonbelievers who are chastised for not facing the consequences of God's demise. Since God is the ultimate symbol of transcendence and foundations, his death is to be praised, but its impact reaches far beyond religion. In the modern world God is no longer the mandated centerpiece of intellectual and cultural life. But historically the notion of God had been the warrant for all sorts of cultural constructs in moral, political, philosophical, even scientific domains—so the death of God is different from atheism, since divinity had been "living" as a powerful productive force. From Plato through to the Enlightenment, a divine mind had been the ultimate reference point for origins and truth. With the eclipse of God, all corollary constructs must fall as well (*TI* 9, 5). The death of God therefore announces the demise of truth, or at least that "the will to truth becomes conscious of itself as a *problem*" (*GM* III, 27). Even though God is no longer at the forefront of culture, we still have confidence in the "shadows" of God (*GS* 108), in supposedly secular truths that have nonetheless lost their pedigree and intellectual warrant.

The consequences of God's death are enormous because of the specter of nihilism, the loss of meaning and intelligibility. The secular sophistication of the modern world has unwittingly "unchained this earth from its sun," so that we are "straying as through an infinite nothing" (*GS* 125). The course of Western thought has lead it to turn away from its historical origins, but the unsuspected result has been that "the highest values devalue themselves" (*WP* 2) and we are faced with a stark choice: either we collapse into nihilism or we rethink the world in naturalistic terms freed from the reverence for being-constructs. "Either abolish your reverences or—*yourselves*! The latter would be nihilism; but would not the former also be—nihilism?—This is *our* question mark" (*GS* 346).

The complex question of nihilism in Nietzsche's thought will be addressed in chapter 3. For now it can be said that the threat of nihilism—the denial of any truth, meaning, or value in the world—is in fact parasitic on the Western tradition, which has judged conditions of becoming in life to be deficient and has "nullified" these conditions in favor of rational, spiritual, or moral corrections. If, in the wake of the death of God, the loss of these corrections is experienced as nihilistic, it is because the traditional models are still presumed to be the only measures of truth, meaning, and value—and thus the world seems empty without them (*WP* 12A). For Nietzsche, philosophers can embrace the death of God with gratitude and excitement, not despair, because of the opening of new horizons for thought (*GS* 343). Various motifs in Nietzsche's texts can be read as antinihilistic attempts to rethink truth, meaning, and value in naturalistic terms, in a manner consistent with conditions of becoming. A central motif in this regard is will to power.

Will to Power

"The world viewed from inside … would be 'will to power' and nothing else" (*BGE* 36). A world of becoming, for Nietzsche, cannot simply be understood as a world of change. Movements are always *related* to other movements and the relational structure is not simply expressive of differences, but rather resistances and tensional conflicts (*WP* 568). Will to power depicts in dynamic terms the idea that any affirmation is also a negation, that any condition or assertion of meaning must overcome some "Other," some obstacle or counter-force. Nietzsche proclaims something quite important that will resonate throughout this investigation: "will to power can manifest itself *only* against resistances; therefore it *seeks* that which resists it" (*WP* 656; my emphasis). A similar formation is declared in *Ecce Homo* in reference to a warlike nature: "It needs objects of resistance; hence it *looks for* what resists" (*EH* I, 7; emphasis in text). What is crucial here is the following: Since power can *only* involve resistance, then one's power to overcome is essentially related to a counter-power; if resistance were eliminated, if one's counterpower were destroyed or even neutralized by sheer domination, one's power would evaporate, it would no longer *be* power. Power is *overcoming* something, not annihilating it: "there is no annihilation in the sphere of spirit" (*WP* 588). Will to power, therefore, cannot be understood in terms of individual states alone, even successful states, because it names a tensional force-field, *within which* individual states shape themselves by seeking to overcome other sites of power. Power cannot be construed as "instrumental" for any resultant state, whether it be knowledge, pleasure, purpose, even survival, since such conditions are epiphenomena of power, of a drive to overcome something (*GM* II, 12, 18). For this reason, Nietzsche depicts life as "that which must always overcome itself" (*Z* II, 12). This accounts for Nietzsche's objections to measuring life by "happiness," because the structure of will to power shows that *dissatisfaction* and *displeasure* are intrinsic to movements of overcoming (*WP* 696, 704), and so conditions of sheer satisfaction would dry up the energies of life.

According to Nietzsche, any doctrine that would reject will to power in his sense would undermine the conditions of its own historical emergence as a contention with conflicting forces. All scientific, religious, moral, and intellectual developments began as elements of dissatisfaction and impulses to overcome something, whether it be ignorance, worldliness, brutality, confusion, or competing cultural models. Even pacifism—understood as an impulse to overcome human violence and an exalted way of life taken as an advance over our brutish nature—can be understood as an instance of will to power.

Agonistics

A prefiguration of will to power can be found in an early text, *Homer's Contest* (*KSA* 1, 783–92). Arguing against the idea that "culture" is something antithetical to brutal forces of "nature," Nietzsche spotlights the pervasiveness in ancient Greece of the *agōn*, or contest for excellence, which operated in all cultural pursuits (in athletics, the arts, oratory, politics, and philosophy). The *agōn* can be seen as a ritualized expression of a worldview expressed in so much of Greek myth, poetry, and philosophy: the world as an arena for the struggle of opposing (but related) forces. Agonistic relations are depicted in Hesiod's *Theogony*, Homer's *Iliad*, Greek tragedy, and philosophers such as Anaximander and Heraclitus.[5] In *Homer's Contest*, Nietzsche argues that the *agōn* emerged as a *cultivation* of more brutal natural drives in not striving for the annihilation of the Other, but arranging contests that would test skill and performance in a competition. Accordingly, agonistic strife produced excellence, not obliteration, since talent unfolded in a struggle with competitors. In this way, the Greeks did not succumb to a false ideal of sheer harmony and order, and thus insured a proliferation of excellence by preventing stagnation, dissimulation, and uniform control. The *agōn* expressed the general resistance of the Greeks to "unified domination" (*Alleinherrschaft*) and the danger of unchallenged or unchallengeable power—hence the practice of ostracizing someone too powerful, someone who would ruin the reciprocal structure of agonistic competition.

The Greek *agōn* is a historical source of what Nietzsche later generalized into the dynamic, reciprocal structure of will to power.[6] And it is important to recognize that such a structure undermines the idea that power could or should run unchecked, either in the sense of sheer domination or chaotic indeterminacy. Will to power implies a certain measure of oppositional limits, even though such a measure could not imply an overarching order or a stable principle of balance. Nevertheless there *is* a capacity for measure in agonistic power relations. Nietzsche tells us (*KSA* 8, 79) that Greek institutions were healthy in not separating culture from nature in the manner of a good-evil scheme. Yet they overcame sheer natural energies of destruction by selectively ordering them in their practices, cults, and festival days. The Greek "freedom of mind" (*Freisinnigkeit*) was a "measured release" of natural forces, not their negation. Accordingly, Nietzsche's concept of agonistic will to power should not be construed as a measureless threat to culture but a naturalistic redescription of cultural measures. The reciprocal structure of agonistic relations means that competing life forces productively delimit each other and thus generate dynamic formations rather than sheer dissipation or indeterminacy.[7]

Psychology and Perspectivism in Philosophy

A central feature of Nietzsche's naturalism, which distinguishes it from scientific naturalism, is that his diagnosis of the philosophical tradition goes beyond a conceptual critique of beliefs and theories: "the path to fundamental problems" is to be found in psychology (*BGE* 23). Nietzsche maintains that the origins of problematic constructs of "being" are not to be found in mistaken beliefs but in psychological weakness in the face of a finite world, an *aversion* to the negative conditions of life, which he describes as "decadence, a symptom of the *decline of life*" (*TI* 3, 6). Thus a certain kind of psychological strength is needed to affirm life and rethink it in ways that are more appropriate to its natural conditions of becoming. What follows is that Nietzschean psychology does not suggest a universal human nature, but a delineation of *types* along the lines of weakness and strength—hence Nietzsche's notorious objections to human equality[8] and his promotion of a hierarchical arrangement of types: "My philosophy aims at an ordering of rank" (*WP* 287).

Nietzsche rejects the notion that philosophy is an "impersonal" pursuit of knowledge; philosophy so conceived conceals a "personal confession," an "unconscious memoir," and so a philosopher's thought bears "decisive witness to *who he is*—that is, in what order of rank the innermost drives of his nature stand in relation to each other" (*BGE* 6). In considering a philosophical claim, one should ask: "What does such a claim tell us about the man who makes it?" (*BGE* 187).[9] The turn to psychology means that knowledge cannot be based in an absolute, fixed, objective standard, but in a pluralized perspectivism: "There is *only* a perspective seeing, only a perspective 'knowing'" (*GM* III, 12). There are many possible takes on the world, and none could count as exclusively correct. And one's perspective can never be separated from one's existential interests, so "disinterested knowledge" is a fiction (*BGE* 207; *GM* III, 12, 26). Perspectives of value are more fundamental than objectivity or certainty. There is no being-in-itself, only "grades of appearance measured by the strength of *interest* we show in an appearance" (*WP* 588). Perspectivism entails that we exchange the connotations of strict knowledge and "facts" for the more open concept of "interpretation" (*GS* 374). Interpretation is the "introduction of meaning (*Sinn-hineinlegen*)" and not "explanation (*Erklärung*)" (*KSA* 12, 100).[10] Different, even conflicting positions can no longer be ruled out of play. Nietzsche expresses his outlook as follows: "Profound aversion to resting once and for all in any one total view of the world. Enchantment (*Zauber*) of the opposing point of view; refusal to be deprived of the stimulus of the enigmatic" (*WP* 470).

I will have more to say on perspectivism in a later chapter. For now it should be noted how Nietzsche's turn to psychology reflects his naturalistic revision of philosophy. The logical limits of answers to the deepest intellectual questions are an obvious feature of the history of thought, given the endurance of unresolved critiques and countercritiques in philosophy. Rather than give up on such questions or resort to mystical, transcendent, even relativistic solutions, Nietzsche focuses on philosophy as an embodied expression of psychological forces. Critical questions that follow such a focus would no longer turn on cognitive tests (How can you prove x?) but on psychological explorations and probes (Why is x *important* to you?). Accordingly, for Nietzsche, philosophy is always value-laden and cannot be reduced to descriptive, objective terms or to a project of logical demonstration; and he is consistent in recognizing this in the course of his own writing: "What have I to do with refutations!" (*GM* P, 4). He often enough indicates that philosophy, including his textual work, is a circulation of writing and reading that stems from, and taps into, personal forces and dispositions toward life.

That is why we must engage Nietzsche's texts in their "addressive" function, because "reader response" is inseparable from the nature of a written text. Nietzsche's stylistic choices—hyperbole, provocation, allusions, metaphors, aphorisms, literary forms, and historical narratives not confined to demonstrable facts or theories—show that he presumed a reader's involvement in bringing sense to a text, even in exploring beyond or against a text. Nietzsche's books do not presume to advance "doctrines" as a one-way transmission of finished thoughts. Good readers must be active, not simply reactive; they must think for themselves (*EH* II, 8). Aphorisms, for example, cannot merely be read; they require an "art of exegesis" on the part of readers (*GM* P, 8).[11] Nietzsche wants to be read "with doors left open" (*D* P, 5). This does not mean that Nietzsche's texts are nothing but an invitation for interpretation. Nietzsche's *own* voice is central to his writings, and in the matter of eternal recurrence, my study is dedicated to giving *his* voice a hearing.

How should one read Nietzsche? I might suggest the following hermeneutical method. Ask yourself five questions (some may not always apply): (1) What is the context of the discussion? (perspectivism); (2) What contest is at issue? (agonistic will to power); (3) What psychological factors are in play? (philosophy as value-laden); (4) What typological issues are involved? (pluralism and rank); (5) What are *my* interests operating in my response to the texts? (the addressive function).

I should mention one further (quite important) methodological implication stemming from Nietzsche's naturalism. I call it a *presumption of immanence*. We can only think in terms of how we are *already* existing in the midst of forces not of our choosing and not imaginable as stemming from, or implying, some other realm beyond the lived world. This mandates that we accept as *given* all forces that we can honestly recognize at work in our lives, from instinct to reason, from war to peace, from nature to culture, and so on. This includes the abiding *contest* between such forces, which undermines traditional projects of "eliminative" opposition (which can arise in any sphere, from religion to science). For Nietzsche, all evident forces play a role in cultural life, and a failure to embrace the whole package betrays weakness and the seeds of life-denial.

The Meaning of Life

Often when I meet someone and tell them I am a philosophy professor, I hear: "Ah, the meaning of life, right?" I usually smile and nod, deflect a discussion by claiming to be off-duty, and duly note to myself that this familiar question usually does not come up in my classes (if it did it might get bogged down in classic professional analytics—What is the meaning of life? It all depends on what the meaning of "meaning," "life," or "is" is). Yet it is clear to me that Nietzsche's philosophy, in all its elements, is focused on the question of the meaning of life—not in the sense of finding a decisive answer to "Why are we here?" but rather the *problem* of finding meaning in a world that ultimately blocks our natural interest in happiness, preservation, knowledge, and purpose. To be precise, the question is not "What is the meaning of life?" but "Can there be meaning in life?" So the question that preoccupies Nietzsche's investigations runs: Is life as we have it meaningful, worthwhile, affirmable *on its own terms*? No culture, no form of thought has ever denied (how could it?) that our "first world," immediate existence, is constituted by negative limits—mystery, change, suffering, loss, and death—as checks on all positive possibilities in life. In the end one must confess that life as we have it is tragic, measured against our highest aspirations.

Nietzsche's diagnosis of the Western tradition is that, in one form or another, the answer to this question of meaning in life as we have it has been: No. "Concerning life, the wisest men of all ages have judged alike: *it is no good*" (*TI* 2, 1). Whether in scientific, rationalistic, religious, or moralistic terms, initial conditions of existence have been judged to be deficient, confused, fallen, alien, or base, and thus in need of correction or transcendence altogether. Nietzsche judges all such judgments as implicitly nihilistic, and sees as his task the aim for an affirmative revaluation of a necessarily tragic existence: "I want to learn more and more to see as beautiful what is necessary in things; then I shall be one of those who make things beautiful. *Amor fati*: let that be my love henceforth…. And all and all and on the whole some day I wish only to be a Yes-sayer" (*GS* 276).

Here we are in transition to the next chapter on Greek tragedy. But it is important to establish that life-affirmation, in response to the *question* of meaning in life (and the danger of nihilism after the death of God), is the core issue in Nietzsche's thought, which lies behind and animates all of his supposed "doctrines," such as will to power, perspectivism, and especially eternal recurrence.[12] Accordingly, Nietzsche's texts cannot be reduced to doctrines or positions that call for assessment as philosophical "propositions" according to conceptual, empirical, or logical criteria.[13] Nietzsche's philosophical work always bears on the existential *task* of coming to terms with the meaning and value of life, in one way or another. This is why Nietzsche will honor life-denying outlooks (*EH* I, 7) even when attacking them, because they at least confront the meaning question in a deep and honest manner (*GM* III, 26), unlike outlooks that ignore it or conceal its import by relegating it to "merely" subjective concerns that have no bearing on truth.[14] A notable instance in the tradition of a deep engagement with meaning is the perennial concern in Christian thought with "theodicy," the attempt to justify God's creation in response to the question: Given that the world is imperfect, why would a perfect God have created it? Of course, Nietzsche sees all projects of theodicy as bankrupt and ultimately life-denying (which explains his admiration for Schopenhauer's pessimism), despite their authentic recognition of the *problem* of meaning measured against perfectionist ideals. In the wake of the death of God, the problem of meaning turns on the choice between a looming nihilism or a revaluation of life. One could, then, call Nietzsche's project a "biodicy."[15]

In sum, it must be established that Nietzsche's philosophy is based in two notions that he claims to have made inseparable: *becoming* and *the value of existence*, "both brought together by me in a *decisive* way" (*WP* 1058). His guiding concern, contrary to the tradition, is to promote the meaning and value of becoming.

2
Retrieving Greek Tragedy

The Birth of Tragedy not only serves to introduce pivotal themes for our discussion; historically it prepared and influenced Nietzsche's entire philosophical journey, culminating in eternal recurrence. No work is more crucial for a proper understanding of Nietzsche than *The Birth of Tragedy*.[1] If one does not begin here, there is little chance of perceiving the cohesive (though unsystematic) whole that Nietzsche's writings offer. Far from being merely a philological thesis, this book planted the seeds for every issue that Nietzsche subsequently undertook, from the critiques of Christianity, morality, science, and philosophy to the notions of *Übermensch*, rank, the death of God, will to power, and eternal recurrence. All are either a variation or direct culmination of themes established in Nietzsche's first published book, themes revolving around the central issue of the affirmation of becoming. Nietzsche calls *The Birth of Tragedy* "my first revaluation of all values," and the "soil" for his intention to be the "disciple for the philosopher Dionysus" and "the teacher of eternal recurrence" (*TI* 10, 5). This book sets up the historical character of Nietzsche's engagement with the Western tradition, in the way he calls for a retrieval of something at the heart of culture that has been lost or suppressed.

Dionysus and Apollo

In *The Birth of Tragedy*, Nietzsche focuses on the Greek deities Apollo and Dionysus in order to understand the meaning of tragic drama.[2] Tragedy, for Nietzsche, was far more than a literary form; it reflected and consummated an early Greek worldview that was more faithful to the finite conditions of life than subsequent developments in philosophy, especially as represented by Socrates and Plato. Early Greek myth and religion were quite different from religions that promote transcendence of earthly existence in favor of eternal conditions and salvation from suffering. Greek mythopoetic works and various cults expressed a religious outlook that sacralized the conditions of concrete life, celebrating all its forces, both benign and terrible, constructive and destructive.[3] Early Greek religion was (1) pluralistic, in not being organized around, or reduced to, a single form or deity; (2) agonistic, in that its sacred stories exhibit a tension between opposing forces; and (3) fatalistic, in that mortality and loss are indigenous to human existence, not to be repaired, reformed, or transcended. Human beings must always confront a negative fate that limits their power and ultimately brings death.[4]

Greek religion divided the world into Olympian and Chthonic powers: the bright, beautiful deities of Olympus and the dark, more brutal deities of the Underworld. Humans dwell in between these realms and experience the tension of their alternating force: life and death, measure and excess, intelligence and raw passion. Nietzsche understands tragedy as the culmination of this early Greek worldview, and the figures of Apollo and Dionysus can be understood as paradigmatic of the dualities and tensions of Greek religious experience, displayed together on the same stage in tragic drama. With the narrative portrayal of a noble hero experiencing an inevitable downfall, tragedy expresses the unfolding of a meaningful but finite life limited by a negative fate.[5]

Nietzsche's interpretation of tragedy is markedly different from traditional treatments. Beyond Aristotle's formal treatment of tragedy as a literary genre and his promotion of poetry as pertaining to ethical life, Nietzsche wants to emphasize the deep religious significance of tragic drama (BT 9), especially its connection with Dionysian worship and festivals.[6] Contrary to the Christian European interpretation, which took tragic destruction to be a consequence of a moral character flaw in the hero, Nietzsche spotlights the inevitability of the downfall and the implication of divine forces in this ruination. And most telling, as opposed to Schopenhauer, who saw tragedy as the highest artistic expression of a pessimistic denial of life, Nietzsche stresses the life-affirming implications of tragic drama, especially by linking it with revered divine forces and with the exuberant spirit of artistic production.

It is generally thought that tragedy had its origins in the dithyramb and the satyr play, both of which were connected with the cult worship of Dionysus. Nietzsche recognizes that mature Attic tragedy introduced non-Dionysian elements, particularly mythical references drawn from Homeric poetry. For hermeneutical purposes, Nietzsche selects Apollo to represent this counterpart to Dionysus, and he maintains that the confluence of these two deities can best illuminate the meaning and significance of tragedy. Apollo and Dionysus represent two fundamental elements of the Greek spirit (the Olympian and the Chthonic) that are initially in opposition but that become reconciled in mature tragedy (BT 1).

Dionysus was a deity of earth forces and his mythos expressed the natural cycle of birth, death, and rebirth: in various versions the god suffers a cruel death and dismemberment, but is restored to life again.[7] The early form of Dionysian worship did not involve a belief in personal immortality,[8] but rather an immersion in the overall power of nature that both bears and destroys its offspring. The earliest cult was composed of women, and the god's devotees would experience wild erotic feasts and also dark rites of animal sacrifice (representing the dismemberment and death of the god), in order to experience a cathartic communion with forces of life and death. In this way Dionysian worship promoted ecstatic self-transcendence, where all boundaries between self and nature are dissolved. As portrayed in Euripides' *The Bacchae*, the message of Dionysian religion was that a "civilized" separation from, or denial of, natural forces and passions generates an unhealthy alienation. To lose oneself in the amorphous surgings and shatterings of the life cycle is to gain a kind of peace and union with what is ordinarily "other" to the self. For this reason, Nietzsche selects the analogy of frenzied intoxication (*Rausch*) to express Dionysian experience (*BT* 1).

Apollo was an Olympian god representing light, beauty, measure, prophecy, poetry, and plastic arts. For Nietzsche, Apollo expresses the "principle of individuation" (*BT* 1), meant to counteract the dissolving flux of Dionysus by setting boundaries of form, the measured shaping of individual entities and selves. But because of the primal power of Dionysus that animates tragedy, the forming power of Apollo is only temporary and it must yield to the negative force of Dionysian flux. For this reason, Nietzsche designates Apollonian forms as analogous to "dreams" (*BT* 1), in that individuated states of being are "appearances" in the midst of a primordial becoming that will reabsorb formed states in a continual cycle of emergence and destruction.[9]

In abstract terms, the confluence of Apollo and Dionysus represents a finite flux of forming and deforming that never rests or aims for a finished state or preserved condition. Nietzsche sees this ineluctable becoming as the essence of Greek fatalism expressed in tragic drama.[10] The early Greeks, especially in Dionysian religion, experienced nature as a fatal paradox in that the forces of life involve both self-generation and self-destruction: life begets life and yet life can thrive only by consuming other life forms. The paradoxical self-consumption at the heart of nature helps illuminate the predominance of family killings in tragic drama and indeed in most Greek mythical narratives (e.g., Hesiod's *Theogony*).[11] The paradox becomes sharpened even further in tragic themes of individual self-destruction, where a hero brings about his own ruin (e.g., Oedipus). Rather than interpret Greek tragedy in mere social or psychological terms, Nietzsche insists on highlighting the deep mythico-religious resonances in tragic narratives. The self-destructive hero is simply an Apollonian mask of Dionysus (*BT* 10), an individuated image reflecting a global insight into the ambiguity of life's generative-degenerative whirl.

Not Dionysus Alone

Although the Dionysian has a certain primacy in Nietzsche's interpretation of tragedy (in that forms must always yield to formlessness), nevertheless the Apollonian is of equal importance; tragedy is not a purely Dionysian phenomenon. As a sophisticated art form, the Apollonian forces of poetry and plastic imagery are essential to the meaning and significance of tragedy. It can be said that the Apollonian brings a more "cultural" shape to the more "natural" force of sheer Dionysian experience. In itself, Dionysian experience is unrestrained and indeterminate, with convulsive whirling, shrieking, howling, lewdness, and the dissolution of identity in violent chaos.[12] Tragic drama, with its Apollonian artistic constructions, transforms amorphous Dionysian experience into an articulated cultural world. Poetry brings shape to Dionysian energy through language, measured rhythm, character formation, and plot structure. Unrestrained whirling is organized into dance. Ecstatic cries become song. Sheer chaos is shaped into a cultural *situation* ruined by fateful destruction. And the dissolution of self becomes a sharply characterized self *confronting* that loss, so that individuation is maintained, but still in the midst of negativity. Such is the essence of tragedy, which has a greater depth and impact than pure Dionysian experience because it presents the *tension* between form and formlessness rather than either side by itself.

Tragic drama constructs and sustains an Apollonian world, in which artistic contours and cultural meanings are portrayed in an unfolding narrative. But behind the social, political, and psychological foreground of tragic poetry, the power of inevitable fate that brings destruction bespeaks a Dionysian truth. In this way the dyadic nature of the Greek sense of the sacred embodied in the Olympian-Chthonic division is organized in a single mythical setting, with both spheres given their respective importance.

For this reason, Nietzsche celebrates tragedy as the consummating synthesis of early Greek cultural forces and insists that the Apollonian is just as important to culture as the Dionysian. In *The Birth of Tragedy*, Nietzsche calls tragedy a mediating mixture of the Dionysian and the Apollonian. Tragedy presents a negative limit, but "without denial of individual existence" (21). Pure Dionysian experience would preclude the awareness and comprehension of cultural production, and so the formative and educative capacity of mythical symbols "would remain totally ineffective and unnoticed." Apollonian art allows us to "find delight in individuals," it "satisfies our sense of beauty which longs for great and sublime forms," it "presents images of life to us, and incites us to comprehend in thought the core of life they contain." With the force of sensuous imagery, intelligible ideas, and sympathetic emotions, the Apollonian prevents a collapse into the "orgiastic self-annihilation" of sheer Dionysian abandon. The Dionysian, by itself, entails the *danger* of nihilism and pessimism, voiced by the "Wisdom of Silenus": It is best "not to be born, not to *be*, to be *nothing*. But the second best for you is—to die soon" (*BT* 3). It is the *pain* of individuated states (intrinsically subject to dissolution) that prompts an interest in dissolution as a (worldly) *deliverance* from pain. Thus, the force of Apollonian individuation is the deliverance not from pain but from the danger of life-denial (*BT* 7).

And yet, the power of Dionysus still holds sway because of tragic limits on formed conditions. So cultural forms and negative limits both have equal status in tragedy: "Thus the intricate relation of the Apollonian and the Dionysian in tragedy may really be symbolized by a fraternal union of the two deities: Dionysus speaks the language of Apollo; and Apollo, finally the language of Dionysus; and so the highest goal of tragedy and of all art is attained" (*BT* 21).[13] *Both* forces "must unfold their powers in a strict proportion" (*BT* 25). Accordingly, it must be said in passing that Nietzsche's later promotion of the Dionysian should not be taken to exclude the Apollonian. Nietzsche remained a philosopher of culture, rather than sheer chaos or unrestrained license. For this reason, I agree with Walter Kaufmann that the later designation of the Dionysian should be taken as shorthand for the earlier tragic dyad of Apollo and Dionysus.[14]

An excellent example of the Apollonian-Dionysian confluence can be found in the figure of Oedipus in Sophocles' Theban Trilogy. Sophocles presents a fully developed heroic individual who exemplifies all the excellences valued in the Greek world: courage, intelligence, strength, and leadership. Oedipus displays a sure sense of self-directed agency on behalf of political responsibilities, and yet the drama unfurls a dark, divinely ordained fate that dictates his doom and that is *brought about* by Oedipus's own decisions and actions.[15] Here the ambiguity of the Dionysian self-generating/self-consuming dialectic is acutely compressed into a single heroic figure who both achieves high station and precipitates his own ruin—*by way and because of* his high achievement. In order for Oedipus to *be* Oedipus he had to act in such a way as to simultaneously elevate and desolate himself (*Oedipus the King* 1197–1207). As indicated in the famous choral speech in *Antigone* (332–360), human existence is marked by an ambiguous element captured in the word *deinon*, meaning wondrous, awful, skillful, terrible, and mighty. In general terms, every human advancement is coextensive with a fateful limit. The world both supports and undermines human achievement. What makes Sophocles' drama deep and interesting is that the plot and the character of Oedipus articulate a rich array of ambiguous juxtapositions that constitute human life: construction and destruction, knowledge and ignorance, success and failure, power and impotence, home and homelessness, familiarity and strangeness, convention and taboo, guilt and innocence. The most telling ambiguity of all is Oedipus's relentless drive for truth that leads to blind darkness. In all, the narrative presents a full dramatic rendering of the complex existential matrix that displays the sacred confluence of Apollo and Dionysus at the heart of tragedy.

Both the content of tragedy and its form (a creative artistic production not grounded in "real" conditions) reveal that life forms are beautiful and meaningful, and yet temporary and insubstantial. Oedipus lived an exalted life and even in ruin he exhibited a noble bearing of his terrible fate. *Oedipus at Colonus* shows Oedipus departing life without rancor or resentment. Such was the element of Greek tragedy that excited Nietzsche so much (and that perplexed Schopenhauer), namely an affirmative bearing in the midst of a tragic worldview. Indeed, Nietzsche went so far as to say that Greek tragedy in the end was life affirming and not a sign of pessimistic life-denial. With tragedy, the Greeks *overcame* pessimism (*EH* III, *BT*, 1; see also *BT* ASC, 1).

Tragedy and Life Affirmation

There are two senses in which we can understand the affirmative posture of Greek tragedy with respect to Nietzsche's interpretation: an aesthetic sense and a religious sense. First, Nietzsche sees the artistic Apollonian elements in tragedy as essential to the life-affirming spirit of the Greeks. The very act of fashioning a beautiful portrayal of a dark truth shows that the Greeks even here were delighting in the power of artistic imagery to display the attractions of the life-world, as opposed to withdrawing into quietism, pessimistic denial, or hopes for another world. For Nietzsche, pessimistic art is a contradiction (*WP* 821). In addition, Apollonian art forms shape a world of meaning in which the Greeks could dwell, and through which they could bear the terrible truth of Dionysian deformation, thus avoiding the danger of self-abnegation.

Second, the historical association of tragedy with the worship of Dionysus, together with Nietzsche's articulation of a divine dyad at the core of tragedy, indicates that the Greeks (and Nietzsche) experienced tragedy as expressive of certain truths about existence that call for responsive reverence. In other words, the disclosures of tragedy, stemming from "divine" sources, are not simply "human" meanings, but rather elements of the world *to* which humans must respond, and which they are called to affirm. The effect of tragedy is the simultaneous affirmation of human life and its ultimate dissolution (Apollo and Dionysus). It should be said that the sacred element of tragic negation is more truly extra-human than other religious narratives predicated on some kind of human salvation or transformation. This would help explain Nietzsche's comfort with early Greek divine references, because Greek tragedy did not fall prey to the common propensity in other religions to surpass finite life conditions and their pervasive threats to human interests.

Moreover, a certain extra-human significance would accord with an aspect of Nietzsche's analysis of tragedy that is often ignored, namely his refusal to reduce Apollonian and Dionysian powers simply to human artistic production. Prior to the discussion of tragic art, Nietzsche refers to the Apollonian and Dionysian as "artistic energies that burst forth from nature herself," and he suggests that human artistry is a "mediated" relation to this natural energy, an "imitation" of immediate creative forces in nature (*BT* 2). Moreover, even regarding human artistic production, Nietzsche suggests that art is not grounded in the individual will and subjectivity of the artist, that humans are not "the true authors of this art world" (*BT* 5). Such suggestions would certainly fit well with Nietzsche's sympathetic treatment of Greek deities and in a general sense with Nietzsche's emphasis on art as not simply a human artifact, but as disclosive of the *world's* meaning and significance: "for it is only as an *aesthetic phenomenon* that existence and the world are eternally justified" (*BT* 5). What is "saved" by art is not only human meaning, but *life* (*BT* 7).

Therefore we can conclude that the "divine" references that exceed humanity and suggest the "true author" of the art world point to primal forces in natural life. This is consistent with Nietzsche's claim that culture arises *out of* nature and it compels us to realize that the baseline reference for Nietzsche is not humanity or even art, but life (*BT* ASC, 2).

Nietzsche's thought, of course, is not overtly religious in any customary way, and yet his early interest in Apollo and Dionysus and his continued reference to Dionysus in later texts show at least that a "deity," in the sense of an extra-human (*Übermenschlich*) site of meaning and significance, would not be anathema to his purposes. This is especially true if we notice the connection between early Greek religion and a Nietzschean affirmation of finite life conditions, which becomes fully dramatized in the "narrative" of eternal recurrence.

We can here revisit the question of truth that was implicated in the death of God. For Nietzsche, a significant feature of the Dionysian aspect of tragedy is that it "educated" the Greeks about inevitable limits and the true meaning of "myth." In *The Birth of Tragedy*, Nietzsche says that the Dionysian disrupted the common tendency to take religious myths as "real" accounts referring to actual events or conditions, that is, as a kind of "juvenile history" (10). The Dionysian spirit of self-consuming flux teaches that mythical forms are creative emergences of meaning that must yield to a negative force. The truth of myth is the truth of becoming, a forming-in-the-midst-of-formlessness, and not a discovery of substantive foundations that surpass or rectify the variety and fluidity of experience. As was said earlier, both the form and content of tragedy exhibit an ungrounded dynamic that fits a world of becoming. Therefore, from a performative standpoint, tragic drama displays a self-consuming narrative consistency in that it both advances and retracts itself. Myth, for Nietzsche, is a self-limiting presentation that does not presume to be the "truth" in a foundational sense. That is why Nietzsche says that through tragedy, "myth attains its most profound content, its most expressive form" (*BT* 10). We must note, however, that because of the formless background, mythical forms, though not foundational, are still "irreducible" in that they do not hide or point to some other *content* outside their presentations.[16]

Socrates and the Philosophical Ideal

Tragic myth preceded the advent of philosophy in the Greek world. In *The Birth of Tragedy*, philosophy is embodied by Socrates, the third important voice in that text. Socrates sought logical consistency, precise definition, and conceptual universals secured in the conscious mind. With such powers of rational thought, humans could overcome confusion, mystery, and limits, and thus come to "know" the true nature of things. Now truth is no longer mythical emergences associated with a negative force, but rather general, fixed ideas that ground knowledge and surpass the life-world. Such a transformation is clinched in Plato's designation of eternal Forms as the ground of "being" that transcends negative conditions of "becoming." In light of Nietzsche's analysis of tragedy, the Socratic-Platonic developments at the beginning of Greek philosophy can be said to represent a reductive restriction to formed conditions without the Dionysian generative-degenerative formlessness that creates, dissolves, and renews forms. For Nietzsche, the Apollonian-Dionysian confluence of mythopoetic forces offers a prephilosophical precedent for his own challenges to the Western philosophical tradition.

It is important to stress that the Apollonian, for Nietzsche, is not equivalent to the rational (a frequent misreading). The Apollonian presents *aesthetic* form, not conceptual or logical form. For instance, art forms display sensuous particulars, not universals (e.g., Oedipus, not the "human"). And narrative structure is not the same as logical structure. Moreover, Nietzsche's correlation of the Apollonian and Dionysian helps articulate the creative, emergent, contingent, and therefore *ungrounded* quality of artistic forms, as opposed to rational presumptions of stable, necessary truths. Even the frequent association of the Apollonian with knowledge should be taken with some suspicion. Apollo's maxim "know thyself" is often taken as a precursor of the Socratic ideal of self-knowledge and rational inquiry. However, the original meaning of the maxim is more in line with the notion of tragic limits: it really says "know your place, know that you are not a god," and as such the maxim is more constraining than progressive.[17]

Plato's seeming transcendent aims brought him to critique tragic art precisely because of the characteristics that Nietzsche considers life-affirming. In books 2, 3, and 10 of the *Republic*, Plato attacks tragic poetry because it falsely portrays the divine as unstable, dark, immoral, and unjust; and the sensuous pleasures of artistic works prompt the passions and seduce us to the attractions of bodily life, which block the higher possibilities of intellectual and spiritual transcendence. Although the *Republic* is a complex text susceptible to a wide array of readings, it is plausible to say that the entire dialogue is a confrontation with the Greek tragic tradition. The frequent references to tragic poetry and its defects can be said to focus the guiding narrative context that launches the extensive "digression" into political structures as a "large scale" image aid in coming to understand justice in the soul (II, 368–69). The appointed task of Socrates is to respond to the daunting challenge in Book 2: defend the idea that the just man will be *happier* that the unjust man, even if worldly forces of power work against the just man; indeed he is charged to defend the worst case scenario: that the just man is despised by everyone as unjust and the unjust man is revered by everyone as just (361). The course of the dialogue is meant to show that the soul should choose justice despite its sacrifices because of its intrinsic worth *and* its compensations after death (expressed in the myth of Er at the end of the work; note that the stipulated challenge is retrieved in this context at 612). A crucial flaw in tragedy is the uncompensated suffering of good people (III, 392b). The *Republic* can be read as a countertragic narrative, a new *mythos* (see *BT* 14) to promote the philosophical life in the face of a tragic mythical tradition, and especially in the face of the obvious "tragedy" of self-inflicted ruin if Socrates' trial and death were the last word.

The Death of Tragedy

Tragic truth expresses an ever-annihilating Dionysian flux. But this flux, in itself, is indeterminate and meaningless. Meaning is achieved through the individuation of this flow, the gathering of images in the midst of perpetual becoming. But because Dionysus must always reabsorb these images, Apollonian individuation is characterized as appearance, since individuated images have no ultimate, permanent reality as such. But Nietzsche considers appearance to be a highly positive phenomenon, as the appearing of the world, the meaning of the world. World imagery is not appearance in the sense of being "false," but in the sense of being a creative emergence. As Nietzsche came to put it, the apparent world is not a fiction (the "true world" is), but a *livable truth* (*WP* 568). The apparent world entails irreducible perspectives of value, and the alternative to appearance is not a "true world" but *no* world (*WP* 567). Apollonian individuation emerges as aesthetic, created imagery that in the end must relinquish itself and recognize the power of Dionysus. Tragic wisdom reflects individuation in the midst of flux, which does not attempt to still the flux. But Nietzsche saw that such wisdom required a great deal of strength, since it simultaneously affirmed life and relinquished fixed individuation. Tragic wisdom did not last. In the absence of strength, the tendency toward individuation would attempt to resist and suppress the presence of Dionysus and maintain itself against the terror of dissolution. Nietzsche locates this development in the twin forces of Socratic logic and its artistic counterpart in Euripidean tragedy.

Tragic wisdom died by its own hands, by way of Euripides, the last tragic poet. Euripides undermined tragedy by abandoning Dionysus and stressing Apollonian individuation, conscious knowledge, and reflection. The eclipse of the Dionysian was the working of a new god, not Dionysus or Apollo, but Socrates, masked by Euripidean characters (*BT* 12). Tragedy died as a result, because in abandoning Dionysus, Euripides also lost Apollo. Apollo offers aesthetic appearance *as* appearance, necessarily related to the annihilating force of Dionysus.

What comes from the loss of this mythical fraternity? For Euripides, the new evaluation is "to be beautiful, everything must be intelligible," which is the aesthetic counterpart of the Socratic dictum "knowledge is virtue" (*BT* 12). Conscious knowledge is now the measure of value, no longer artistic instinct or mysterious powers of fate. Apollonian individuation is severed from its relation to the Dionysian; so Apollo no longer relates to Dionysus but only to himself (as the boundary maker). But he no longer manifests *aesthetic* individuation; individuated form now opens the door to fragmentation and reification, and thus to conscious knowledge and reason.

Nietzsche cites Euripides' prologues as an example of the new reflective ideal. Here the poet maps out the tragedy in advance, giving the background meaning and course of events in the drama. But in this way, the spontaneity and suspense of direct dramatic effect is lost. Euripidean poetry thus esteems conscious knowledge and aligns itself with Socrates, who opposed Old Tragedy and its fatalism, who fought against instinct and the power of illusion in Greek life. Socrates wanted to reform life through the power of reason. Tragedy did not "tell the truth" and was an obstacle to knowledge and justice. With the Euripidean-Socratic axis, philosophical thought now overcomes art through dialectical thinking. Apollo's force is transformed into logical schematism, which is in fact an overextension and disguise of the Apollonian that pretends to be nothing like Apollonian art and that winds up ruining tragic sympathy (*BT* 14). Euripidean heroes defend their actions with arguments and counterarguments, and continually give forth heated analyses of their fate and resistance from the standpoint of their own subjectivity. This dialectical tactic destroys tragic emotion and reverence. Dialectic implies optimism: conclusions must be conscious to be true; humans can come to rationally comprehend the meaning of life.

> Who could mistake the optimistic element in the nature of dialectic, which celebrates a triumph with every conclusion and can breathe only in cool clarity and consciousness—the optimistic element which, having once penetrated tragedy must gradually overthrow its Dionysian regions and impel it necessarily to self-destruction. (*BT* 14)

Optimism means that one has the power to *know* life, not that things will necessarily turn out well. It dictates that the way to *approach* well-being is through conscious knowledge. But optimism destroys Dionysian wisdom. The "tragic" end of Euripidean plays merely indicates the failure of conscious knowledge and control, not the restorative *emergence* of Dionysus. Euripidean heroes are merely blocked and cannot experience Dionysian joy because they are bound by an interest in conscious knowledge. They are trapped in subjective consciousness, and therefore their relation to fate must now be one of struggle rather than transformative integration. We can see that, for Nietzsche, the tragic is not confined to the negative outcome of a drama, but is concerned with how life is *engaged* in tragic drama.

Nietzsche sees Socrates as a profound turning point in history. He represents a *type*, the theoretical life, the faith that thought can penetrate the depths of reality, can know it and correct it (since blocks to conscious knowledge are seen as faults). The artist experiences joy in appearances, coverings, and veils. The theoretical type takes joy in unveiling, in stripping appearances, because what is veiled is "truth" in the form of concepts. The highest powers of the spirit are to be found in concept formation, judgments, and inferences. Knowledge of truth is the good, appearances and error are evil (hence the shift from a tragic to a moral stance). Bad outcomes in life are not the result of tragic fatality but of "errors in logic" (*KSA* 1, 546). Accordingly, theoretical knowledge destroys tragic myth; it seeks comfort not in the play of fatal appearances, but in its optimistic view that it can correct existence, guide life by reason, and "confine the individual within a limited sphere of solvable problems, from which he can cheerfully say to life: 'I desire you; you are worth knowing'"(*BT* 17).

Socratic logic and dialectic also transform the agonistic spirit that Nietzsche admired in early Greek culture. Contestation is certainly the life-blood of Platonic dialogues in testing and challenging received opinions. But the ground rules of dialectic (one's beliefs must be clearly defined and justified by adherence to principles of universality and consistency) introduce a change. The older agonistics, for Nietzsche, reflected an ongoing interplay of conflicting forces in competitions that were open-ended, revisited, and ungoverned by any overarching order or presumption of final victory. Socratic dialectic undermines this agonistic structure by setting rules that predetermine successful outcomes and presume the possibility of utter victory: rational argumentation aims to *defeat* opponents by stripping their positions of validity and significance, by working for abdication, even self-abdication when internal inconsistencies are uncovered.[18]

For Nietzsche, the theoretical man is a *noble type*, as opposed to more vulgar, common forms of life, exemplified in egotism and physical power (*BT* 18). Noble types create *cultural value and direction*. Nietzsche summarizes that culture is either Socratic, artistic, or tragic (*BT* 18); the tragic is artistic, but it goes deeper than other forms of art. Modern culture is Socratic because of the predominance of knowledge and science. The tragic and the artistic are now "tolerated, but not intended" (*BT* 18). Modern culture is also optimistic, due to its delusion of limitless power. For this reason, Nietzsche praises Kant and Schopenhauer for demonstrating the limits of science and rational knowledge, thus opening the door for a retrieval of tragic culture (*BT* 18).

Tragic Wisdom and Philosophy

I close this chapter with two discussions drawn from *The Birth of Tragedy* that will have a bearing on the course of this investigation: the relationship between philosophy and preconceptual, tragic sources; and the deconstructive role of certain philosophical critiques in preparing a tragic worldview.

Nietzsche tells us that the *meaning* of tragic myth was not directly expressed in the "word drama" of poetry, and that his own conceptual efforts are initiating such an understanding: "the structure of the scenes and the visual images reveal a deeper wisdom than the poet himself can put into words and concepts" (*BT* 17). It should be clear that tragic poetry by itself would not suffice for Nietzsche's intellectual tasks. Philosophical concept formation (e.g., "the tragic") provides a deepened and enhanced comprehension of the meaning and purpose of cultural phenomena. Indeed, Nietzsche maintains that the emergence of theoretical reason and science in the Greek world was not the elimination of aesthetic, creative forces, but their modification (*BT* 15); witness the artistic elements in Platonic dialogues (*BT* 14).

Nietzsche here announces something that continues to resonate in his writings: philosophical understanding is valuable, but it has to "distance" itself from prephilosophical, preconceptual cultural forms. Such distance harbors the danger of philosophical alienation from, even hostility toward, preconceptual culture (this may even rise to the level of a tragic dilemma). The advent of philosophy in the Greek world is the original case study. Pre-Socratic philosophy in many ways was reflective of tragic meanings (see *PTAG*). But later philosophy, perhaps as an inevitable consequence of its need to shape its own contours, became antagonistic toward tragic myth. Concept formation resisted the force of becoming to create structures of "being" that could quell or govern flux for the purpose of secured knowledge and conscious mastery of life. But in this way philosophy suppressed its *own* creative, and thus *apparent* and *tragic* character.

In *The Birth of Tragedy,* Nietzsche aims for much more than a historical analysis of Greek culture; he is meditating on the very nature of philosophy and its future prospects, indeed the coming of a new tragic age (*EH* III, BT, 4). Philosophy must always draw on preconceptual sources—in terms of preexisting artistic cultural productions and by way of philosophy's own creative impulses that cannot be reduced to its conceptual products. The problem, as Nietzsche sees it, is that Platonic philosophy and its inheritors represent an antagonistic, eliminative disposition toward preconceptual, aesthetic, tragic origins. In *The Birth of Tragedy,* Nietzsche poses the question of whether this antagonism between the theoretical and the tragic worldview is inevitable and beyond resolution (*BT* 17). He thinks not, and suggests an image for reconciliation in the figure of an "artistic Socrates" (*BT* 14, 15, 17), a thinker who is not averse to aesthetic modes, who indeed can employ such modes in the practice of philosophy. One naturally thinks of the deliberate deployment of literary and artistic devices in the course of Nietzsche's philosophical writings.

It is not enough, however, to coordinate conceptual and artistic production in philosophy. Such coordination implies a tragic limit because of the indigenous abyss at the heart of philosophy (indeed all cultural production) owing to its "creative," rather than "foundational," base. Reflecting back on *The Birth of Tragedy,* Nietzsche claims that in this work he had discovered the *concept* of the tragic, and that he sees himself as "the first *tragic philosopher,*" the first to offer a "transposition of the Dionysian into a philosophical pathos" (*EH* III, BT, 3).[19] Moreover, tragic philosophy is here called the "antipode" to a pessimistic philosophy because it says Yes to becoming in all its constructive-destructive energies, it embraces "the eternal joy of becoming," and its "Dionysian philosophy" entails the "doctrine of the 'eternal recurrence,' that is, of the unconditional and infinitely repeated circular course of all things."

The second point I want to emphasize is that *The Birth of Tragedy* establishes a certain agonistic, deconstructive operation within philosophy itself, which can provide clues for understanding Nietzsche's own textual development (and especially his various approaches to eternal recurrence). Because of the dominance of theoretical Socratism and scientific optimism in the modern world, Nietzsche surmises that the possibility of a "rebirth" of tragic culture and artistic philosophy can only arise once "the spirit of science has been pursued to its limits, and its claim to universal validity destroyed by the evidence of these limits" (*BT* 17). In other words, scientific rationality must (tragically) deconstruct *itself* to break its hold and open the door to tragic philosophy. Nietzsche thus applauds Kant and Schopenhauer for initiating the *self-overcoming* of reason by way of their limiting rational constructs to "appearances" that cannot comprehend noumenal "reality" (*BT* 18). In this way, philosophical optimism dies at its own hands; such self-limitation even amounts to a "Dionysian wisdom comprised in concepts" (*BT* 20). The path is now open for a more comprehensive wisdom that can embrace the whole of life, including the terrors of nature. The self-critique of reason causes the theoretical type to shudder before an abyss. He is so nurtured on optimism that "he feels that culture based on the principles of science must be destroyed when it begins to grow illogical, that is, to retreat before its own consequences" (*BT* 18). But Nietzsche thinks that such a self-consuming anxiety harbors the healthy prospect of overcoming optimism and cultivating a tragic disposition that can *recover* prephilosophical origins in a new way.

It is crucial to recognize that this motif of a self-consuming-prelude-to-recovery operates throughout Nietzsche's writings, and it shows that his critique of the Western tradition is not conceived as an alien invasion or a brand new, revolutionary conversion. The critique works within imminent developments in the history of thought and it calls for a retrieval of forces that were operating at the origins of Western culture.

Nietzsche says that "all great things bring about their own destruction through an act of self-overcoming" (*GM* III, 27). Such events abound in Nietzsche's texts: for instance, the self-overcoming of morality (*EH* IV, 3), the death of God as a culmination of the Christian ideal of truthfulness (*GM* III, 27), and bad conscience turning against itself (*GM* II, 24). Moreover, I think we should apply this motif to the role of Kantian/Schopenhauerian philosophy in *The Birth of Tragedy* and to subsequent developments in Nietzsche's work. The question pertains in part to the so-called periodic nature of Nietzsche's writings: an early metaphysical period (1872–1878), a middle positivist, scientific period (1878–1882), and a later antifoundational, transformational period (1882–1889). There is some truth in this picture of a movement from an early idealism inspired by Schopenhauer, to a more skeptical, scientific outlook, to the disruptive, prophetic later works. But the picture is misleading. There is much continuity and cross-referencing throughout Nietzsche's career, and I maintain that the affirmation of becoming and a tragic worldview are central to all of Nietzsche's thinking.

In addition, I think one can read Nietzsche's so-called middle period as analogous to the role of Kantian/Schopenhauerian philosophy in preparing a rebirth of tragic culture.[20] *Human All Too Human*, for example, is rife with scientific and naturalistic debunkings of human ideals and spiritualistic interpretations of culture, tracing them to "all too human" pretenses that have no validity beyond serving human needs. Such critiques amount to unmasking the "anthropomorphic" misconceptions of natural conditions. Yet, rather than view this period as a discrete interlude between early and later reflections on history and culture, we might see it as a preparatory deconstruction of traditional beliefs by way of one of modernity's own preferred measures of truth, scientific naturalism. In this way, traditional constructs can self-destruct under the weight of their own historical momentum. But then (in the manner of *The Birth of Tragedy*) Nietzsche's later works can be seen to fill in this emptied space (and its nihilistic dangers) with his more positive reconstructions of culture along the lines of his own version of naturalism (which is not purely scientific).[21]

Evidence for such an account is found in *Ecce Homo*. Nietzsche tells us that *Human All Too Human* represented a liberation from idealism, including his own in *The Birth of Tragedy* (*EH* III, *HAH*, 1). He aimed to reduce all "idealistic higher swindles" to mere human propensities (5). He restricted himself to "nothing more than physiology, medicine, and natural sciences," to exchange youthful, academic "idealities" for more hard-headed "realities" (3). Yet in this same passage Nietzsche says that this period preceded a compelled "return" to "properly historical studies." Indeed, Nietzsche depicts his transitional text, *The Gay Science*, as stemming from the "gratitude of a convalescent," as the "saturnalia of a spirit" who has endured hopelessness, who now has a "reawakened faith in a tomorrow," who anticipates "goals that are permitted again, believed again" (*GS* P, 1). The roles of the historian and psychologist are touted to engage the primal question of the *value* of existence, a question that lacks "any grain of significance when measured scientifically" (*GS* P, 2). The range of Nietzsche's texts might have to be seen in terms of a tensional structure that manifests a simultaneous forward-backward posture, which can explain his reference to a "Janus face which all great insights share" (*EH* III, *HAH*, 5).

I think it is plausible to see the movements between (and even within) Nietzsche's texts as exhibiting a structure of deconstructive, agonistic tension, wherein certain perspectives perform a corrective, delimiting role that is meant to *open* thought and prepare new movements, rather than exchange one form of thinking for another. We find Nietzsche engaging in this tensional dynamic all the time, either in stages of his writing or within a given text. Scientific, religious, artistic, psychological, historical, moral, and political perspectives are continually deployed to check each other at appropriate points of analysis, and sometimes this cross-checking includes the self-limitation of a perspective's own self-exceeding implications. Yet all of this is a circulating process meant to enrich and advance cultural life, rather than a purely destructive dispersion.

Moreover, the claim of my book is that the course of Nietzsche's thinking was always animated by the core question of the value of a finite, tragic world, which came to a head in the notion of eternal recurrence. *The Gay Science*, a transitional work, advanced the first overt formulation of eternal recurrence, and the text is specifically linked to his next work, *Thus Spoke Zarathustra* (a narrative thoroughly engaged with eternal recurrence), with a reference to tragedy (*GS* 342). In this regard, I mention finally the tactical reasons for stressing the productive/tensional structure of Nietzsche's cross-checking circulation of thought perspectives: I want to suggest an answer to why Nietzsche experimented with a "cosmological" version of eternal recurrence. Such a version should be read, neither as the definitive model for understanding eternal recurrence, nor as an utterly dispensable scheme rejected by Nietzsche; rather, it can be understood as a tensional, perspectival *participant* in the baseline question of the *meaning and value* of a tragic existence, and in Nietzsche's affirmative response to this question.

3
Morality, Nihilism, and Life Affirmation

This chapter articulates themes that will be essential for coming to understand the place of eternal recurrence in Nietzsche's thought and for engaging persistent critical discussions of this doctrine.[1] We begin with Nietzsche's adoption of a genealogical method, which drove his return to historical/cultural questions after the middle period. He deploys quasi-historical, genealogical discussions to subvert the confidence of traditional belief systems (not to refute them). Genealogy shows that revered doctrines are not fixed or eternal: they have a history and emerged as a contest with existing counterforces; indeed, they could not avoid being caught up in the conditions they were opposing. Such analysis reveals the complexity of cultural beliefs and undermines the presumed stability and purity of long-standing measures of thought. Genealogy, then, is a kind of history different from those that presume discrete origins or simple lines of development.

Some writers think that Nietzsche's genealogy implies a nostalgia for a more noble original condition.[2] But Nietzsche does not advocate a return to past circumstances (see *GS* 377 and *WP* 953). Genealogy is a strategy for critique in the face of hardened convictions (*GM* P, 6) and a preparation for something new (*GM* II, 24). Attention to the complexities of historical emergence destabilizes foundationalist models and transcendent warrants; and the agonistic crossings intrinsic to this history tear at the clear boundaries of conceptual categories. In this way, genealogy is simply disruptive and preparatory for new ventures.

A Genealogy of Morality

In his genealogical treatment of moral ideals, Nietzsche aims to ruin the pretense of moral purity by suggesting a different look at the historical context out of which certain moral values arose. Ideals such as neighbor-love, peacefulness, and humility were not derived from some transcendent source, but from the interests and needs of particular types of human beings, weaker peoples suffering at the hands of stronger types. Hierarchical domination was the ruling condition of early human societies (*BGE* 257). What has been exclusively called "morality" was originally only a particular kind of morality, one quite different from another kind of morality that reflected the interests of stronger, master types: "There are *master morality* and *slave morality*.... The moral discrimination of values has originated either among a ruling group whose consciousness of its difference from the ruled group was accompanied by delight—or among the ruled, the slaves and dependents of every degree" (*BGE* 260).[3]

Nietzsche distinguishes master and slave morality according to two sets of estimation: good and bad in master morality, and good and evil in slave morality. Master types discover what is good out of their own condition of strength; they experience pleasure and exaltation in their victories and their distance from the powerless. Characteristics such as courage, conquest, aggression, and command that produce the feelings of power are deemed "good," while traits of weaker types such as cowardice, passivity, humility, and dependence are deemed "bad." Nietzsche finds support for his analysis in the etymology of ancient words for good and bad, which generally connoted "noble" and "base," "superior" and "inferior" (*BGE* 260; *GM* I, 5). What is important for Nietzsche here is that good and bad are not absolutes. What is good is good only for the master; what is bad in the slave arouses embarrassment and contempt in the master, but not condemnation or denial. In fact the existence of the slave is essential for maintaining the master's sense of distance, rank, and thus "goodness." The condition of the slave is not esteemed but at the same time it is not annulled, since it provides the master with psychological (and material) benefits. In sum, what is good for the master is something active, immediate, and spontaneous, arising directly out of the master's accomplishment; what is bad is a *secondary* judgment in contrast to an antecedent experience of self-worth.

In relation to master morality, slave morality is constituted by a number of reversals. What the master calls "bad" is deemed good by the slave, and what is good for the master is called "evil" by the slave. The difference between "bad" and "evil" is important for Nietzsche. What is evil is absolutely negative and must be annulled if the good is to endure. Nietzsche traces this different kind of judgment to the existential situation of the slave: The *immediate* condition of the slave is one of powerlessness and subservience; the master is a threat to the very existence and well-being of the slave; in effect the slave lacks agency and so the initial evaluation is a negative one: the "evil" of the master is in the foreground, while what is "good," the features of the slave's submission, is a reactive, secondary judgment.

According to slave morality, anything that opposes, destroys, or conquers is evil and should be eliminated from human relations. In master morality, however, strife, opposition, and danger are essential to the feelings of power and accomplishment that spawn a sense of goodness (one thinks of the warrior ideals in Homer's *Iliad*). Harmlessness and security, which are good for the slave, are an embarrassment and encumbrance for the master. Slave morality reverses master morality and recommends humility, selflessness, and kindness as the measure for *all* human beings, but only out of a condition of weakness and as a strategy for self-protection and self-enhancement. Slave morality seeks the simultaneous exaltation of the weak and incapacitation of the strong; but in doing so, slave types find enhancement not through their own agency but through the debilitation of others.

Nietzsche's target here is generally the Judeo-Christian ethic. The stories and exemplars embodying this moral outlook have promoted the ideal of supplanting worldly power with "justice" and "love." In the context of cultural history, however, Nietzsche sees in this ideal a disguised form of power, in that it is meant to protect and preserve a certain type of life; even more, the images depicting divine punishment of the wicked suggest to Nietzsche that the slave type has simply *deferred* its own interest in conquest (*GM* I, 15). Both master and slave moralities, therefore, are expressions of will to power. A current distinction in the literature draws from Nietzsche's differentiation of *aktive* and *reaktive* attitudes (*GM* II, 11) and stipulates that the master expresses active will to power, while the slave expresses reactive will to power. The slave has no genuine agency and therefore can compensate only by reacting to an external threat and attempting to annul it. For Nietzsche, slave morality is not immediately an affirmation of a good, but a denial of something dangerous and fearful, and he grounds this evaluation-by-negation in the psychological category of resentment.[4]

> The slave revolt in morality begins when *ressentiment* itself becomes creative and gives birth to values: the *ressentiment* of natures that are denied the true reaction, that of deeds, and compensate themselves with an imaginary revenge. While every noble morality develops from a triumphant affirmation of itself, slave morality from the outset says No to what is "outside," what is "different," what is "not itself"; and *this* No is its creative deed. This inversion of the value-positing eye—this *need* to direct one's view outward instead of back to oneself—is of the essence of *ressentiment*: in order to exist, slave morality always first needs a hostile external world; it needs, physiologically speaking, external stimuli in order to act at all—its action is fundamentally reaction. (*GM* I, 10)

For Nietzsche, the difference between active and reactive will to power, between affirmation and resentment, is a fundamental issue that bears on *all* intellectual and cultural topics. The general question is the ability or inability to affirm a finite world of limits, losses, conflicts, and dangers (see *Z* II, 20 and *TI* 2, 1). His analysis of the social arena targets the concrete soil out of which grew a host of intellectual movements. Nietzsche is trying to subvert long-standing social values that are animated by notions of universality, equality, harmony, comfort, protection, and the like—seemingly positive notions that Nietzsche insists are connivances of negative attitudes: fear of danger and difference, hatred of suffering, resentment and revenge against excellence, superiority, and domination. In the ascendancy of the slave mentality, Nietzsche sees three lower types of life (the oppressed, the mediocre, and the discontented) retaliating against and subduing three successful types of life: the ruling class, exceptional individuals, and the high-spirited (*WP* 215).[5]

With literal slavery disappearing,[6] Nietzsche tends to designate this condition of weakness and its voluntary perpetuation of the slave attitude as the "herd instinct," which is continually seeking to exercise its own mode of power by enforcing conformity and comfort; in so doing it protects the self-esteem of ordinary humans by neutralizing differences and denigrating excellence. It is in this light that we can better understand Nietzsche's blistering attacks on democratic egalitarianism.[7]

It must be stipulated that Nietzsche's genealogical analysis is not meant to reject or even regret the slave/herd mentality, as much as to redescribe the environment of moral values. In doing so Nietzsche aims to disarm the high-minded pretense of egalitarian thinking by contextualizing it and showing it to be no less interested in power and control than aristocraticism (*BGE* 51; *GM* I, 15). Moreover, for Nietzsche, slave morality is no less *creative* than master morality; it is the *motive* behind creative forming that differentiates master and slave (*GM* I, 10).

A careful reading of the texts does not support the thesis that Nietzsche's genealogy is exclusively a defense of crude physical power or overt social control. Throughout the writings, the meaning of weakness, strength, and power is polymorphous and far from clear. For instance, Nietzsche calls the values he criticizes necessary for life. Consider the value of rationality:

> If the majority of men had not considered the discipline of their minds—their "rationality"—a matter of pride, an obligation, and a virtue, feeling insulted or embarrassed by all fantasies and debaucheries of thought because they saw themselves as friends of "healthy common sense," humanity would have perished long ago! The greatest danger that always hovered over humanity and still hovers over it is the eruption of madness—which means the eruption of arbitrariness of feeling, seeing, and hearing, the enjoyment of the mind's lack of discipline, the joy in human unreason. (*GS* 76)

Morality also has been essential for human development in its contest with nature and natural drive and for this it deserves gratitude (*WP* 403–4). The exceptional individual is not the only object of honor for Nietzsche; conditions of the rule are equally important for the species (*GS* 55). The "weakness" of the herd mentality turns out to be a practical advantage, since it has prevailed over the strong: "The weak prevail over the strong again and again, for they are the great majority—and they are also more intelligent" (*TI* 9, 14). Indeed, the higher types of creative individuals that Nietzsche favors are more vulnerable and perish more easily, because of their complexity, in contrast to the simplified order of herd conditions.

> The higher the type of man that a man represents, the greater the improbability that he will turn out *well*. The accidental, the law of absurdity in the whole economy of mankind, manifests itself most horribly in its destructive effect on the higher men whose complicated conditions of life can only be calculated with great subtlety and difficulty. (*BGE* 62)
>
> The higher type represents an incomparably greater complexity—a greater sum of coordinated elements; so its disintegration is also incomparably more likely. The "genius" is the sublimest machine there is—consequently the most fragile. (*WP* 684)

So we can see that "weak" and "strong" are anything but stable signifiers in Nietzsche's discourse. We will revisit this complex issue later in the chapter.

The Ascetic Ideal

The climax of Nietzsche's genealogical analysis of morality is his focus on the ascetic ideal. The slave mentality, owing to its external impotence, turns power *inward* and crafts a new ideal to combat worldly expressions of power; it crafts the power of the self to renounce its natural impulses and strive for "supernatural" transformations based in transcendent expectations (*GM* II, 16). Bad conscience (*GM* II) is the expression of this self-consuming battle with natural life (and the tactic for seducing the master mentality into renouncing its natural dominance). The ascetic ideal (*GM* III) is Nietzsche's term of choice for confronting the development in Western culture of life-negating forces that came to dominate the tradition.

The ascetic ideal in its purest form has manifested itself in religious expressions of saintly and monastic self-renunciation. Yet Nietzsche wants to focus on the intense feelings of power and exaltation accompanying such projects (*GM* III, 11). The priest, who creatively fashions the projects of natural self-transcendence, introduces potent new ideals that provide lowly types a way to affirm their dispossessed condition as chosen and admirable. In fact, the ascetic ideal is not life-denying in the strict sense; it reflects the instincts of a certain *kind* of life (degenerating life) to preserve itself through meaning creation (*GM* III, 13). We will return to this important point shortly.

Most dramatically, Nietzsche does not limit his discussion of the ascetic ideal to morality and religion. Even philosophy has been a continuation of this ideal in its promotion of a "reality" independent of sensuous nature (*GM* III, 10, 12). Even modern science is the "latest and noblest form" of the ascetic ideal (*GM* III, 23). Not done, Nietzsche goes on to say that the supposed "free thinkers" of his day (atheists, skeptics, immoralists, nihilists) are still in the service of asceticism. Why? Because they are not true "free spirits" in Nietzsche's sense: "they still have faith in truth," in the "*metaphysical* value" of truth (*GM* III, 24). To understand this we can recall that metaphysics, for Nietzsche, is the faith in opposite values. If, from the standpoint of modern belief in science and free inquiry, one champions these perspectives as correcting the superstitious "errors" of the past, one is still caught up in the problem of truth as diagnosed by Nietzsche: the discontent with agonistic becoming and the impulse to surmount such tensional existence by way of a secure warrant, in *whatever* form this may take, whether it be religious, philosophical, scientific, skeptical, or even the posture of the "free individual."

Before continuing, something important must be stressed. Nietzsche's genealogical analysis is through and through an engagement with the question of *meaning* in life, even with respect to the life-denying beliefs he attacks. Ascetic ideals are profound responses to the problem of meaning in a finite world. Even Schopenhauer's pessimism (which argues that all positive possibilities in life are for naught and that wisdom entails the self-abnegation of the will) was not life-denying in an absolute sense. His enemies (the optimists) seduced him into a *life* of pessimism, the vigorous assault upon optimism (*GM* III, 7). His rich, productive output of writings suggests that he found *meaning* in promoting the meaninglessness of existence. As Nietzsche put it in a general way, humans would "rather will nothingness than not will" (*GM* III, 1). And ascetic ideals are *honored* by Nietzsche (*GM* III, 26) precisely because of the honest confrontation with the meaning problem, even if the response is to find no meaning in finite life. Nietzsche highlights this point when discussing science as an instance of the ascetic ideal. Such an ideal is *lacking*, not in science per se, but in modern scholarly work that is *not* animated by deep ideals of meaning, namely in the dispassionate "objectivity" and professionalism of scholars who see and feel nothing beyond their narrow work of problem solving (*GM* III, 23, 26). Nietzsche surely opposes the ascetic ideal, but he recognizes its importance as *engaged* with the problem of meaning and meaning creation. *How* meaning is created and how it accords with finite becoming will distinguish Nietzsche's approach from others.

Life-Affirmation and Life-Enhancement

It is central for my purposes to clarify something that might mislead or confuse readers of Nietzsche. He espouses life-affirmation, and at the same time, throughout his writings he discusses beliefs that are life-preserving, life-enhancing, and life-promoting; and yet often these beliefs are the ones he attacks as life-denying. What is going on here? For the sake of economy, I want to suggest a distinction between *life-affirmation* and *life-enhancement*, where the former is Nietzsche's ideal and the latter can be attributed even to ideals that are life-denying in Nietzsche's sense.[8] This distinction will be crucial for coming to terms with eternal recurrence. In order to build this distinction I must back up a bit and return to the genealogy of master and slave values, where *both* are instances of creative will to power; indeed, the slave mentality is essential for the creation of an advanced culture.

I offer what I call the *creativity thesis* to address the complex features of Nietzsche's genealogy. The outline of the thesis is as follows: the kind of artistic, cultural, and intellectual creativity championed by Nietzsche was made possible by the slave mentality. Outwardly thwarted and powerless, the slave turned to the inner realm of imagination. Cultural creativity is the internalization or spiritualization of more overt and brute manifestations of power (the condition of the original master). This greatly expands the possibilities of innovation (since it is not completely bound by external conditions) and so cultural invention is set loose as a contest with existing conditions (*GM* III, 4). Accordingly, cultural creators, like the original master, will be perceived as threats, as destroyers, as evil. In this light, the genealogy of morals is a complex code for understanding the dialectics and dynamics of cultural development.

Let me fill out this thesis by citing texts that help build its features. Will to power is connected with creativity, with "spontaneous, aggressive, expansive, form-giving forces that give new interpretations and directions" (*GM* II, 12). The slave can exercise will to power only in the inner domain of imagination.

> All instincts that do not discharge themselves outwardly *turn inward*—this is what I call the *internalization* (*Verinnerlichung*) of man: thus it was that man first developed what was later called his "soul." The entire inner world, originally as thin as if it were stretched between two membranes, expanded and extended itself, acquired depth, breadth, and height, in the same measure as outward discharge was *inhibited.* (*GM* II, 16)[9]

The slave mentality is the prerequisite for spiritual cultivation (*BGE* 188); the "weak" represent a positive power of spirit (*TI* 9, 14) because their resentment of the strong opens up the possibilities of a higher culture, which is based on *der Vergeistigung und Vertiefung der Grausamkeit,* "the spiritualization and deepening of cruelty" (*BGE* 229). Such a turn begins to make mankind "an interesting animal," because the most ancient cultural concepts were "incredibly uncouth, coarse, external, narrow, straightforward, and altogether *unsymbolical* in meaning" (*GM* I, 6). Now higher culture is possible, since "human history would be altogether too stupid a thing without the spirit that the impotent have introduced into it" (*GM* I, 7).[10]

So the master-slave distinction may have clear delineations at first, but it begins to get complicated in the context of cultural creativity and Nietzsche's brand of higher types, who should be understood as an "interpenetration" of master and slave characteristics combined in a "single soul" (*BGE* 260). To be precise, Nietzsche distinguishes slave *instincts* that are "instruments of culture" from *bearers* of these instincts who are not (*GM* I, 11); so only certain individuals will carry slave instincts in a higher direction. For instance, the priest type, though weak in a worldly sense, is strong in will to power by *creating* values that promote the sick and castigate the healthy (*GM* III, 15). Nietzsche tells us that the *conflict* between master and slave forces is the most decisive mark of a higher, more spiritual nature (*GM* I, 16). As a result, the "evil" that designated the destructive threat of the master is now recapitulated in creative disruptions of established conditions.

> The strongest and most evil spirits have so far done the most to advance humanity: again and again they relumed the passions that were going to sleep—and they reawakened again and again the sense of comparison, of contradiction, of the pleasure of what is new, daring, untried; they compelled men to pit opinion against opinion, model against model. Usually by force of arms, by toppling boundary markers, by violating pieties—*but also by means of new religions and moralities* [my emphasis]. In every teacher and preacher of what is *new* we encounter the same "wickedness" that makes conquerors notorious, even if its expression is subtler and it does not immediately set the muscles in motion, and therefore also does not make one that notorious. What is new, however, is always *evil*, being that which wants to conquer and overthrow the old boundary markers and the old pieties. (*GS* 4)

Innovators are the new object of hatred and resentment (*Z* III, 12, 26), they are the new "criminals" (*TI* 9, 45), the new "cruel ones" (*BGE* 230), the new perpetrators of "war" (*GS* 283).

In sum, cultural creativity is made possible by a dialectic of master and slave characteristics, so that not everything in the latter is "slavish" and not everything in the former is "noble." In the end, therefore, the creator-herd distinction is *not* equivalent to the master-slave distinction; there are overlaps, but the crude domination found in the original condition of the master cannot be considered the primary focus of Nietzsche's analysis of creative types.

There are comparable complications in certain other phenomena supposedly denigrated by Nietzsche, such as bad conscience (resentment turned inward against the self) and the ascetic ideal (the self-destructive denial of nature). Both are conditions of denial that nevertheless also serve culture and have great potential for a higher order (*GM* II, 16 and III, 27). Specifically, for Nietzsche, these instincts of hatred and denial can perhaps be turned against themselves, where nihilism can be despised and then overcome in the spirit of affirmation. We should notice a general insight operating here: for Nietzsche, *any* development of culture out of natural conditions and any innovation will require a dynamic of discomfort, resistance, and overcoming—a contest with some Other. Nietzsche forces us not only to acknowledge this dynamic but to be wary of its dangers, which are indicated in traditional constructs and their *polarization* of a conflicted field into the oppositions of good and evil, truth and error. The ascetic ideal in the end represents the desire to escape the difficulty of incorporating the Other (*as* other) into one's field of operation. Affirmation, for Nietzsche, is anything but comfortable and pleasant; it means the capacity to take on the difficulty of *contending the Other without wanting to annul it.* The bottom line in Nietzsche's genealogy, then, is that *every* perspective is mixed with its Other. Such a mixture has two components: first, a perspective needs its Other as an agonistic correlate, since opposition is part of a perspective's constitution; second, a perspective can never escape a certain complicity with elements of its Other. Conflict, therefore, is not simply to be tolerated; affirming oneself requires the affirmation of conflict, since the self is not something that is first fully formed and then, secondarily, presented to the world for possible relations and conflicts. The self is formed *in* and *through* agonistic relations. So in a way, openness toward one's Other is openness toward oneself.

Life-affirmation, in Nietzsche's sense, requires an affirmation of otherness, which is consistent with the agonistic structure of will to power. Life-denial stems from weakness in the face of agonistic becoming; yet life-denying perspectives are life-enhancing because they further the interests of certain types of life who have cultivated their own forms of power that have had an enormous effect on world history. So, for example, Christianity is life-enhancing (see *A* 34–35, 39–40) but not life-affirming. Life-denying perspectives exhibit *local* affirmations of their form of life; the priest, for instance, in his posture of denial is still a powerful "conserving and yes-creating force" (*GM* III, 13). As we have seen, even philosophical pessimism is a stimulus for (a certain kind of) life. The sheer absence of life-enhancement would amount to *suicidal* nihilism (*GM* III, 28). Short of suicide, then, all forms of life aim to will their meaning, even if that meaning is a conviction about the meaninglessness of (natural) life. This helps explain an interesting fact: religions that yearn for a deliverance from earthly life still forbid suicide. Even Schopenhauer, who saw life as an absurd error, argued against suicide.[11]

Nietzsche's conception of life-affirmation goes far beyond life-enhancement; it aims for a *global* affirmation of all life conditions, even those that run counter to one's interests (including, as we will see, Nietzsche's own philosophical interests). To sort all this out, we need to keep in mind the following distinctions: (1) that between life-enhancement and suicidal nihilism, and (2) that between life-affirmation and life-denial. Nietzsche can extol the value of life-denying perspectives because of their life-enhancing power.[12] But he can challenge these perspectives as falling short of life-affirmation.[13]

The Problem of Nihilism

Some further discussion of nihilism is in order now. There is some ambiguity (especially in the notebooks) as to whether Nietzsche is promoting or rejecting nihilism, defined as "the radical repudiation of value, meaning, and desirability" in life (*WP* 1.1). To clarify, I think we can say that Nietzsche welcomes nihilism as a denial of *traditional* constructs (i.e., the death of God), but only as a transition to revaluation, which would overcome the deep danger of nihilism.[14] Philosophies of "being" are diagnosed as moralistic masks of pessimism. Overcoming these philosophies requires an intermediary period of nihilism that amounts to a *denial* of "being," which is preparatory for the strength to reverse values and "deify becoming and the apparent world as the only world, and to call them good" (*WP* 585A).

As we have seen, nihilism is a consequence of the tradition's own self-deconstruction. Accordingly, Nietzsche declares that nihilism shows itself as the heretofore *concealed* essence of the tradition, an annulment of finite becoming stemming from weakness in the face of life. Yet in keeping with tradition, nihilism becomes its own kind of dogma, a peculiar form of certainty that simply reverses traditional doctrines while covertly retaining their confidence in achieving a fixed position. Nihilism is a "belief in unbelief" (*GS* 347). In a time of cultural upheaval and uncertainty, nihilism amounts to a preference for the certainty of nothingness over conditions of uncertainty. No matter how courageous it might appear, nihilism is still a sign of weakness and despair (*BGE* 10).

Nietzsche holds that traditional constructs are *implicit* forms of nihilism, because they seek to deny the life-world. But since this is the only world, for Nietzsche, the "positive" postures of the tradition are in fact creative ornaments for *nothingness* (*GM* III, 17, 25; *TI* 3, 6). The denial of traditional beliefs (without revaluation) is simply *explicit* nihilism, an honest confession. This is why Nietzsche admired Schopenhauer so much. His unflinching pessimism was the secret code for deciphering the motives of Western philosophy and religion.[15] Nihilism is more realistic and beneficial in dismantling the past; it rightly recognizes that we have no right to posit a divine, moral, or rational transcendence. But its conclusion is the "absolute untenability of existence" (*WP* 3). Accordingly, it turns out that traditional optimism was a disguised nihilism and that nihilism is simply a disenchanted or failed optimism. Schopenhauer's pessimism, for instance, must be explained as follows: the world *should* provide salvational meaning but *cannot* (without the "should," how could pessimistic life-denial follow?). For Nietzsche, nihilism admits radical becoming as the only reality but cannot endure it; without the categories of purpose, unity, truth, and being, the world now "looks valueless" (*WP* 12A). A nihilist is someone who believes that the world as it *ought* to be does not exist and that the world as it *is* ought not to be (*WP* 585A). Nihilism can be beneficial, but only as a transitional stage, the overcoming of tradition that permits a new advance (*WP* 7, 111–12). Devaluing the tradition is "no longer any reason for devaluing the universe" (*WP* 12B). There is an urgent need for new values, wherein the world can be seen as "far more valuable than we used to believe" (*WP* 32). What is required is a form of thinking that is liberated from both the tradition and its nihilistic core (whether implicit or explicit). Those capable of such thinking will accomplish a "redemption" of the life-world:

> a redemption from the curse that the hitherto reigning ideal has laid upon it. This man of the future, who will redeem us not only from the

hitherto reigning ideal but also that which was bound to grow out of it, the great nausea, the will to nothingness, nihilism; … this Anitchrist and antinihilist; this victor over God and nothingness—*he must come one day.* (*GM* II, 24)

Nietzsche's antidote to nihilism is spotlighted in his ideal of *amor fati*, which is surely an echo of Greek tragic fate, but which concentrates on the affirmation of all elements of existence:

My formula for greatness in a human being is *amor fati*: that one wants nothing to be different, not forward, not backward, not in all eternity. Not merely bear what is necessary, still less conceal it … but *love* it. (*EH* II, 10)

Nietzsche even calls *amor fati* his "innermost nature," in terms of not being hurt by what is *necessary* in life (*EH* III, CW, 4). The meaning of "necessity" in Nietzsche's thought is tricky, and we will engage it in due course. For now we can notice how *amor fati* and necessity point toward eternal recurrence as the precise and articulated antidote to nihilism and life-denying attitudes. Before moving to a treatment of eternal recurrence, two final discussions must be established because of their significant role in the course of my interpretation.

Nietzsche and Individuality

Contrary to many readings, it must be said that Nietzsche does not advance a philosophy of individualism. He does extol creative individuals, but in a selective manner not applicable to all human selves; and the creative individual cannot be called an autonomous, discrete, self-originating locus. We can begin the discussion by considering Nietzsche's sustained critique of liberalism, which was born out of Enlightenment paradigms. Throughout many of his writings, Nietzsche attacks liberal notions of egalitarianism, individualism, rationalism, optimism, emancipation, and human rights.[16]

There are a number of deep currents in Nietzsche's objections to liberalism, which mainly concern the central modernist categories of equality, freedom, subjectivity, and agency. In liberal theory, equality and freedom seem to have a comfortable association, but a socio-psychological doctrine of equality is ruinous for Nietzsche's peculiar version of freedom, which reflects the *disequilibrium* of a struggle against an opposing force, of a creative overcoming that achieves something in and through this strife.

How is freedom measured in individuals and peoples? According to the resistance which must be overcome, according to the exertion required, to remain on top. The highest type of free men should be sought where the highest resistance is constantly overcome. (*TI* 9, 38)

Liberalism conceives freedom politically as state-guaranteed liberty to pursue individual self-interest. Philosophical justifications for political freedom have flowed from a modernist picture of human nature: all human beings share a common general structure as individual subjects grounded in reflective consciousness; each individual has a definable nature, a unified order of needs and faculties that can be discovered by rational examination and actualized by powers of agency that purposive, regulatory reason gives to the subject. Any conflicts in the self can in principle be resolved by the individual's rational deliberation and orchestration, and so happiness is within the reach of people if not constrained by outside forces. With such a picture of human nature, all persons are *entitled* to freedom from social control. Another feature of the modernist paradigm subsequently informs the rhetoric of liberalism: the subject as a discrete, enduring "substance," the unified foundation for attributes and faculties, the site of identity, and the causal source of action.

Nietzsche rejects this modernist model of an individual, unified, substantive, autonomous, rationally ordered human nature. The self is not an enduring substance, not a unified subject that grounds attributes, that stands "behind" activities as a causal source (*BGE* 19–21). In Nietzsche's outlook, there is no substantive self behind or even distinct from performance: "There is no 'being' behind doing, effecting, becoming; 'the doer' is merely a fiction added to the deed—the deed is everything" (*GM* I, 13).

More than anything it is language that subsidizes these mistaken models of selfhood. Human experience and thinking are decentered processes, but the "grammatical habit" of using subjects and predicates, nouns and verbs, tricks us into assigning an "I" as the source of thinking (*BGE* 17). Human experience is much too fluid and complicated to be reducible to linguistic units (*BGE* 19), and the vaunted philosophical categories of "subject," "ego," and "consciousness" are nothing more than linguistic fictions that cover up the dynamics of experience and that in fact are created to protect us from the precariousness of an ungrounded process.

Nietzsche (before Freud, and borrowing from Schopenhauer) dismisses the centrality of consciousness and the long-standing assumption that the conscious mind defines our identity and represents our highest nature in its capacity to control instinctive drives. According to Nietzsche, consciousness is a very late development of the human organism and therefore it is not preeminently strong or effective (*GS* 11). If we consider ourselves as animals, we should be suspicious of the claim that consciousness is necessary for our operations.

> The problem of consciousness (more precisely, of becoming conscious of something) confronts us only when we begin to comprehend how we could dispense with it; and now physiology and the history of animals place us at the beginning of such comprehension … we could think, feel, will, and remember, and we could also "act" in every sense of that word, and yet none of all this would have to "enter our consciousness" (as one says metaphorically). The whole of life would be possible without, as it were, seeing itself in a mirror. For even now, for that matter, by far the

greatest portion of our life actually takes place without this mirror effect; and this is true even of our thinking, feeling, and willing life, however offensive this may sound to older philosophers. (*GS* 354)

I must note here that by "consciousness" Nietzsche does not mean simple "awareness" but rather self-consciousness, a reflective "mirror." Accordingly, nonconsciousness would not mean "unconsciousness" but simply non-reflective activity, since he includes *thinking* in what can operate without (self-) consciousness. In addition, consciousness is not the opposite of instinct, but rather a refined *expression* of instincts; even the reflective thinking of a philosopher "is secretly guided and forced into certain channels by his instincts" (*BGE* 3).

Since consciousness seems to arise in *internal* reflection, the emphasis on consciousness has been coordinated with atomic individualism, the idea that human beings are discrete individuals and that social relations are secondary to the self-relationship of consciousness. For Nietzsche, however, the notion of an atomic individual is an error (*TI* 9, 33; *BGE* 12). "Individuality" is not an eternal property, but a historical development; and even consciousness itself is a social and linguistic construction. Nietzsche's argument is that consciousness is a function of language, and in language understood as *communicative* practice, a *common* apprehension of signs goes all the way down.

> Today one feels responsible only for that which one wills and does, and one finds one's pride in oneself. All our teachers of law start from this sense of self and pleasure in the individual, as if this had always been the fount of law. But during the longest period of the human past nothing was more terrible than to feel that one stood by oneself. To be alone, to experience things by oneself, neither to obey nor to rule, to be an individual—that was not a pleasure but a punishment; one was sentenced "to individuality" (*verurteilt "zum Individuum"*). (*GS* 117)
>
> Consciousness is really only a net of communication (*Verbindungsnetz*) between human beings; it is only as such that it had to develop; a solitary human being who lived like a beast of prey would not have needed it. That our actions, thoughts, feelings, and movements enter our own consciousness—at least a part of them—that is the result of a "must" that for a terribly long time lorded it over man. As the most endangered animal, he *needed* help and protection, he needed his peers, he had to learn to express his distress and to make himself understood; and for all of this he needed "consciousness" first of all, he needed to "know" himself what distressed him, he needed to "know" how he felt, he needed to "know" what he thought. For, to say it once more: Man, like every living being, thinks continually without knowing it; the thinking that rises to *consciousness* is only the smallest part of all this—the most superficial and worst part—for only his conscious thinking

takes the form of words, which is to say signs of communication, and this
fact uncovers the origin of consciousness.

In brief, the development of language and the development of consciousness (*not* of reason but merely of the way reason enters consciousness) go hand in hand. Add to this that not only language serves as a
bridge between human beings but also a look, a pressure, a gesture. The
emergence of our sense impressions into our consciousness, the ability
to fix them and, as it were, exhibit them externally, increased propor-
tionately with the need to communicate them to *others* by means of
signs. The human being inventing signs is at the same time the human
being who becomes ever more keenly conscious of himself. It was only
as a social animal that man acquired self-consciousness. (*GS* 354)

If Nietzsche is right, then even *self*-consciousness, perceived as a kind of
internal representation or dialogue, is a function of social relations and the
commerce of common signs. Accordingly, even "self-knowledge" (a crucial
ingredient in traditional philosophical and political strategies) is in fact only a
function of the internalization of socio-linguistic signs that operate by fixing
experience into stable and common categories. What is truly "individual,"
then, is *not* indicated even in self-reflection, because the *instruments* of
reflection are constituted by the *omission* of what is unique in experience.

... given the best will in the world to understand ourselves as individu-
ally as possible, "to know ourselves," each of us will always succeed in
becoming conscious only of what is not individual but "average."
... Fundamentally, all our actions are altogether incomparably personal, unique, and infinitely individual; there is no doubt of that. But as
soon as we translate them into consciousness *they no longer seem to be.*
(*GS* 354)

This helps explain an otherwise perplexing pronouncement: "To become
what one is, presupposes that one not have the faintest notion *what* one is"
(*EH* II, 9).

For Nietzsche, "individualism" is disrupted by the fact that most of what
we recognize as human is a *social* phenomenon; at the same time, we can not
ultimately *reduce* "human nature" to conscious linguistic and conceptual
categories, even when such structures have been appropriated by individuals
in their own self-regard, because there is an element of experience that eludes
these structures. It is also important to recognize how the delimitation of
consciousness figures in Nietzsche's call for life-affirmation. In *The Will to
Power*, Nietzsche claims that the belief in conscious values, that is, values
intended by an originating self, is the source of the notion of God creating the
world according to a conscious plan (707). But (in view of the intractable
"problem of evil") such an extension of values to the heart of things would
make life a "monstrosity" and would surely justify pessimism. Liberating

ourselves from conscious values as the core of life allows us to escape from pessimism.

Finally, for Nietzsche the self is not an organized unity, but an arena for an irresolvable contest of differing drives, each seeking mastery (*BGE* 6, 36). There is no single subject, but rather a "multiplicity of subjects, whose interplay and struggle is the basis of our thought and our consciousness" (*WP* 490). Nietzsche's agonistic psychology does not suggest that the self is an utter chaos. He does allow for a shaping of the self, but this requires a difficult and demanding procedure of countercropping the drives so that a certain mastery can be achieved. This is one reason why Nietzsche thinks that the modernist promotion of universal freedom is careless.

> "Freedom which I do *not* mean." In times like these, abandonment to one's instincts is one calamity more. Our instincts contradict, disturb, destroy each other; I have already defined what is *modern* as physio-logical self-contradiction. Rationality in education would require that under iron pressure at least one of these instinct systems be paralyzed to permit another to gain in power, to become strong, to become master. Today the individual first has to be made possible by being pruned (*beschneidet*): possible here means *whole*. The reverse is what happens: the claim for independence, for free development, for *laisser aller* is pressed most hotly by the very people for whom no reins would be too strict. This is true in *politics*, this is true in art. But that is a system of decadence: our modern conception of "freedom" is one more proof of the degeneration of the instincts. (*TI* 9, 41)

Contrary to modernist optimism about the rational pursuit of happiness, Nietzsche sees the natural and social field of play as much more precarious and demanding. So according to Nietzsche (and this is missed in many inter-pretations) freedom and creative self-development are not for everyone: "Independence is for the very few; it is a privilege of the strong" (*BGE* 29). Simply being unconstrained is not an appropriate mark of freedom; being free should only serve the pursuit of great achievement, a pursuit that most people can not endure.

> You call yourself free? Your dominant thought I want to hear, and not that you have escaped from a yoke. Are you one of those who had the *right* to escape from a yoke? There are some who threw away their last value when they threw away their servitude. Free *from* what? As if that mattered to Zarathustra! But your eyes should tell me brightly: free *for* what? (*Z* I, 17)

Nietzsche does not regret that most people are bound by rules and are not free to cut their own path. The "exception" and the "rule" are *both* important for human culture, and neither one should be universalized. Although exceptional types further the species, we should not forget the importance of the rule in *preserving* the species (*GS* 55). The exception as such can never become the rule, can never be a model for all humanity (*GS* 76). Absent this provision, Nietzsche's promotion of "creative individuals" is easily misunderstood. The freedom from constraints is restricted to those who are capable of high cultural achievement. Nietzsche therefore believes that freedom is a privilege of rank and should not be generalized to all individuals: "My philosophy aims at an ordering of rank: not at an individualistic morality. The ideas of the herd should rule in the herd—but not reach out beyond it" (*WP* 287).

With respect to all these questions, I must engage Nietzsche's figure of the *souveraine Individuum*, the "sovereign individual" (*GM* II, 2). Virtually all commentators have assumed that the sovereign individual expresses in some way Nietzsche's ideal of a self-creating individual in contrast to the herd.[17] I have yet to be convinced, however, that any of this is accurate.[18] The sovereign individual (in its lone appearance in the context of the genealogy of morals) names, I think, the modern ideal of subjective autonomy, which Nietzsche *rejects*. The sovereign individual is the result of a long process of making people calculable, uniform, and morally responsible (*GM* II, 2). This process culminates in the power of *reason* to control the affects (*GM* II, 3). When the sovereign individual is called "supra-moral," the German term is *übersittlich*, which is more in line with the modernist notion of liberation from custom and tradition (*Sitte*), and therefore it is closer to the modern construction of rational morality (*Moralität*).[19] Later in the same passage, the sovereign individual is described as claiming power over fate, which surely does not square with Nietzsche's insistence on *amor fati*. "Autonomy" is something that Nietzsche traces to the inversion of master morality; freedom in this sense means "responsible," "accountable," and therefore "reformable"—all in the service of convincing the strong to "choose" a different kind of behavior (*GM* I, 13).[20]

The meaning of freedom in Nietzsche's thought is not at all clear, but it *is* clear that it does not reflect the modern ideal of "free will." At the same time, Nietzsche does not opt for a mechanistic determinism either.[21] In *Beyond Good and Evil*, Nietzsche rejects both free will and unfree will: the former because of his dismissal of atomic individualism, and the latter because of his voluntaristic alternative to mechanistic causality (21). Nietzsche's self-creating individual can not be associated with autonomy in the strict sense. Nietzsche's dictum, "Become what you are" (*GS* 270, 335), is ambiguous regarding the freedom-necessity scale (in effect it connects with the atmosphere of eternal recurrence, in the sense of willing to be what you have always been). It may be that the figure of the sovereign individual does foreshadow in some way Nietzsche's creator type, but my point here is that such a connection is quite problematic because of the meaning of "sovereignty," its textual association with morality, and Nietzsche's critique of modernist freedom and individualism. In chapter 7, I will return to the question of freedom in Nietzsche and argue for a kind of "middle voice" conception that is neither active nor passive in the strict sense. But for now it must be established that Nietzsche questions *any* sense of "sovereignty" or self-sufficiency in accounting for human action (in keeping with *amor fati*): "Nothing is self-sufficient, neither ourselves nor things" (*KSA* 12, 307); "we are not the work of ourselves" (*HAH* I, 588).

The Übermensch

At this transitional point we consider the sense and significance of Nietzsche's notorious *Übermensch*, which figures prominently in *Thus Spoke Zarathustra* (indeed this is the only text where it functions as a specific term). Kaufmann's translation of "overman" has displaced the completely inadequate "superman," which distorts the German and misleads readers in English. But even "overman" does not do full justice to this enigmatic term, and for that reason I think it is preferable to leave it untranslated. *Übermensch* should not be taken as a hyperextension of the master type or as the promise of a higher, progressive type of human being (an association that Nietzsche repudiates in (*EH* III, 1). I read *Übermensch* as a more anonymous, structural concept that prepares the possibility of life-affirmation and eternal recurrence. It should be noted that in the passage repudiating higher-type interpretations (*EH* III, 1), Nietzsche three times refers to *Übermensch* as a *word*; it *names*, not a human type, but a "type of highest achievement and success (*Wohlgeratenheit*)." When the figure is first announced (*Z* P, 3), it is connected with the "overcoming" (*überwinden*) of the human, and it is directly named *der Sinn der Erde*, "the meaning of the earth," not someone who affirms the meaning of the earth, but the meaning itself. In fact, Zarathustra says that human existence so far is "*unheimlich* and still without meaning." The *Übermensch* will "teach humans the meaning of their existence" (*Z* P, 7).

Übermensch calls us to remain "faithful to the earth" (*Z* P, 3). This of course fits with Nietzsche's naturalistic alternative to otherworldly doctrines, an alternative that mandates an affirmation of finite, earthly conditions. Such affirmation requires that we "get over" humanity (*Überwinden* can mean getting over something, like a cold), that we "recover" from the polar opposition of "human" and "world" that has fostered the self-serving constructs in the tradition, the attempts to rescue us from finitude.

> *Man*! What is the vanity of the vainest man compared with the vanity possessed by the most modest who, in the midst of nature and the world, feels himself as "Man"! (*WS* 304)

Nietzsche directly calls into question the dyadic human-world distinction (*GS* 346); and the various "crossing" motifs in *Zarathustra* (*über* can mean "across") suggest that *Übermensch* names a break with the past that will integrate humanity with the tragic character of natural earthly life. What distinguishes the *Übermensch* from previous examples of high achievement in history (masters, creators) is the full scope of its affirmation and the extent to which the rethinking of existence is measured by that affirmation (which is expressed in eternal recurrence).

Übermensch, therefore, is better rendered as a structural model for a new way of *experiencing* the world, rather than a new type of person or entity. It suggests what I call "world-experience," which indicates an extra-human-experience-of-meaning that is no longer "fixed" either in the human "subject" or in "objects" independent of human meanings; it is rather a fluid circulation of intersecting forces that undermines *any* locus of fixed identity, either in "us" or in "reality" (hence its tragic implications). Evidence for my suggestion of world-experience can be found in a notebook entry, which also touches on Nietzsche's critique of the individual: "*Stop feeling like such a fantastic ego! Learn to throw off, step by step, your alleged individuality! ...* Go beyond 'me' and 'you'! *Experience cosmically!*"(*KSA* 9, 443).

How can we characterize world-experience, especially since "characteriz-ing" it requires a reflective partition that the model undermines? I think a helpful analogy can be found in creative, artistic experience, which Nietzsche, as we have seen, insists should not be construed as grounded in the conscious self, but rather as a *process* that is wider and deeper than conscious intention and reflection (witness the ancient association of poetry with the Muses, and even modern artists who often speak of the creative process as having a life of its own, *in* which they find themselves immersed). For Nietzsche, creative activity is *übermenschlich* in being a *release* into creative powers that reach beyond normal conditions (conscious "experience" of evident "things"). In a notebook passage Nietzsche associates the *Übermensch* with an activity that exceeds ordinary human experience (again expressed in anonymous, imper-sonal terms). He speaks of a *countermovement* to the average man, a "luxuri-ous surplus (*Luxus-Überschusses*) of mankind," where a "stronger way (*Art*), a higher type (*Typus*) steps into the light, which possesses different conditions of origin and maintenance than the average man. My concept, my *parable* for this type is, as one knows, the word '*Übermensch*'" (*KSA* 12, 462).

Moreover, since for Nietzsche, all our understandings of the world origi-nate in the "abnormal" production of innovators, then the *übermenschlich* structure of creative world-experience is "closer" to the world's nature than is normal experience. Indeed, the world exceeds our customary delineations in being "a work of art that gives birth to itself" (*WP* 796). What follows from the *übermenschlich* structure of world-experience is Nietzsche's unsettling move to link it intrinsically with eternal recurrence.

4
Eternal Recurrence in Nietzsche's Texts

This chapter provides an analysis of Nietzsche's discussions of eternal recurrence, but it is important to keep preceding chapters in mind so that my argument in this book can be properly engaged. My aim is to make sense out of Nietzsche's serious interest in eternal recurrence as essential to his philosophical project. Without qualification Nietzsche calls himself "the teacher of eternal recurrence" (*TI* 10, 5). With life-affirmation as the central focus, eternal recurrence is called the "highest formula of affirmation that is at all attainable" (*EH* III, Z 1). Nietzsche directly associates eternal recurrence with two fundamental notions he claims to have reconciled: becoming and the value of existence (*WP* 1058), thus overcoming the traditional attempt to separate these ideas for the purpose of finding meaning only in "being."

Many have recognized and granted the essential connection between eternal recurrence and life-affirmation. But I want to go further in showing how eternal recurrence functioned in Nietzsche's overall philosophical enterprise. For Nietzsche, *all* philosophical and cultural questions turn on or stem from the problem of finding existential meaning in a finite world of becoming. Meaning questions are always prior to "objective explanations" (since one must first be *interested* in such accounts as valuable for giving intellectual bearings in a confusing world). Finding meaning is the primal task of life, and the tensional features of this task make it a form of will to power: "all meaning is will to power" (*WP* 590). Even when questions of meaning seem absent, it is a consequence of a concealed suppression of the interests that promote the absence. With Nietzsche's stipulation of the death of God, tragic finitude is now shown to be the "brute given," and all cultural issues will have to be traced back to this abyssal base. The question now is: *Can* meaning be found in tragic finitude? If it can, what could be its measure? I argue that, for Nietzsche, these questions can only be answered adequately in the light of eternal recurrence, which amounts to the only *positive* expression of meaning that is not susceptible to *flinching* from finite becoming. My point is that eternal recurrence is far more than simply a psychological or personal call for life-affirmation. Since the meaning question is at the heart of all cultural matters, the powerful concentrating effect that eternal recurrence has in forcing attention on the meaning of finitude presents an unavoidable test for *any* kind of intellectual project. Accordingly, I think that Nietzsche's challenge to tradition and his revaluation project would, in his eyes, *rise or fall* with eternal recurrence, because its significance is implicated at every level of human endeavor.

To set the stage for my analysis, I take up two important background questions: the problem of time and Nietzsche's critique of teleology.

The Redemption of Time

In this section I offer a very brief sketch of how time has been understood in Western thought.[1] I begin with the Greeks, for whom time was unending and therefore eternal, with no conception of an absolute beginning or end to time. We have already seen how the early Greeks saw existence as an agonistic movement of strife emerging out of a "negative" force. The tragic implications of time's course are dramatically expressed by Sophocles: "Strangely the long and countless drift of time brings all things forth from darkness into light, then covers them once more" (*Ajax* 645–47).[2] Early Greek philosophy can be seen as conceptualizing this tragic model as a continual construction/destruction of forms, which must always recede back to formlessness to perpetuate an ongoing flux. Anaximander associates time with a "fateful necessity" (*chreōn*), the ceaseless coming-to-be and passing-away of all things out of and back to an "indefinite nature" (*phusin apeiron*).[3] Heraclitus articulates a similar view with his concept of the *logos*, an ordered exchange between opposite conditions that never comes to rest in a fixed state. In this respect the course of time is an unending governance of world activity, which is why Heraclitus associates time with a "kingship."[4]

Later philosophers, as we have seen, moved away from the tragic character of early Greek culture, but the eternity of time was never displaced. Plato's *Timaeus* offers a definition of time as the "moving image of eternity" (37d–38c). Time is "eternal but moving according to number," while eternity itself "rests in unity." Here we have a distinction between *timeless eternity* and *eternal time*; the former is utterly outside time and movement, while the latter is movement without beginning or end. Plato's larger project in the *Timaeus* goes beyond a so-called physics to address the existential problem of living in a temporal (tragic) world. Temporal states, as "images" of eternal Forms, reveal that existence in time is a corrupt approximation of true reality (46b), which can prompt the soul to recall and anticipate its eternal (timeless) condition (69a, 90d).

Aristotle's analysis of time in the *Physics* departs from Plato's existential problematic and offers a more formal account in terms of a science of nature. Nature (*phusis*) is essentially identified with movement and change (200b12); and nature itself never comes to be, since Aristotle's god is not a creator but simply a timeless reference for intelligibility (*Physics* 8.6). So time is intrinsically related to motion, but it is not motion alone; it is the *measure* of motion with respect to before and after according to the governing concept of presence in the "now" (219b1–5). Aristotle constructs the (now) familiar model of time as a series of now-points: the present now, the future not-yet-now, and the past no-longer-now. Time is a measure of movement according to quantified now-points. Although Aristotle does not share Plato's existential hopes for deliverance from the temporal world, the intrinsic negativity of temporal movement has him agreeing with Plato's contention that reality must contain *some* locus of timeless eternity if we are to ever satisfy our interest in "grasping" reality by way of a stable reference (see *Metaphysics* 1139b15–25).

An interesting summation of the ancient view of time for our purposes can be found in the Stoics. The ancient world understood time in cyclic terms, at least compared with later views of time as a linear path between an absolute beginning and end. There are some references in Heraclitus, Empedocles, and Plato to the idea of cosmic periods, where world conditions wind down and reconfigure themselves in endless cycles of return. Some Stoic thinkers, following a rationalized model of the cosmos, gathered and concentrated the ancient predilection for cycles into a full-fledged theory of cosmic repetition that went beyond generalized notions of return to insist on the identical character of each cycle, down to every specific detail.[5] Such a recurrence scheme was based on a strict causal determinism and the notion of an immanent divine providence.

The Judeo-Christian worldview introduced something new: a linear/historical model of time based on a once-only creation of the world with an absolute beginning and end. The salvational scheme perfected in Christianity marks the direction of time between divine creation, the fall of humanity, and the immortal destiny of the soul according to God's judgment at the end of time. The Christian account of time amounts to the invention of "history" in the sense of a global conception of the singular importance of events in the world scripted by the irreversible and nonrepeatable course of time directed toward salvation. The ancient idea of eternal, cyclic time would dictate entrapment within a fallen world, and events in time would never intimate anything decisive beyond the endless succession of similar conditions. This is why the Christian view attaches infinite importance to the course of time and the specific tasks of each soul's life in time. Every soul is unique and valuable because each is meant for salvation and capable of achieving immortal perfection. The entry of God into time in the person of Christ dramatically captures the concrete sense of historical direction and promise at the heart of the Christian viewpoint; its linear scheme is driven by the unique historical value of events in time, a value (it must be added) marked by the directional anticipation of the *end* of time and history.

The Christian view of time is shaped philosophically by Augustine in Book 11 of the *Confessions*.[6] Following Aristotle, Augustine analyzes time as the measure of motion according to now-points; but he adds and stresses the psychological aspects of past, present, and future in terms of the soul's memory, attention, and anticipation. The soul's true nature is outside time, in God's eternal presence, a "now" that never "passes." The soul's "fall" into time stems from its prideful interest in the world and concealment of God's call away from the world. Following Plato, Augustine says that the soul possesses an "image" of God's eternal presence: the "now" that the soul uses to measure the passage of time (from a not-yet-now to a no-longer-now). Far from simply a philosophical analysis, Augustine's account is animated by the ultimately unsatisfying character of a fallen, temporal life, and by the possibility of breaking one's attachment to earthly life by the force of God's promise of deliverance. The linear structure of Augustine's model of time is directly described in Book 12 of *The City of God*, where he argues against the Greek model of eternal, cyclic repetition because it entails the return of the fall after the achievement of blessedness (ch. 13). In this same chapter he cites a scriptural passage describing the birth and death of Christ as a unique, unrepeatable event. Cyclic repetition would render the *effort* for salvation meaningless and absurd. Augustine defines religious truth as the "straight path" to salvation, as opposed to a "godless" circularity (ch. 20).[7]

Modern philosophy was launched as a departure from ancient and medieval thought in the light of the new mechanistic science of nature. Newtonian time, for instance, perfected the ancient idea of numerical measure by seeing time *exclusively* in terms of quantified measures of the movements of bodies in space, deployed to discern the mechanical relations of cause and effect. Human meanings or purposes would no longer function in accounts of nature (Aristotle had understood temporal movement as the purposeful direction toward a thing's completed state). Time relations are restricted to the necessary causal effects of the past on the present and the subsequent power of predicting future states on the basis of past patterns. Newtonian time is also absolute and uniform, independent of things in time (which guarantees the causal necessity discoverable in physics). The common approach to time in modern philosophy follows this scientific detachment from the existential *meaning* of time (and its tragic implications); it is confined to objective explanations concerning *how* things in nature move through successive states (not *why* they do in terms of larger purposes or meanings).[8]

Kant departs from Newtonian "realism" by restricting time to appearances grounded in the subject's a priori constructs. Science can still provide necessary causal knowledge of natural events, but only from the standpoint of the rational subject. Hegel recovers a temporal realism that also reaches back to Aristotle's teleology. Time, for Hegel, is not only an objectively measurable feature of nature; it is also the intrinsic aiming of Spirit toward the world-historical development of an integrated whole. Hegel returns to the existential meaning of time, yet he rejects an otherworldly escape from tragic temporality in favor of an immanent resolution: the negative force of time and becoming is *productive* of an emergent order *by way of* dialectical conflicts (struggles that lead to advanced conditions). For Hegel, time does not come to an end, but "history" does when the course of dialectical movements is consummated in an integrated world governed by reason and social justice. Time, therefore, is driven by an intrinsic spiritual force, which is eternal and unified, but which is utterly worldly in its purpose and manifestations.

Schopenhauer despised Hegel's optimistic teleology. For Schopenhauer, an analysis of time cannot be separated from the problem of meaning. Following Kant, scientific explanations only supply appearances, yet "reality" (the Will) for Schopenhauer cannot be associated with any worldly or otherworldly resolution of tragic finitude. The Will is eternal and unified, but only as a blind and aimless force. The "apparent" nature of time is the source of fictional dreams of purpose and salvation, which must be unmasked and renounced by philosophical wisdom.

To sum up for our purposes, after the Greeks time was primarily understood in linear and/or teleological terms, either in the sense of scientific analysis of causal relations or in aims toward completed states.[9] The Greek idea of temporal circularity was eclipsed. Yet the Greek introduction of a timeless eternity continued to play a role in Western intellectual movements, especially in the predilection for absolute, fixed warrants at the heart of knowledge. It is only in *early* Greek thought that we find the absence of an utterly time-surpassing eternity (one reason for Nietzsche's interest in that period).

The Critique of Teleology

Nietzsche opposes all forms of global teleology, where the linear course of time is directed toward a resolution of tragic negativity, either in terms of religious deliverance or worldly forms of progress. Any world-historical teleology—whether in social-political projects, utopian dreams, or even visions of scientific-technological advances over ignorance and subjection to nature—is, for Nietzsche, one of those "shadows" of God that can no longer be sustained after God's demise. The deconstruction of teleology can even be ascertained by considering the Christian worldview, where the ultimate *telos* or purpose of life can only be realized by overcoming the temporal world. The "end" or purpose of life can only be achieved by the *ending* of time, otherwise tragic forces or cyclic repetition will render such a goal impossible or futile. This is why early Christianity saw life in this world pessimistically, as having in itself no meaning (and why Nietzsche admired Schopenhauer's honest exposure of pessimism and his willingness to embrace it in the absence of transcendent purposes). The problem with worldly forms of teleology is that they have *converted* a transcendent *telos* into an immanent scheme of progress, forgetting that the conversion loses its directional reference in the face of radical becoming (see *WP* 339).

It would be a mistake, however, to think that Nietzsche rejects any form of purpose. Humanity cannot live without some sense of purpose and meaning in life (*GS* 1). Nietzsche endorses the creation of *local* forms of purpose while denying any *global* purpose in existence. The overall course of things is an unstructured chaos (*GS* 109) and is governed by chance (*Z* III, 4). But he defines strength of will as the capacity to *endure* a meaningless world "because one organizes a small portion of it oneself" (*WP* 585A). Due to the perspectival character of meaning, Nietzsche forcefully challenges any attribution of meaning to life itself as a whole: "the value of life cannot be estimated" (*TI* 2, 2). That this sentence should be read in a global sense is indicated in a contemporaneous note: "the total value (*Gesamtwert*) of the world cannot be evaluated" (*WP* 708).

The basic reason for Nietzsche's opposition to global or progressive teleology is that a purpose implies an end point that resolves becoming into a state of "being" (*WP* 708). How else could a directional line "toward" something be shaped without some "point" of arrival that does not admit further movement? For all its recognition of movement, teleological development amounts to a self-consuming movement, because an *achieved* purpose is no longer an "end" as an aim, but the *ending* of movement, the cessation or restriction of development. In this regard Nietzsche calls his antiteleological posture a primal affirmation of creative freedom: "The absolute necessity of a total liberation from ends (*Zwecken*): otherwise we should not be permitted to try to sacrifice ourselves and let ourselves go. Only the innocence of becoming (*die Unschuld des Werdens*) gives us the *greatest courage* and the *greatest freedom!*" (*WP* 787). The innocence of becoming is Nietzsche's alternative to all Western moralistic scripts that portray the life-world as a fallen or flawed condition, which would require reparation according to transcendent or historical forms of transformation.

In a more formal analysis (*WP* 708), Nietzsche claims that if the world aimed at a final state, it would have been reached; but since no final state has been achieved, none should be inferred. Becoming cannot be explained or justified in terms of something "other" than its immediate conditions. We cannot leap outside becoming and justify in linear terms the present according to the future or the past according to the present. The "self-justification" of becoming is what Nietzsche here calls *necessity*. We will consider this important term more fully in a later discussion, but for now it can be said that necessity, for Nietzsche, is not equivalent to causal or logical necessity, or the necessary teleological force of an intended beginning or an inevitable end. Such notions account for temporal movement in terms of something *other* than immediate conditions of temporal flux. Nietzschean necessity simply captures the idea of "no alternative," but *without* recourse to some fixed explanatory scheme that constructs necessity by bracketing temporal events as such. This is why Nietzsche can say in stark terms that "event and necessary event is a tautology" (*WP* 639). Necessity also figures in Nietzsche's approach to the meaning question and his call for affirmation, which entails the capacity to say Yes to the necessity of all events in themselves, that is, *only* in terms of how they emerge immediately in time, with no mandate for grounding them in causes, purposes, or fixed references.

Saying Yes, for Nietzsche, is a call to *live* affirmatively, not merely to *think* affirmatively. This is why Nietzsche will differ from certain other approaches that seem to be in his company. He recognizes that the Stoics advanced a cosmic model of eternal recurrence (*EH* III, BT 3), but the causal determinism operating in their accounts and their "cool" posture of accepting things by overcoming the passions are not amenable to Nietzsche (see *BGE* 9, 198). Nietzsche also had great admiration for Spinoza, especially because of his radical identification of God with nature and his dismissal of teleological thinking.[10] But Nietzsche finds Spinoza's *amor intellectus* too thin a form of affirmation, and he derides his geometrical method as the "hocus-pocus of mathematical form" (*BGE* 5).

Necessity for Nietzsche is bound with affirming all elements of existence, including those that exceed rational models of necessity. One must also affirm the conditions of tensional will to power, a dynamic negativity that cannot be reduced to fixed results or governing orders. Embracing becoming and destruction is essential for the creative openness that animates life and culture. Yet Nietzsche points to a dangerous ambiguity in the embrace of destruction. It can stem from two very different kinds of desire: it "can be an expression of an overflowing energy that is pregnant with a future (my term for this is, as is known, 'Dionysian'); but it can also be the hatred of the ill-constituted, disinherited, and underprivileged, who destroy, *must* destroy, because what exists, indeed all existence, all being, outrages and provokes them" (*GS* 370). Nietzsche does not espouse the second kind of *eliminative* destruction, but rather a creative, agonistic destruction that advances *over* something without annihilating it. Any purely destructive outcome violates a baseline agonistics because it aims for the *elimination* of conflict rather than a creative *perpetuation* of conflict in relation to existing counterforces.

In this same passage Nietzsche also cites an ambiguity in "eternalization" (which will bring us to eternal recurrence). Eternalization can be a sign of "love and gratitude" for life. The "eternal" in Nietzsche's eyes is more an evaluative than a conceptual term (timeless presence). It is prompted by *joy* over the self-presenting necessity of unmitigated worth: "all joy wants eternity" (*Z* III, 15, 3). But eternalization can also arise from an unhealthy *suffering* from life that finds solace in an eternal sphere beyond life in this world. Such solace is nothing more than a concealed pessimism, a yearning for nothingness. Nietzsche advances an antipessimistic ideal in line with the first form of eternalization: "the ideal of the most high-spirited, alive, and world-affirming human being who has not only come to terms and learned to get along with whatever was and is, but who wants to have *what was and is* repeated into all eternity" (*BGE* 56).

Textual Settings of Eternal Recurrence

Eternal recurrence expresses a radical affirmation of time and becoming: everything, all aspects of existence, are *worthy* of eternal repetition, in the same way. In this respect, *what* eternal recurrence represents is simple enough: there is infinite time and a finite number of events; and events, having run their course, will repeat themselves ad infinitum. But *why* Nietzsche advanced eternal recurrence and what it means for a world interpretation is the perplexing question that guides this investigation. Eternal recurrence must be seen in the light of Nietzsche's entire philosophical enterprise and his reaction to the tradition, the groundwork for which has been our purpose thus far. Understood in this light, we can see that Nietzsche's thinking, too often thought to be disconnected, possesses a rigorous (albeit unsystematic) unity, based in eternal recurrence.

My aim in what follows is to adopt an "affirmative" posture toward Nietzsche's writings on eternal recurrence, that is, to presume an acceptance of this notion on its own terms, *as* it functions in the texts, without trying to explain it (away) in terms of something outside the presentation. Of course, my approach does not presume to argue that Nietzsche gives us the truth about existence with eternal recurrence; it is simply an exegetical principle of charity that has rarely, if ever, been granted to Nietzsche on this matter. Virtually all interpreters of Nietzsche, friends and foes alike, find eternal recurrence problematic in one way or another. Nietzsche, however, stood by it decisively on its own terms. Coming to terms with eternal recurrence should be the first order of business in engaging Nietzsche philosophically, to understand why this notion was not problematic for *him*. To be precise, however, we will have to recognize that in advancing eternal recurrence decisively, Nietzsche anticipates, even celebrates its problematic *effects*, its unsettling force. In this respect, interpretive resistance to the direct terms of eternal recurrence would be perfectly in keeping with its intended force. Nietzsche scholars have rarely faced up to this aspect of engaging eternal recurrence philosophically. I am trying to face up to it.

To begin, I reiterate that the "eternal" for Nietzsche is more an evaluative than a conceptual term.[11] The "factual" sense of eternal recurrence is not the primary concern, despite the fact that Nietzsche experimented with "scientific justifications" for the idea. The repetition of the course of occurrences can neither be proven nor disproven (no "law" *within* the process can really determine whether the process itself will or will not repeat itself).[12] For Nietzsche, I think, the baseline sense of eternal recurrence is its desirability (or undesirability), its effect as a world interpretation that draws out one's overall response to the meaning of existence. But in demoting the factual sense of eternal recurrence, it is important to avoid the other extreme of assuming it to be some sort of cryptic metaphor that really has nothing to do with identical repetition; in other words, that Nietzsche did not intend eternal recurrence to be taken literally. To gather Nietzsche's serious interest in this most troublesome thought, I suggest that eternal recurrence be read literally, but not factually. This admittedly tenuous distinction is meant to show that eternal recurrence has significance *as written*, but that the task is not to determine whether or not it is objectively "true," but *how* it is apprehended in existential terms (which also suggests an alternative sense of "truth"). My case will hopefully become clearer as we proceed to examine the references to eternal recurrence in Nietzsche's writings.

We will engage the sequence of three textual presentations of eternal recurrence in *The Gay Science, Thus Spoke Zarathustra*, and notebook entries gathered in *The Will to Power*. *The Gay Science* expresses the "existential" version of eternal recurrence, in the sense of being a test for the affirmation of life in the wake of nihilistic threats to meaning that follow the death of God. *The Will to Power* offers the "cosmological" version, in the sense of a "factual" account of world events that would dictate repetition by way of intrinsic properties in natural forces, which can be discerned by scientific analysis. The treatment in *Thus Spoke Zarathustra*, I suggest, stands in between the existential and cosmological versions by presenting a "descriptive" account of eternal recurrence in terms of the temporal course of events, but thoroughly embedded in the existential foundation of the textual narrative, Zarathustra's task of affirming earthly life. I hope to show that this sequence of texts suggests a *literal* meaning of eternal recurrence, in between, and thereby modifying, the *existential* and *cosmological* versions. And yet, the existential version (the first published formulation) will always be the animating heart of all discussions of eternal recurrence in Nietzsche's texts.

The Gay Science

The first instance of the phrase "eternal recurrence" (*ewige Wiederkunft*) appears in section 285 of *The Gay Science*, the textual context of which is important for my analysis. Section 283 highlights an agonistic image, an "age that will carry heroism into the search for knowledge and that will *wage wars* for the sake of ideas and their consequences." The agonistic sense of "overcoming" is expressed, not in terms of sheer destruction, but rather creative productiveness that will make human beings *happier*. Nietzsche sums up the point in strong terms: "The secret for harvesting from existence the greatest fruitfulness and the greatest enjoyment is—to *live dangerously*." Then: "Send your ships into uncharted seas! Live at war with your peers and yourselves!" It should be noted that the image of embarking by ship into an infinite ocean (*GS* 124) directly precedes the madman passage announcing the death of God. Freedom from being bound to any "land" is the counterimage to the tradition's emphasis on fixed stability. What section 283 adds is that instability is understood in agonistic/productive terms. Then section 285 talks of willing "the eternal recurrence of war and peace." Section 288 discusses the value of elevated moods and the possibility of something heretofore unknown: "to be a human being with one elevated feeling—to be a single great mood incarnate."

Section 289 follows with the heading, "To the Ships!" and begins by citing the importance to all human beings of an overall "philosophical vindication" for their ways of living and thinking. Different types of people "should all have their philosophy," exceptional and unexceptional types alike.

I include all this as preparation because the contexts of open seas, agonistics, elevated moods, and plural philosophies of meaning are important for understanding the second textual appearance of eternal recurrence in the dramatic section 341:

> *The Greatest Weight.*[13] What if some day or night a demon were to sneak after you in your loneliness and say to you: "This life as you now live it and have lived it, you will have to live once more and innumerable times more; and there will be nothing new in it, but every pain and every joy and every thought and sigh and everything immeasurably small or great in your life must return to you, all in the same succession and sequence—even this spider and this moonlight between the trees, and even this moment and I myself. The eternal hourglass of existence is turned over and over, and you with it, a speck of dust."
>
> Would you not throw yourself down and gnash your teeth and curse the demon who spoke thus? Or did you once experience a tremendous moment when you would have answered him: "You are a god, and never have I heard anything more godly." If this thought were to gain possession of you, it would change you, as you are, or perhaps crush you. The question in each and every thing, "Do you want this again and innumerable times again?" would weigh upon your actions as the greatest weight. Or how well disposed would you have to become to yourself and to life to *desire nothing more* than this ultimate eternal confirmation and seal?

In this passage eternal recurrence is expressed in evaluative rather than factual terms. It is not presented as a "theory" but as a *call* to one's ability to affirm the world as a necessary self-repetition; and its personal address is evident in Nietzsche's use of the *du* form.[14] This thought will "change" or "crush"; it is not based in a reflective intellectual exercise. And it is clearly related to Nietzsche's ideal of *amor fati*, where one wants nothing different, not in all eternity (*EH* II, 10).

The existential version of eternal recurrence comes across as a measure for the capacity to affirm life. Nietzsche seems to take it as a powerful device for drawing out fundamental reactions to the question of meaning, in such a manner that it will *force* us to face the collapse of all traditional constructs by way of a concentrated restriction within life *as it is*. Later we will explore this effect in more philosophical terms, but an essential import of eternal recurrence is, I think, its effect as a test for life affirmation (or life denial). Even if it were only a "prospect" not susceptible to proof, eternal recurrence "can devastate and reconfigure us, not just feelings or specific expectations! What an effect the *prospect* of eternal damnation has had!" (*KSA* 9, 523).

In this respect, eternal recurrence is less an examination of the world and more an examination of *ourselves*, a "final exam," if you will, in our schooling on the meaning of life. And like any examination, grades of success and failure will be handed out. Nietzsche therefore deploys eternal recurrence as a selective principle (*WP* 1053, 1056, 1058). The affirmation exam will sort out those who can love life on its own terms from those who cannot (and who have been "cheating" in the past by masking their life-denial with "positive" projects that can no longer hold up).

Despite the fact that eternal recurrence is primarily an existential call and test, it should not be reduced to mere psychological states because the "subject matter" is *life*, the life-world in which we find ourselves. Eternal recurrence, I think, reflects Nietzsche's own appropriation of the Greek tragic worldview, which presented an affirmative response to a self-limiting world that ultimately consumes human interests. It is noteworthy that section 341 is directly preceded by a section headed "The Dying Socrates," where Nietzsche highlights his suspicion that Socratic philosophy saw life as a disease for which death is the cure (*GS* 340). And the succeeding section 342, which was the conclusion of the first edition of 1882, is headed "The Tragedy Begins," and it contains almost verbatim the first section of his next published work, *Thus Spoke Zarathustra*, which is the second and most important text animated by eternal recurrence.

The Setting of *Thus Spoke Zarathustra*

This text, as we have seen, begins with the figure of Zarathustra, who announces the task of being faithful (*treu*) to the meaning of the earth, which entails an *Übermenschlich*, and therefore tragic, worldview. Parts 1 and 2 articulate this task and diagnose the various traditional failures to live up to it. The text itself is an existential narrative, rather than a treatise, and the figure of Zarathustra is the central character in this drama portraying the *task* of affirmation. That is to say, Zarathustra is not some prophetic sage who from the standpoint of achieved wisdom simply proclaims a task that *we* must undergo; he himself must go through the task and experience the full range of its difficulties.

The first intimation of eternal recurrence in the light of this difficult task is found in the section "The Soothsayer" in Part 2. The soothsayer tells Zarathustra of a great sadness and exhaustion that befalls humanity, which I think expresses the nihilistic disposition in the wake of the death of God and the prospect of eternal recurrence. The best have grown weary of their works, and a doctrine appears announcing: "All is empty, all is the same, all has been!" Indeed, "we have become too weary even to die. We are still waking and living on—in tombs." The soothsayer's speech has a powerful effect on Zarathustra: it "touched his heart and changed him. He walked about sad and weary; and he became like those of whom the soothsayer had spoken." Zarathustra tells his disciples that this empty condition is inevitable (it "will come"), and he worries about succumbing to it. But he declares hopefully that his spirit "must not suffocate in this sadness."

After three days of grief and incapacity, Zarathustra falls into a deep sleep and awakens to tell his disciples of a dream he had, the meaning of which is unclear to him. He had turned his back on life and became a guardian of tombs at the castle of death. Coffins contained the forces of life that had been overcome by denial. Then, a powerful wind broke open a coffin, which spewed out a mocking laughter embodied in a thousand different forms. The force of the mockery terrified Zarathustra and caused him to cry in horror as he had never cried before.

His most beloved disciple then offers an interpretation of the dream, wherein the forces of laughter are Zarathustra himself and the Zarathustra in the dream represents his enemies, who are subjected to his deconstructive mockery. But Zarathustra shakes his head at the disciple, after suggesting a "plan to atone for bad dreams" and a good meal at which the soothsayer shall eat and drink at Zarathustra's side and be shown "a sea in which he can drown." I think it is clear that Zarathustra was dreaming of himself, not his enemies, and that he is going through the first of the necessary challenges forced by eternal recurrence: that life not only can but apparently *will* seem meaningless in the face of the eternal repetition of identical events.

The very next section is called "On Redemption." Zarathustra declares the essential importance of a future vision that can open beyond the actualities of the present and the past. Zarathustra sees himself as a bridge to a future, a vision that can "compose (*dichten*) and bring together into One what is fragment and riddle and dreadful accident. And how could I bear to be a man if man were not also a creator and guesser of riddles and redeemer of accidents?" He then defines redemption (*Erlösung*) as the task "to redeem everything in the past and to recreate (*umschaffen*) all 'it was' into a 'thus I willed it.'" Will is a creative liberator and bringer of joy, but thus far it has been constrained by a "most secret melancholy," an anger toward the past because it cannot be undone. Unable to will backwards, the will is faced with irreversible events that stand fixed as the concrete contents of life. Suffering from this incapacity to undo or revise life conditions, the will takes revenge on temporal life.[15] Revenge is defined as "the will's ill will against time and its 'it was.'" The spirit of revenge "has so far been the subject of man's best reflection." The tradition has taken vengeance on life and has even seen existence as a form of punishment. The passing of things is understood as *deserved* owing to a primal flaw in life, and redemption is sought beyond a corrupt world of flux. Zarathustra reminds his followers that he has taught them to renounce such pseudo-redemptive "fables of madness." True redemption would have to overcome the spirit of revenge:

I led you away from these fables when I taught you, "the will is a creator." All "it was" is a fragment, a riddle, a dreadful accident—until the creative will says to it, "But thus I willed it." Until the creative will says to it, "But thus I willed it; thus shall I will it."

Zarathustra then associates this redemptive will with will to power, but he indicates that such a self-redemptive will and bringer of joy has yet to overcome the spirit of revenge. Zarathustra asks if such overcoming is possible, if the will, in effect, can learn to will backwards.

The textual references so far point to a crucial element in Zarathustra's engagement with the task of affirmation. The possibility of redemption clearly expresses his hope that he can overcome his experience of the soothsayer's nihilism. But why should Zarathustra, the great proponent of earthly life, have been susceptible to nihilism? Not simply because eternal recurrence triggers a bout with the meaninglessness of existence in general terms. Any affirmation of life would have to confront the *specific* contents of one's own particular life, a specific set of irreversible past events, which would spawn one's *own* wrath at not being able to undo them. The redemptive possibility of actively willing *every* "it was" just *as* it was can only be truly tested by facing one's own specific repulsions that would have to be actively willed. Zarathustra's own despair at the prospect of eternal recurrence would have to be understood in terms of his specific revulsion. And what is it that Zarathustra reviles? The very spirit of vengeful revulsion that has marked past accounts of life! Zarathustra denies the life-deniers and wants them to be overcome. But if redemption from revenge requires willing *every* "it was" as "thus I willed it," then Zarathustra must confront the paradoxical task of affirming life-denial, of willing the eternal return of the life-negating forces he most despises.

The task of affirmation, therefore, is confronted with a fundamental challenge sparked by eternal recurrence, a challenge with both a general and specific character: the looming *meaninglessness* of life prompted by the radical *inclusiveness* of eternal recurrence. Inclusiveness forces one's attention on specific regret or disdain one has about how life has unfolded, and the eternal repetition of these life conditions spawns the disposition of meaninglessness about life in general. The overall force of eternal recurrence mandates the threat of meaninglessness in the following way: the only way to affirm life as measured by eternal recurrence is to confront the necessity of elements that run *counter* to specific meanings that animate one's life. Life affirmation, then, would require the necessary confluence of "meaning" and "unmeaning," and only by force of specific conflicts in this confluence. Zarathustra himself must confront this apparent paradox in a most dramatic way: his impulse to affirm earthly life must include the affirmation of life-*denying* outlooks. We will see how the text confirms this scenario in Zarathustra's experience. The overall message fleshed out in this narrative is a perplexing answer to the question of meaning in life. How is it that anything in life can be meaningful and therefore life-sustaining in some sense? Only by way of a necessary correlation with what *threatens* that meaning. Zarathustra too must encounter this paradox with respect to beliefs that run counter to his life-affirming ideal.

The Vision and the Riddle

The second section of Part 3 is called "On the Vision (*Gesicht*) and the Riddle." It begins with Zarathustra on a ship manned by the kind of danger-seekers he so admires. After lauding their preference for *guessing* riddles over transparent deductions, he tells them of a puzzling vision he experienced (not a dream). He had gone through a terrible gloom, incarnated by a dwarf perched on his body, the "spirit of gravity (*Schwere*)," a word connotating heaviness, difficulty, and melancholy. The creature mocks Zarathustra with the dictum that every stone cast high must fall: "Sentenced to yourself …, far indeed have you thrown the stone, but it will fall back on yourself." To fend off this oppressive force of gravity, Zarathustra summons his courage, which has so far won over every setback. Human courage is said to exceed that of all other animals in its capacity to "overcome every pain and sorrow (*Schmerz*)," and especially because "human pain is the deepest pain." Humans are distinctive in confronting *abysses*, because of their awareness of suffering and death at the heart of life. But courage can overcome a "dizziness at the edge of abysses" that brings on pity and gloom. Courage "is the best slayer—courage which attacks: which slays even death, for it says, 'Was *that* life? Well, then! Once more!'" With that Zarathustra proclaims his power over the spirit of gravity because of an "abyssmal thought" marking his divergence from life-denying gloom. Immediately Zarathustra and the dwarf come upon a gateway (which stands for this abyssmal thought).

Zarathustra directs the dwarf to look at the gateway. It has "two faces (*Gesichter*)," a Januslike *vision* in two directions, a present focal point on two paths that stretch eternally into the past and the future. Zarathustra declares that the two paths "contradict each other" at this bidirectional gateway. On the gateway is written its name: Moment (*Augenblick*). Zarathustra asks the dwarf if he believes that the two paths contradict each other eternally. The dwarf replies: "All that is straight lies. All truth is crooked; time itself is a circle." Zarathustra angrily chides the dwarf: "Do not make things too easy for yourself!" Zarathustra then proceeds to offer a descriptive account of eternal recurrence implied by the "contradictory" locus of the moment:

> Behold this moment! From this gateway, Moment, a long eternal lane leads *backward*: behind us lies an eternity. Must not whatever *can* walk have walked on this lane before? Must not whatever *can* happen have happened, have been done, have passed by before? And if everything has been there before—what do you think, dwarf, of this moment? Must not this gateway too have been there before? And are not all things knotted together so firmly that this moment draws after it *all* that is to come?

Therefore—itself too? For whatever *can* walk—in this long lane out *there* too, it *must* walk once more.

And this slow spider, which crawls in the moonlight, and this moonlight itself, and I and you in the gateway, whispering together, whispering of eternal things—must not all of us have been there before? And return and walk in that other lane, out there, before us, in this long dreadful lane—must we not eternally return?

In speaking thus, Zarathustra's words become softer and softer, because of being "afraid of my own thoughts and the thoughts behind my thoughts."

Why is Circularity too Easy?

Before going on with the text, I want to explore an important question: Why does Zarathustra balk at the dwarf's proposal that time is a circle, especially since Nietzsche does associate eternal recurrence with a circular sense of time (*Z* III, 13, 1; *EH* III, BT 3)?[16] I want to suggest two reasons, both having to do with the limitations of a *formal* scheme of circularity, limitations that unfold in comparison with a linear model of time and in relation to the existential basis of eternal recurrence. First it is important to establish that a straightforward sense of eternal repetition is the only way to comprehend Zarathustra's claim that the moment *is* a "contradictory" present locus between the past and the future. The eternal paths of the future and past can only "offend each other face to face" if the present is eternally repeated ("Must not this gateway too have been there before?"), necessarily following from what has been and "drawing after it all that is to come." In this way, at any present point, its future is *also* its past and its past is *also* its future, because with endless identical repetition, what "will be" will "lead to" and therefore "precede" the present, and what "has been" awaits and therefore "succeeds" the present. If the moment were interpreted apart from identical repetition—as simply a focal reference for the passing character of time or a looser sense of repetition (e.g., the present as a reciprocal gathering of the future and past)—then the language of the text, which clearly advances the moment as a *contradictory* interface of the paths, would make no sense. I presume a certain straightforward sense of eternal repetition for textual and interpretive reasons, as we will see. But I add that the contradictory implications in the text do not suggest some logical deficiency that must be solved or overcome, something which has spawned a host of critical discussions of eternal recurrence.[17] The gateway image "contradicts" in a *productive* way previous rational and existential models of time that have been complicit with nihilism. Life affirmation will "resolve" the contradiction by *embracing* the unsettling effects of its "counter-speaking." More on this in due course.

For now, I want to suggest why Nietzsche chose a model of "pathways" stretching on indefinitely without including a circular arc; indeed, the figure of a circle is rebuked. Recall that the linear-teleological concept of time in Christianity was predicated on the eternal and infinite *value* of moments in time, albeit in terms of their position on a line of movement that will overcome time and *preserve* the human soul by delivering it from temporal finitude. Did Nietzsche want to borrow something from this linear model of time, namely the eternal value of moments in time? If so, the value of moments would no longer be conceived as an irreversible transition to something extra-temporal. The value of moments, as eternally repeated, would now be registered in their *concrete finitude*, in *just the way* that they manifest themselves. Consider this notebook entry:

> A certain emperor [Marcus Aurelius] always bore in mind the transitoriness of all things so as not to take them *too seriously* and to remain calm among them. To me, on the contrary, everything seems far too valuable to be so fleeting: I seek an eternity for everything: should one pour the most precious salves and wines into the sea?—My consolation is that everything that has been is eternal: the sea will cast it up again. (*WP* 1065)

Here again eternalizing is linked to valuing, and seeking "an eternity for *everything*" includes temporal events *as such*, which entails the eternal value of all their concrete and tensional features. Such affirmation is markedly different from aiming to overcome termporal flux or disengaging from it (not taking it too seriously) in order to gain calm over its effects.

What is "too easy" in the model of circular time may refer to previous motifs of recurrence that either generalized beyond event-specific repetition or, like the Stoics, deduced identical repetition from a presumption of rational necessity and cosmic providence. Such recurrence schemes completely bypass the existential element that is so central for Nietzsche: the *value* of temporal events *as they are*. Again, is Nietzsche deploying a certain feature of the Christian view (the eternal value of events) completely beyond its own agenda, in order to inject a value-specificity into previous recurrence models that missed or recoiled from the concrete affirmation of life exactly as lived?

I am not denying that an image of circularity functions productively in Nietzsche's texts; the idea of repetition certainly prompts it and repetition *is* essential to the sense of eternal recurrence. I am simply suggesting that a discrete, formal conception of time is not the bottom line for Nietzsche. The gateway image can be said to "mix" the implications of linear and cyclical time. Moreover, "deciding" between a linear and a cyclical course of time—indeed the very assumption that some kind of objective, conceptual "model" of time must be implicated in the account of eternal recurrence—seems to me *unnecessary* in coming to terms with Nietzsche's thinking on this matter, at least with respect to the published accounts. We are simply told of a finite set of possible events repeating itself in an infinite procession of becoming.

Even more, in confronting eternal recurrence, it turns out that the very technique of picturing time as a circle *itself* creates the puzzles that have preoccupied many commentators, but that Nietzsche for some reason did not entertain. For instance, repeated cycles are pictured graphically as succeeding circles, one after (next to) the other. Then questions are raised governed by the principle of "identity of indiscernibles."[18] Two "identical" events pictured apart graphically encourages the charge that genuine identity is lacking here (*e* in cycle *n* compared to *e* in cycle *n+1*). Or if we settle for simply one circle to capture eternal recurrence, puzzles arise about "points" on the circle in relation to each other: a future point both is and is not identical with a past point; when the "next" cyclic set of events unfolds, "where" can we locate the point at which one set "ends" and another "begins"? The difficulty with this approach is twofold: (1) Nietzsche did not exhibit a concern with such problems (he certainly could have); (2) the mental picture of the totality of events encouraged by a graphic placement before our gaze violates a central tenet of Nietzsche's immanent naturalism: there can be *no* "extra-cyclic" vantage point from which to grasp the whole in some way, no "God's eye" standpoint that could discern comparative relationships "between" finite sets in one way or another.[19] If there were a graphic representation that would least violate a Nietzschean immanence, one might imagine (impossibly) being *within* an infinitely stretching concentric "tube" (or maybe a mobiuslike "slinky").

This brings us to the second reason why Zarathustra may have chastised the dwarf's proffer of the circle as "too easy." Picturing time as a circle completely bypasses (or suppresses) the profound existential task at the heart of eternal recurrence.[20] The gateway passage harks back to (repeats) section 341 of *The Gay Science* in designating "this spider" and "this moonlight" as returning, including "this moment" (*dieser Augenblick*) of encountering the prospect of eternal recurrence itself. Section 341 also speaks of a "tremendous moment" where one might greet the demon's offer as a divine blessing. What the gateway passage adds to this "momentous" encounter is the image of *walking* on the path and through the gateway, which points to a concrete, embodied *movement* entailed by eternal recurrence. The spatial image of a circle cannot capture the moment as something seen (*Gesicht*), something *experienced*, rather than something merely conjured up mentally.

In addition, the experience of the gateway moment, as we have seen, brings with it the force of an abyss, since every moment is caught up in an eternal stretching that (1) exceeds the moment's form because of its necessary placement within a chain of temporal movements, and (2) compresses attention on the moment *as lived* because of repetition, with no alternative hopes for resolving tragic finitude. Eternal recurrence cannot be engaged without confronting an existential abyss that shakes us to the core because it denies us any escape from concrete temporal finitude. Zarathustra's "moment of vision" forbids any stabilization or reformation of the momentary and tragic character of factical life.

Creative Moments and Will to Power

It is helpful here to recall the tragic confluence of Apollonian and Dionysian forces in connection with an 1881 note (composed right after Nietzsche's first mention of eternal recurrence) that takes up an important sense of the "moment" (*KSA* 9, 50ff.). Nietzsche distinguishes between three degrees of "error" in relation to an eternal flux: "the crude error of the species, the subtler error of the individual, and the subtlest error of the creative moment (*Augenblick*)." This distinction articulates something implicit in *The Birth of Tragedy*, that "form" can have differing degrees of openness (or closure) to the Dionysian formlessness tearing at the edges of form. Species-form is the crudest error because it corrals differences into a common universal. The assertion of the individual is a "more refined error" that comes later, rebelling against commonality in favor of unique forms. But then the individual learns that it itself is constantly changing and that "in the smallest twinkling of the eye (*im kleinsten Augenblick*) it is something other than it is in the next [moment]." The creative moment, "the *infinitely small moment* is the higher reality and truth, a lightning image out of the eternal flow."

This passage is important for understanding Nietzsche on the question of formative powers in the midst of flux (and the creative moment as a "higher reality and truth" should warn us against reading Nietzsche's rhetoric of "error" in a one-dimensional manner). Moreover, the association with momentariness, the proximity of eternal recurrence, and the gradations of form together provide significant hermeneutical guidance in comprehending the gateway passage. *All* formings are "creative" in the sense of shaping a primal becoming that cannot be reduced to *any* form. This includes Nietzsche's own philosophical shapings in his texts. Primal becoming presents an "abyss" in two senses: (1) the sheer groundlessness (*Abgrund*) of the flux as such; and (2) The specter of meaninglessness haunting the existential encounter with tragic finitude. The "measuring" of formative powers turns on the extent to which they either conceal or reflect the abyssal limits of form. Eternal recurrence provides such a measure by bringing us "face to face" with this abyssal environment of meaning-creation.

Recalling Zarathustra's mention (in "On Redemption") of will to power in connection with creating and the "recreating" of "it was" into "thus I willed it," we can surmise the link between (1) will to power as a tensional productive force, and (2) the "creative moment" and its closer proximity to abyssal becoming. Especially relevant is Nietzsche's claim in the notebooks concerning "the absolute momentariness of the will to power" (*KSA* 11, 655). Will to power, as tensional becoming, "names" an essentially momentary structure that cannot be fixed or separated from competing moments. Will to power is therefore a nominal, linguistic "formation" that is essentially self-limiting, in that the metaphysical emphasis on stable "nouns" is deconstructed into a "verb-al" environment of movement and countermovement. As Nietzsche puts it, willing "is a unity only as a word" (*BGE* 19). At the same time, will to power is not simply a gesture toward instability but a radically productive concept, because the dream of an achieved actuality freed from negativity would spell the *end* of creative production by cancelling out creative *potential*, which is always open to "more" work and is thus inexhaustible. Temporal moments therefore embody what I would call a *momentous momentum*. The intrinsic links between power, potential, capacity, and openness should always be kept in mind in addressing will to power. Once again, we notice Nietzsche's forceful deconstructive critique of traditional projects aiming to still the flux of life or to transcend time. Historically, such projects are themselves creative (emergent) formations that nevertheless set out conditions that would obviate creative movement and thus undermine their own origins.

When Nietzsche charges the West with being nihilistic, he is referring to much more than simply psychological attitudes of life-denial. He is also working to defend, restore, and encourage cultural life. Time-transcending formations are structurally incoherent and they foster (if they do not stem from) a disinhibition of creative *work* that can further life. In this respect, Nietzsche's approach to time, in whatever conceptual form we might take it to be, is inseparable from the *productive* capacity of temporal movement.[21] It was typical of the tradition to conceive time as a degenerative force, as the undoing or destruction of formed states (see Aristotle, *Physics* 222b30). Nietzsche retrieves something evident in early Greek thinkers (Anaximander and Heraclitus) where time is also a generative force that brings forth things into being (and that therefore is not a result of creation or a mere format for created conditions). The internal correlation of temporal passing *and* emerging is the key to understanding Nietzsche's affirmation of time and becoming, which says Yes simultaneously to both passing-away and coming-to-be. Moreover, the productive side of temporality may provide clues for comprehending the strange conceptual picture of time in the gateway passage. Governed by the scheme of repetition, the future is also the past (the coming repetition of what has preceded the present). Time in this sense is generative, in that what lies ahead of the present (the future) will also *bring about* the present again (as past).

Among the many puzzles in the gateway passage, the most perplexing concerns how the identical repetition of the past can square with creativity. We will address this important question further in due course, but for now, a few remarks are in order. Zarathustra clearly identifies affirmation, willing, and creating. In "On Redemption," the notion of repetition is not put forth as a "description" of time relations, but as *re-creating* "it was" into "thus I willed it; thus shall I will it." Eternal recurrence, therefore, involves a creative reorientation toward temporal movement, rather than some presumed factual account. And yet, since *everything* in life is a creative product, for Nietzsche, we cannot assume that the creative element in eternal recurrence robs it of any "descriptive" significance (there is *no* free-standing reference that could render a formation as "merely" creative). In any case, would not the creative formation of identical repetition completely undermine the presumption of novelty and openness indigenous to creativity? Perhaps. But we must always keep in mind that Nietzsche refuses to examine anything in purely abstract terms. Creativity always involves *this* creative moment in relation to *these* surrounding forces. The concrete circumstances of life are the bottom line. And too many philosophical notions suppress or wish away concrete circumstances, precisely because their embedded, finite, and tragic elements are the primary "data" of experience and the primal challenge that usually prompts resentment and fugitive dreams. Although the gateway passage certainly seems paradoxical, for Nietzsche it may represent a productive paradox in the following way: "Re-creating" the past as repetitive and therefore proclaiming the "necessity" of past creative events may, for Nietzsche, indicate the *least* fugitive way of depicting creative moments. Eternal recurrence may embody the affirmation of creative moments *as* necessarily tensional and tragic in *the very way* they unfold, and thus not susceptible to reform, rectification, or even the seeming openness of an *abstract* conception of novelty. For Nietzsche, "necessity" seems to function in existential terms as an antidote to various poisonous dispositions that want life to be "otherwise" in some way.

We now return to the text of *Thus Spoke Zarathustra* and its powerful depiction of eternal recurrence as an abyssal existential task.

Who is the Shepherd?

In the gateway passage, Zarathustra continues his account of his vision to the sailors. Right after his fearful response to eternal recurrence, suddenly a howling dog alerts him to a young man in a terrible scenario. I quote this important passage in full:

> A young shepherd I saw, writhing, gagging, in spasms, his face distorted, and a heavy black snake hung out of his mouth. Had I ever seen so much nausea and pale dread on one face? He seemed to have been asleep when the snake crawled into his throat, and there bit itself fast. My hand tore at the snake and tore in vain; it did not tear the snake out of his throat. Then it cried out of me: "Bite! Bite its head off! Bite!" Thus it cried out of me—my dread, my hatred, my nausea, my pity, all that is good and wicked in me cried out of me with a single cry. You bold ones who surround me! You searchers and researchers, and whoever among you has embarked with cunning sails on unexplored seas. You who are glad of riddles! Guess me this riddle that I saw then, interpret me the vision of the loneliest. For it was a vision and a foreseeing. *What* did I see then in a parable? And *who* is it who must come one day? *Who* is the shepherd into whose throat the snake crawled thus? *Who* is the man into whose throat all that is heaviest and blackest will crawl thus?
>
> The shepherd, however, bit as my cry counseled him; he bit with a good bite. Far away he spewed the head of the snake—and he jumped

up. No longer shepherd, no longer human—one changed, radiant, *laughing*! Never yet on earth has a human being laughed as he laughed! O my brothers, I heard a laughter that was no human laughter; and now a thirst gnaws at me, a longing that never grows still. My longing for this laughter gnaws at me; oh, how do I bear to go on living! And how could I bear to die now!

I think it is clear from the ensuing text that the shepherd—the man gripped by a great nausea, who viscerally fights it off and, transformed, issues a radiant *Übermenschlich* laughter—symbolizes the condition and hopes of Zarathustra himself, a dramatic portrayal of the wrenching existential task at the heart of eternal recurrence.

In the next section ("On Involuntary Bliss"), Zarathustra recovers from his pain at the vision, but he realizes that his happiness is premature because it blocks the full test for a life-affirming creative will (the title of the section is "*Von der Seligkeit wider Willen*," more literally, "On the Bliss against the Will"). With the image of a stormy sea, Zarathustra talks of a "testing and knowledge" that requires "day and night watches," that can prepare a "companion" for Zarathustra, one who, interestingly, is associated with future writing: "a fellow creator and fellow celebrant of Zarathustra—one who writes my will on my tablets to contribute to the fuller perfection of all things."[22]

For the sake of this possibility, Zarathustra says: "I must complete myself; therefore I now evade my happiness and offer myself to all unhappiness, for my final testing and knowledge." He mentions pains hidden in tombs that now burst out alive. Then, with clear reference to the shepherd and the spirit of gravity, Zarathustra speaks of *his* particular abyss and abysmal thought:

> Thus everything called out to me in signs: "It is time!" But I did not hear, until at last my abyss stirred and my thought bit me. Alas, abysmal thought that is *my* thought, when shall I find the strength to hear you burrowing, without trembling anymore? My heart pounds to my very throat whenever I hear you burrowing. Even your silence wants to choke me, you who are so abysmally silent. As yet I have never dared to summon you; it was enough that I carried you with me. As yet I have not been strong enough for the final over-bearing, prankish bearing of the lion. Your gravity was always terrible enough for me; but one day I shall yet find the strength and the lion's voice to summon you. And once I have overcome myself that far, then I also want to overcome myself in what is still greater; and a victory shall seal my completion.

Still adrift in uncertain seas, looking "forward and backward" still with no end, Zarathustra declares: "The hour of my final struggle has not come to me—or is it coming just now?" Casting off his premature bliss, Zarathustra claims that he is "willing to suffer my deepest pain." His bliss "came at the wrong time."

Zarathustra's Abysmal Thought

After deriding the traditional doctrine of happiness and speaking of a "great love" mixed with "great contempt" (*grosse Verachtung*: *Z* III, 5), Zarathustra comes across his "ape" (*Z* III, 7), a fool who has appropriated Zarathustra's rhetoric. The fool beseeches Zarathustra not to enter a great city, berating its mediocrity, and in shrieking terms he implores Zarathustra to spit on the city and turn back, so as to preserve his greatness. But Zarathustra stops the fool's vitriolic speech, saying "I despise your despising (*Verachten*)." Such contempt by itself is nothing more than another form of revenge. "Out of love alone shall my despising and my warning bird fly up, not out of the swamp."

Later in the text (*Z* III, 12, 2–3), Zarathustra reiterates central elements in the narrative: the spirit of gravity, the "word" *Übermensch* as the sign for overcoming gravity, his creating (*Dichten*) and striving in the name of redemption, the re-creation of accident into necessity, of "it was" into "thus I willed it." Now he waits for his *own* redemption, but for this he must "go under" like the sun in order to prepare "new dawns."[23] At the close of this section of the text, Zarathustra calls out: "O will, the turning-around (*Wende*) of all distress (*Not*), you my *own* necessity (*Notwendigkeit*)! Save me for a great victory!"

The very next section is a crucial one, "The Convalescent." Resting in his cave with his animal companions, Zarathustra awakens and roars with a terrible voice: "Up abysmal thought, out of my depth! … For I want to hear you…. And once you are awake, you shall remain eternally awake for me…. I, Zarathustra, the advocate of life, the advocate of suffering, the advocate of the circle; I summon you my most abysmal thought!" (*Z* III, 13, 1). Overcome with nausea, Zarathustra crashes deadlike for seven days. After he recovers, his animals speak to him and encourage him to overcome his sorrow, because the world longs for him and awaits "like a garden" (*Z* III, 13, 2). Zarathustra is relieved by their chatter-talk (*schwätzen*) and wants to listen:

> It is so refreshing to hear you chattering; where there is chattering, there the world lies before me like a garden. How lovely it is that there are words and sounds! Are not words and sounds rainbows and bridges of shining appearance (*Schein-Brücken*) between things that are eternally apart? … Have not names and sounds been given to things that man might find things refreshing? Speaking is a beautiful prank (*Narretai*): with that man dances across all things. How lovely is all talking (*Reden*) and all the deception of sounds! With sounds our love dances on many-hued rainbows.

The animals then begin to speak and tell of all things dancing on a ring of eternal recurrence: "Everything goes, everything comes back; eternally rolls the wheel of being…. eternally the ring of being remains faithful to itself…. The center is everywhere. Bent is the path of eternity." Zarathustra, smiling at the animals, nevertheless chides them, with a clear reference to the shepherd scene:

> How well you know what had to be fulfilled in seven days, and how that monster crawled down my throat and suffocated me. But I bit off its head and spewed it out. And you, have you *already* made a lyre-song out of this? But now I lie here, still weary of this biting and spewing, still sick from my own redemption (emphasis added).

Then Zarathustra proceeds to articulate his most abysmal thought. Even the small man's accusations against life contain a voluptuous desire and delight (*Wollust*). He questions whether he can be man's accuser, because "only this have I learned so far, that man needs what is most evil in him for what is best in him." Zarathustra now reveals his torturous thought with a reference to the soothsayer's malaise. Even the greatest in man has been all too small. And if the eternal recurrence of the *same* is the path to life-affirmation, even the life-denying force of the small man must return.

> "Eternally recurs the man of whom you are weary, the small man"— thus yawned my sadness…. my sighing and questioning croaked and gagged and gnawed and wailed by day and night: "Alas, man recurs eternally! … the eternal recurrence of even the smallest—that was my disgust with all existence. Alas! Nausea! Nausea! Nausea!" (*Z* III, 13, 2).

The animals repeat their encouragement to Zarathustra, this time emphasizing that he must learn to sing, but not simply a convalescent's song, which is not healthy enough to speak (*reden*). Zarathustra should both speak and sing in a different voice. But Zarathustra once more chastises the animals, again with a smile, yet this time he demands their silence. His suffering and recovery are necessary if he is to sing again. The animals are too quick to overlook this correlation: "Must you *immediately* turn this too into a lyre-song?" (emphasis added).

Disobeying Zarathustra, the animals retort that he should not speak on in this way. He should make himself a new lyre, because "new lyres are needed for your new songs," so that "you may bear your great destiny, which has never yet been any man's destiny." The animals recognize the existential challenge of this destiny, but they stress its life-affirming outcome by force of the doctrine of eternal recurrence.

> For your animals know well, O Zarathustra, who you are and must become: behold: *you are the teacher of eternal recurrence*—that is your destiny! That you as first must teach this doctrine—how could this great destiny not be your greatest danger and sickness too?

The animals then proceed with a descriptive account of eternal recurrence: the identical cyclic return of a finite set of events, a "great year of becoming" that like an hourglass turns itself over and over again, with each and every moment in each cycle being identical (*gleich*). The animals beg Zarathustra not to die yet, and to have patience that his great weight (*Schwere*) can be overcome. They then represent to Zarathustra what his own words to himself at the moment of death would have to be in the light of eternal recurrence:

> "Now I die and vanish," you would say, "and all at once I am nothing. The soul is as mortal as the body. But the knot of causes in which I am entwined recurs and will create (*schaffen*) me again. I myself belong to the causes of eternal recurrence. I come again, … *not* to a new life or a better life or a simliar life: I come back eternally to this same and self-same life, in what is greatest and also in what is smallest, to teach again the eternal recurrence of all things, to speak again the word of the great noon of earth and man, to proclaim the *Übermensch* again to men. I spoke my word, I am broken by my word (*ich zerbriche an meinem Wort*): Thus my eternal lot wants it; as a proclaimer I perish! The hour has now come when he who goes under blesses himself. Thus *ends* Zarathustra's going under."

The animals wait for Zarathustra to say something, but he does not reply to them because he is lying still, eyes closed, in "conversation with his soul" (*Z* III, 13, 2).

Significant elements of this text must be emphasized before following Part 3 to its conclusion. Most important is the centrality of the existential encounter with meaninglessness at the core of eternal recurrence. In keeping with the demand for concrete encounters, it is Zarathustra's *own* challenge that takes center stage: the necessity of the return of the small man, the life condition most deplored by Zarathustra. The implication is that unless one confronts the eternal necessity of one's ownmost aversion, the true force of eternal recurrence as an affirmation test will have been evaded. It is also noteworthy that Zarathustra deliberately *invites* his abysmal thought to awaken and that it will *remain* awake eternally for him, which suggests its ineluctable and ongoing role in addressing eternal recurrence.

The descriptive account of eternal recurrence as a temporal model of cyclical repetition continues to function positively in the text. Zarathustra calls himself the advocate of the circle, and his affectionate chiding of the animals' portrayal of recurrence cannot mean a repudiation of the descriptive version, but rather a warning against its *premature* distance from the existential crisis. Interpreters who downplay the descriptive account because it is voiced by Zarathustra's animals are not on firm ground if they mean to distance Zarathustra (and Nietzsche) from a more literal depiction of eternal recurrence.[24]

Also significant is the rendering of language as a beautiful appearance that "bridges" divisions. In this respect language does not provide substantive truth, but it is indispensable as a *creative* reach that gathers together a host of breaches in temporal life for the purpose of meaning creation and life affirmation—most particularly, ruptures between the past, present, and future, and the binary division between humanity and the life-world.[25] In the text, Zarathustra is clearly working toward a new creative language, which will mix both song and speech; but he is not ready. Zarathustra's destiny is to be the teacher of eternal recurrence, but at this point he retreats into a conversation with his soul (and, as we will see, with life), in preparation for the climax of Part 3.

All Joy Wants Eternity

The next section of the text, "On the Great Longing," portrays Zarathustra's conversation with his soul, which amounts to a summation of Zarathustra's journey thus far. What has been learned includes the following: a round-dance (*Reigen*) that dances across temporal and spatial differences; the right to say Yes and No, described as an illumination within "storms of negation;" freedom over the distinction between "the created and uncreated;" the "loving contempt" that prepares renewal; a destiny given two names: the "turning-around of distress," and the "embracing circumference" (*Umfange der Umfänge*); new names and "multicolored playthings" (*bunte Spielwerke*); the future and past dwelling nearer together owing to the soul being "more loving, comprehensive, embracing, and encircling" (*liebender, umfangender, und umfänglicher*).

Zarathustra's soul still is mixed with smiles and tears, joy and lamentation; yet its creative potential persists, its "over-richness stretches out longing hands." To overcome its distress, the soul must *sing*: "even now your melancholy rests in the happiness of future songs." Zarathustra finally bids his soul to speak forth in song.

In the next section, "The Other Dancing Song," Zarathustra speaks to life, which is depicted as a serpentlike feminine creature who tempts Zarathustra, not to sin, but to embrace the life-world in all its force. Tellingly, Zarathustra confesses the ambivalence of his love for life: "I fear you close by, I love you far away" (*Z* III, 15, 1). Life replies to Zarathustra by echoing his own call at the beginning of the book to remain faithful (*treu*) to the earth: "O Zarathustra, you are not faithful enough to me. You do not love me nearly as much as you say" (*Z* III, 15, 2). Life knows that Zarathustra is thinking of leaving her soon. Admitting such, Zarathustra says that she also knows something else, which he whispers in her ear. Life replies: "You *know* that, O Zarathustra? No one knows that." Then Zarathustra and life weep together, and Zarathustra says that at this point "life was dearer to me than all my wisdom ever was."[26]

The last part of this section of the text simply depicts twelve bell strokes of a clock, each (save the last) followed by a terse proclamation, the most telling of which are that the world's woe is deep, but deeper still is joy; that woe declares "Pass away!" but joy wants eternity, "deep, deep eternity." The twelfth stroke, absent a proclamation, thus points to the concluding section of Part 3, "The Seven Seals or: The Yes and Amen Song."

Zarathustra's Proposal

Two elements of this section should be noted up front. First, the seals (*Siegel*) hark back to the end of section 341 of *The Gay Science*, where affirming eternal recurrence is called a "sealing" (*Besiegelung*) that "confirms" one's ultimate bond with life. Second, Zarathustra's relationship with life is portrayed in conjugal terms of lust, love, marriage, and procreation.

The seven seals pronounce Zarathustra's mood of affirmation in the face of eternal recurrence, amidst various echoes from his journey heretofore. He sings of his love for life, even for "churches and tombs of gods" (2). His existential nausea was in fact a pregnancy that can bear creative offspring (1). His seafarer's delight in open seas now lusts after eternal recurrence (5). He is now ready to sing (7). And each seal ends with the same refrain:

> O, how should I not lust after eternity and after the nuptial ring of rings, the ring of recurrence? Never yet have I found the woman from whom I wanted children, unless it be this woman whom I love: for I love you, O eternity. *For I love you, O eternity*!

Thus ends the first published version of *Thus Spoke Zarathustra*. We will take up the subsequently added fourth part of the text in a later discussion. But it should be noted here that the third part ends, not in a full consummation of Zarathustra's love for life, but in a state of deep desire for that finale, albeit in a condition of consummate readiness for completion. Also noteworthy in the context of desire is the metaphorical mix of the ring of recurrence and the wedding ring. If we think back to "The Convalescent," where words are described as beautiful bridges of appearance between things that are eternally apart (*geschieden*), the image of marriage captures well the creative conjugation marking Zarathustra's passionate, faithful union with the life-world. Indeed, Zarathustra's "marriage" to life would embody the *Übermenschlich* ideal voiced at the beginning of the story: the overcoming, crossing-over, and getting-over the human-world *separation* that has animated life-negating worldviews. Could one even say that, in historical context, Zarathustra's courtship of life yearns for a "remarriage," considering the tradition's nihilistic "divorce" from life?[27]

Before moving on from *Thus Spoke Zarathustra*, one notion drawn from Part 4 can help in understanding the linkages between joy, woe, affirmation, and eternal recurrence. The issue turns on the sense of necessity following from the radical intertwining of all events, which cannot be overcome by a transcendent deliverance or mastered by any immanent scheme of governance. Normally we affirm life in the light of its joys, and so the unavoidable forces of woe prompt us to look beyond life or to reform life in order to affirm meaning. But Nietzsche's immanent naturalism diagnoses such outlooks as *fugitive* dispositions that cannot authentically lay claim to "affirming" life. True life affirmation demands the recognition of intrinsic structural relations between joy and woe. Near the end of Part 4, Zarathustra retrives and embellishes the end of Part 3:

> Have you ever said Yes to a single joy? O my friends, then you said Yes to *all* woe as well. All things are entangled, entwined, enamored; if ever you wanted one occasion twice, if ever you said, "You please me, happiness! flash! moment!" Then you wanted *everything* back. Everything afresh, everything eternally, everything entangled, entwined, enamored—O, then you *loved* the world. Eternal ones, love it eternally and always; and to woe as well, you say: pass on but come back! *For all joy wants—eternity. (Z IV, 19, 10)*

Keeping in mind that this radical correlation of joy and woe cannot be thought in the abstract, the enjoyment of *any* specific moment cannot be separated from its specific relationship with all other moments, hence the need for identical repetition if *earthly* joy is to be fulfilled. In dramatic terms, eternal recurrence plays on our natural interest in certain moments and decrees forcefully that enjoying *this* moment draws with it all other countermoments as well; and conversely, that if we wish *any* of these other moments to be absent or even different, we would unravel and expunge the joy of *this* moment.

This completes the analysis of the existential/descriptive version of eternal recurrence. We now turn to the so-called cosmological version sketched in notes gathered in *The Will to Power*.

Fact and Value in *The Will to Power*

In his notebooks, Nietzsche explored possible connections between eternal recurrence and scientific theories of nature. Yet my contention is that Nietzsche did not, indeed could not, think that eternal recurrence might be "demonstrated" or derived from the sciences of mathematics and physics. At best, I believe he might have hoped that eternal recurrence could be consistent with science, but not deduced from it. Moreover, the notebook entries continue to express in many ways and in strong terms the question of existential meaning as the animating background of eternal recurrence.

The scope of eternal recurrence, for Nietzsche, is philosophically far-reaching because it is intended to replace metaphysics and religion (*WP* 462). It serves as a meta-conception that will concentrate attention comprehensively on the life-world as a whole, and replace all previous models that propose something beyond, ahead of, outside, above, beneath, or even alongside the concrete flux of life. In this respect, as we have seen, Nietzsche's preeminent target is teleological thinking. In section 55 of *The Will to Power*, Nietzsche echoes the soothsayer's nihilism as an inevitable consequence of the death of God. A theocentric worldview is only "one interpretation," but "because it was considered *the* interpretation it now seems as if there were no meaning in existence, as if everything was in vain." As in *Thus Spoke Zarathustra*, eternal recurrence is then implicated (initially) with the thought of nihilism: "Let us think this thought in its most terrible form: existence as it is, without meaning or aim, yet recurring inevitably without any finale in nothingness: *the eternal recurrence.*" But nihilism in this respect simply follows from the *defeat* of teleological prospects of a consummated purpose. It is in this context of nonteleological thinking that Nietzsche calls eternal recurrence "the most *scientific* of all possible hypotheses." This does not mean that eternal recurrence is exclusively a scientific hypothesis but that it magnifies the posture of modern science against attributing purposeful goals to nature.

Yet a nihilistic response to the absence of goals is not the only response. Nietzsche asks: "Can we remove the idea of a goal from the process and then affirm the process in spite of this?" The answer is Yes if we can affirm the necessity of every moment *as such.* Nietzsche mentions Spinoza as having affirmed such a necessity in place of teleology, but only in terms of a "logical necessity." Spinoza is "only a single case." What is missing is experiencing necessity "as good, valuable—with pleasure" (*WP* 55).

Eternal recurrence is simultaneously a worldview and an antinihilistic expression of meaning. The *process* of becoming endures (eternally), but nothing *in* the process endures except as a *repeated* temporal moment. Repetition indicates that becoming is not simply a "formal" concept but a "material" concept inseparable from its specific content.[28] Material repetition forces attention on the *value* of temporal moments, our attitude toward concrete temporal life. Recurrence in its non-nihilistic register affirms the eternal value (and meaning) of temporal moments as such. Eternalizing moments overcomes meaninglessness without positing any ultimate meaning beyond the moment; it attends directly to temporal events "as they are" (as they become), rather than to what could be, should be, or "is" behind momentary conditions.

As we have seen, affirming moments as such includes affirming their temporal, tensional, and fragile nature. Late period notebook entries reiterate Nietzsche's retrieval of Greek tragic experience in this regard, because it embraced all sides of existence, both the benign and the terrible (*WP* 1052). Eternal recurrence fulfills a "tragic truth" that is not strictly cognitive but evaluative, since it is predicated on a confrontation with meaninglessness, which nonetheless can be overcome by an existential courage, *amor fati*, and a Dionysian "worship" of life.

> Philosophy, as I have hitherto understood it and lived it, is a voluntary quest for even the most detested and notorious sides of existence.... I learned to view differently all that had hitherto philosophized: the *hidden* history of philosophy, the psychology of its great names, came to light for me. "How much truth can a spirit *endure*, how much truth does a spirit *dare*?"—this became for me the real measure of value. Error is *cowardice....* Such an experimental philosophy as I live anticipates

experimentally even the possibility of the most fundamental nihilism; but this does not mean that it must halt at a negation, a No, a will to negation. It wants rather to cross over to the opposite of this—to a Dionysian affirmation of the world as it is, without subtraction, exception, or selection—it wants the eternal cycle: the same things, the same logic and illogic of entanglements. The highest state a philosopher can attain: to stand in a Dionysian relationship to existence—my formula for this is *amor fati.*

It is part of this state to perceive not merely the necessity of those sides of existence hitherto denied, but their desirability; and not their desirability merely in relation to the sides hitherto affirmed (perhaps as their complement or precondition), but for their own sake, as the more powerful, more fruitful, *truer* sides of existence, in which its will finds clearer expression. (*WP* 1041)

Eternal recurrence is the antidote to nihilism without traditional metaphysics and religion (*WP* 417). Indeed, nihilism is simply the unveiling of the tradition's "hidden history," its fugitive "annulment" of earthly life in its search for meaning, its turning away from finite temporality. The tradition looked for meaning in "being," and always by "looking away" from immediate becoming. Nihilism simply assumes that traditional eyes are the only means of vision, the only way to look. The loss of those eyes suggests that there is no longer any way to look, that now we can see *nothing.* But the *vision* of the moment entailed by eternal recurrence is a reorientation of human eyes that no longer looks away, that looks directly *at* the temporal moment as such—an "eye-look" (*Augen-blick*) that *is* momentary (*augenblicklich*), that finds meaning directly in the momentous momentum of temporal life.

Nietzsche seems to have regarded eternal recurrence as the *only* way that life can have meaning on its own terms, since all other possibilities amount to *looking away* from the life-world and are thus inseparable from nihilism, whether overtly or covertly. Considering being and becoming, Nietzsche acknowledges that recurrence is a scheme that presents a certain shape to things rather than sheer becoming. But of course nothing in thought and culture could be sustained in sheer becoming. Will to power manifests a creative forming out of tensional conditions, and so "being" in *some* sense is the antidote to radical chaos. But eternal recurrence is a formation that does not oppose itself to tragic forces of becoming. Nietzsche writes: "To imprint (*aufprägen*) upon becoming the character of being—that is the supreme will to power…. That *everything recurs* is the closest approximation of a world of becoming to a world of being" (*WP* 617).[29]

An Argument by Default

Although Nietzsche does not explicitly say so, I think there is in his texts an implicit default argument for eternal recurrence with respect to how time, becoming, and meaning are to be construed. In other words, all other conceivable models fail the affirmation test in one way or another, leaving eternal recurrence as the only alternative.[30] Keeping in mind that, for Nietzsche, the concept of time cannot be separated from the existential meaning of temporal events, there seem to be six conceivable alternative models of time and meaning, all of which would be diagnosed by Nietzsche as fugitive evasions of the life-world. I name these alternative models *positivistic, salvational, teleological, cyclical, pessimistic,* and *novelistic.* With the exception of the last one, an extended treatment of these models is unnecessary, given what has been covered already in previous discussions.

The positivistic model of time can be dismissed because it conceives temporal movement in objective terms as the measurable relations between quantified "points" of past, present, and future "nows." Although Nietzsche appreciates the nonteleological element in scientific thinking, he dismisses its detachment from matters of existential meaning (*GS* 346). Indeed, objective models of time require their own constructions of "being" (the "now," and the cognitive permanence of the measuring principle itself) that look away from becoming. The perceived *value* of such an outlook stems from the sense of detachment and mastery over temporal events. What is dishonest here is the presumption of a value free, objective analysis. At least asceticism is honest in responding to temporal life as an existential problem. Scientific approaches to time ignore (suppress) the deep issues of meaning that are intrinsic to temporal finitude.

The salvational model of time is best illustrated in the Christian view, where the temporal world is a once and for all creation with an absolute beginning and end, consummated by a transformation into eternal perfection. Such a view obviously fails Nietzsche affirmation test and honestly admits as much (recall Augustine on cyclical time).

Teleological models of time modify the trajectory of the salvational view by staying within temporal movement. But time is still conceived as a direction toward completion that will overcome or resolve the temporal finitude and limitations of earlier or present conditions. Nietzsche diagnoses worldly forms of progress as no less moralistic and fugitive than salvational models. For teleological thinking, conditions of temporal becoming can only be meaningful or bearable in terms of something ahead of, other than, immediate experiences of life. As noted, teleological development amounts to a self-consuming movement because of its ideal of completed (finished) movement. Moreover, Nietzsche's repetition scheme would be no less offensive to teleological constructs, because it undermines their moralistic posture of perfecting or resolving deficient conditions.

Certain cyclical views of time seem to avoid the faults of salvational and teleological models by not picturing an end to temporal movement. Yet Nietzsche's proposal of identical cycles would draw out the existential issues that distinguish eternal recurrence from other cyclical views. Even the Stoic model of identical cycles, as we have seen, does not measure up to the existential test: Somewhat like positivistic approaches, repetition follows from a kind of rational necessity; and the posture of Stoic equanimity suggests an avoidance (suppression) of the existential *trauma* intrinsic to the repetition scheme (again, at least the salvational model does *not* evade the trauma).[31]

The pessimistic model of time is well expressed by Schopenhauer. Like the salvational view, pessimism engages the trauma of temporal finitude but rejects the idea of any positive transcendence or transformation. Time simply manifests itself (as appearance) and then ends in nothingness. One might simply shrug and say "So what?" but Schopenhauer (and Nietzsche) would deem this an evasion of the profound importance of the matter. For Schopenhauer, the tragic finitude of existence, surrounded by nothingness, should prompt one to turn against life as an absurd mistake, and to welcome extinction as the only conceivable release. We have seen that Nietzsche admired Schopenhauer's honesty (and even saw in him a clarification of the concealed life-denying impulses in Western thought). So of course Schopenhauer would (willingly) fail Nietzsche's affirmation test. On this score it is interesting to note Schopenhauer's admission of the necessary correlation of joy and woe, and his specific rejection of something like eternal recurrence. A person's will to live naturally embraces the enjoyments of life, but he "does not know that, by this very act of his will, he seizes and hugs all the pains and miseries of life, at the sight of which he shudders."[32] But the correlation of joy and woe, for Schopenhauer, mandates pessimism (and so, from Nietzsche's perspective, this is not really a two-way correlation but a one-way preference for joys that *cannot be sustained*). Schopenhauer, anticipating the prospect of recurrence as a dispositional test, answers clearly: "at the end of his life, no man, if he be sincere and at the same time in possession of his faculties, will ever wish to go through it again. Rather than this, he will much prefer to choose complete non-existence."[33] Although the finale in nothingness in pessimism might seem to be an acutely heroic acceptance of tragic limits, we must remember Nietzsche's distinction between pessimism and tragedy. A tragic disposition does not rest exclusively in Dionysian negation, but rather affirms Apollonian meaning formation in the midst of negation. For Nietzsche, resignation and a yearning for nothingness are opposite to, and a *denial* of, tragic wisdom (*WP* 1029).

The novelistic model is the most interesting case. With the pessimistic model, we can see why Nietzsche would reject a finale in nothingness, even though it might at first seem consistent with a tragic acceptance of destruction. But given Nietzsche's promotion of creativity, one would think that a repetition scheme would not be his preference. Why not a model of eternal novelty, where time neither begins nor ends and issues forth ever new conditions, never to be transcended, transformed, reformed, completed, or annihilated? Would not eternal novelty be the more Nietzschean choice over the seeming constriction of eternal repetition? It certainly would seem so, and yet the case of eternal novelty is specifically rejected by Nietzsche, which helps show why he was convinced of the unique significance of eternal recurrence with respect to the question of life affirmation. In *WP* 1062, Nietzsche reiterates his claim that if the world aimed at some final state of "being," it would have been reached. The immediate fact of becoming is presumed to refute the aim toward a final goal. Moreover:

> The old habit, however, of associating a goal with every event and a guiding, creative God with the world, is so powerful that it requires an effort for a thinker not to fall into thinking of the very aimlessness of the world as intended. This notion ... must occur to all those who would like to force on the world the ability for *eternal novelty*.... The world, even if it is no longer a god, is still supposed to be capable of the divine power of creation, the power of infinite transformations; ... it is supposed to possess not only the intention but the *means* of avoiding any repetition.

Nietzsche attributes such thinking to a residue of theological habits that took solace in God's infinite freedom from earthly constraints: "It is still the old way of thinking and desiring, a kind of longing to believe that *in some way* the world is after all like the old beloved, infinite, boundlessly creative God." The question of God's freedom in relation to the created world had always been a theological puzzle: Was the created world necessarily *grounded* in God's conception of it? If so, would this not be a restriction on God's freedom? If not, does this not render creation arbitrary? Nietzsche is directly pointing at this issue and the notion that, for God to be truly free, the divine will must precede the divine intellect.[34] Nietzsche seems to think that eternal novelty would be a naturalized modification of theological freedom from worldly conditions as they are.

In the light of life affirmation, it seems to me that eternal novelty is the most plausible alternative to eternal recurrence. Yet Nietzsche was convinced that it could not measure up. We will have more to say on this matter in upcoming discussions of freedom and creativity. For now I can say that Nietzsche's attempt to connect eternal novelty with old habits of intention seems to be a stretch. Even if there were some historical link, it would not necessarily follow that the idea of eternal novelty *must* be implicated with even a subliminal sense of intentionality. Nietzsche is in better form when simply tracing eternal novelty to a "desiring" and "longing" that the world be "boundlessly creative." Recalling that Nietzsche will never argue on strictly cognitive grounds, that values, interests, and needs are his first-order concerns, his question would not be "What are your reasons supporting eternal novelty?" but rather "Why is eternal novelty *important* to you? Why are you *interested* in such an idea?" The existential response to the prospect of repetition is the baseline issue. Eternal novelty, in Nietzsche's estimation, is still another form of *looking away* from concrete conditions of life. In rejecting repetition, the novelistic model betrays a dissatisfaction with life as it is, masked by its apparent celebration that the world *will* always be different (better?).

Such is the course of what I have called the default argument for eternal recurrence. Given the question of life affirmation, eternal recurrence comes forth as the only conceivable cosmic model that does not fall prey to a fugitive gaze *away* from life as lived. Moreover, it is important to recognize that the scheme of identical repetition is absolutely essential for the operation of this argument (especially evident in the case of eternal novelty). If eternal recurrence were in any way disengaged from a literal sense of repetition, the force of the default argument would be lost. This central role of repetition in Nietzsche's philosophical enterprise explains, I think, why he explored scientific frameworks in thinking about eternal recurrence: to bolster and complement (at the very least rhetorically) the deeper philosophical function of eternal repetition, a function always and primarily geared toward the existential question of meaning.

The Factual Case for Eternal Recurrence

In the context of critiquing eternal novelty, Nietzsche advances a conceptual point about force. The world is materially finite in the sense that an infinitely manifesting force (eternal novelty) would contradict the meaning of force. If force is to be effective *as* a gathered, concentrated power of finite relations, an infinite force would amount to a dispersal of its essential nature: "we forbid ourselves the concept of an infinite force as incompatible with the concept 'force.' Thus—the world also lacks the capacity for eternal novelty" (*WP* 1062).[35] So Nietzsche allows for a formal infinity of time and becoming but not a material infinity of forces. Although force is essentially temporal and mutable (*WP* 1064), its concrete manifestations cannot tail off into infinity. In fact, Nietzsche believes that "the law of the conservation of energy demands *eternal recurrence*" (*WP* 1063).

In this context Nietzsche provides what certainly sounds like a scientific argument for eternal recurrence:

> If the world may be thought of as a certain definite quantity of force and as a certain definite number of centers of force—and every other representation remains indefinite and therefore useless—it follows that, in the great dice game of existence, it must pass through a calculable number of combinations. In infinite time, every possible combination would at some time or another be realized; more: it would be realized an infinite number of times. And since between every combination and its next recurrence all other possible combinations would have to take place, and each of these combinations conditions the entire sequence of combinations in the same series, a circular movement of absolutely identical series is thus demonstrated: the world as a circular movement that has already repeated itself infinitely often and plays its game *in infinitum.* (*WP* 1066)

Right away, Nietzsche interjects that this account cannot be sufficiently rendered as a mechanistic conception, which he calls "an imperfect and merely provisional hypothesis." Yet surely it comes across as a kind of cosmological thesis stemming from the presumed character of natural forces. I am not going to pursue an examination of the scientific merits or demerits of Nietzsche's position on such topics. I say this for two reasons. First, my competence in this subject is limited, and excellent discussions are already available.[36] Second, I want to argue that a "scientific" account of eternal recurrence, even if it were to be successfully demonstrated, would not be the basis or proving ground for the philosophical issues at hand. Nevertheless, it is clear that Nietzsche was familiar with the science of his day, and that in one way or another he experimented with couching eternal recurrence in the light of that science. Although there are many interesting questions and problems associated with the so-called cosmological version, in the end I do not think that either positive or negative assessments of this version would be *decisive*. One point I do want to make can have a bearing on later discussions. The "extent" of the finite cycles is not intimated at all. Indeed, it seems to be an impossible thought; infinite becoming and time have no boundaries, and the "length" of a cycle could be so extensive as to be functionally worthless in aiming to "grasp" it. As Nietzsche puts it, the set of possible events is finite, but "incredibly large and practically unmeasurable" (*KSA* 9, 523). What is repeated can include so many novel conditions (within the cycle) and even all the slightest possible variations of past conditions (within the cycle) that repetition's supposed oppressive constraint on innovation might betray creative greed (All *that* isn't enough?)

In any case, we turn next to a discussion of how the different versions of eternal recurrence can be hermeneutically orchestrated according to a kind of "existential literalness."

5

Making Belief: Literal Repetition
and Its Existential Force

I want to argue that Nietzsche's commitment to eternal recurrence can best be explained by reading cyclic repetition literally but not factually. A literal account can be seen to cut across the existential, descriptive, and cosmological versions and to stand in between an existential and factual sense of eternal recurrence. The gist of my argument is as follows: the existential meaning of eternal recurrence is its baseline significance, and so a factual account could not be primary or decisive; yet, if recurrence were not taken literally in the way presented in the texts, its existential force would be lost because the power of identical repetition to draw out a response to the meaning question would be neutralized (or avoided) if recurrence were "really" not about reliving one's life, or were somehow symbolic of something *other* than repetition.

In advancing a distinction between literal and factual senses of eternal recurrence, I am pursuing an interpretive strategy that is not directly or formally expressed in Nietzsche's texts. Yet, in accordance with my principle of hermeneutical charity, I think I have found a way to make more sense out of Nietzsche's thinking on this matter; and there *are* elements in his writings that can reinforce such an approach. My book, as I have said, is primarily exegetical in nature. I believe that a literal reading of eternal recurrence is most consistent with the spirit and the letter of Nietzsche's texts. I suppose my question to readers is this: Why *not* read eternal recurrence literally? What would be lost by doing so and what would be gained by reading it in different ways?

At the same time, one can readily pose a question to me: How can I dare to press a sense of literalness on a thinker notorious for rejecting linguistic "accuracy" measured against the flux of experience? Moreover, in both his theory of language and his manner of writing, Nietzsche wants us to recognize that metaphorical tropes and like devices go all the way down in human language and thinking.[1] And what about Nietzsche's admission and celebration of the use of masks in profound thinking (*BGE* 40)? I concede that I may be on thin ice here (not literally), but I have nowhere else to go if my case in this book is to bear any fruit. My venture stems from the following three background assumptions: (1) There is a current tendency to conflate the "literal" and the "factual" in a way, however, that departs from primary and other possible senses of the literal. (2) A clear and substantive division between the literal and the metaphorical cannot be sustained. (3) Although Nietzsche insists on a masking element in philosophy, this does not mean that *everything* in a text is hiding something.[2] In reading Nietzsche on eternal recurrence, I am impressed by how simple and clear the idea is in its presentation (which is a different matter from why he advocated it or whether it has any truth). Moreover, I see no evidence in the texts that Nietzsche was anything other than sincere, straightforward, and committed to the idea of eternal recurrence *as written*.

Words, Facts, and Metaphors

Resistance to a literal reading of eternal recurrence stems not only from a preference for presumably subtler, more interesting (safer?) metaphorical senses; it also reflects epistemological concerns owing to descriptive, referential connotations in common usage: "literally true" can be equivalent to "factually accurate." But a look at the *Oxford English Dictionary (OED)* reveals a complex history of usage that opens up many questions about literal language. The primary meaning of "literal" pertains simply to alphabetic letters, and thus not to a differentiation from metaphor (since metaphors have letters). In this sense, a "literal mistake" would refer not to a descriptive error but a misprint. Other meanings grow out of and modify this primary sense: word for word transcription (e.g., quotation versus paraphrase); taking words in their natural or customary meaning; the primary sense of a word or the direct wording of a passage, as distinguished from metaphorical or suggestive meaning; a matter-of-fact, unimaginative disposition; accurate meaning or reference, free of metaphor, exaggeration, or error. We notice here a shift from "literal" in a *wordly* sense (cf. the German *wörtlich*) pertaining to written words as such, to a *descriptive* sense pertaining to how a text (or the world) is understood.

The tendency to conflate literal descriptions and factual accounts opens up another complex history of usage. The Latin *factum* originally referred to actions and deeds as opposed to words (the Greek *ergon* had the same sense; and consider the German *Tatbestand*). Then fact came to mean an actual event known through direct observation or reliable testimony, as opposed to conjecture, fiction, or misrecollection. For us, a fact mainly denotes the findings of scientific inquiry and its rigorous, controlled methods of testing observations governed by theoretical postulates and mathematical formulas.[3]

My point is that a historical look at language usage shows that current familiar meanings of the literal and the factual have arisen out of linguistic shifts and relations that exhibit anything but clear, direct references, and thus anything but "literal" or "factual" sources. The same holds true for the literal-metaphorical distinction. As Derrida has shown, the distinction between the metaphorical and the literal cannot be drawn in a nonmetaphorical manner.[4]

The distinction itself has a philosophical history within Greek thought, when new frameworks emerged for understanding natural speech and mythopoetic language, frameworks that generally presumed deficiencies in these prior modes of discourse.[5] The problem is that even "metaphor" is metaphorical; *metaphero* in Greek means "to carry over," and so the familiar sense of metaphor—as "combining" one sense with another owing to a similar, though nonequivalent likeness—is itself a metaphorical trope. As we have seen, the connotations of "literal" as univocal (noncombined) meaning and descriptive accuracy are themselves "carried over" from a reference to written letters. One can say then that the former extended senses are no longer "literally" literal (in the primary wordly sense). A similar metaphorical process can be located in the meaning of "factual" as carried-over from doing-versus-speaking. So the familiar connotation of the literal-factual dyad, which presumes a secured, unambiguous actuality (as-is), is itself an ambiguous extension of even more direct meanings (as-written, as-done). Consequently, it is hard to avoid the conclusion that indirect, nonliteral forces such as metaphor go all the way down in human language, thus undermining the presumed privilege bestowed on the literal-factual dyad. Indeed, in cases where metaphorical uses might be irreducible, and thus indispensable in expressing a meaning (e.g., the concept of "force" in physics), we could say that a metaphor can be "literally" true in terms of its linguistic necessity.[6]

It is well known that Nietzsche insists upon and celebrates a nonfoundational perspective on language. For Nietzsche, language by its very nature is a formative, creative shaping of the unstable flux of experience. Language cannot be understood as a representational description of nonlinguistic "facts" presumed to be independent of metaphorical, rhetorical, and imaginative forces in language (see *OTL*). Nietzsche's linguistic theory and his own textual practices presume and portray a radical undecidability between literal and figurative meanings in philosophical language.[7]

For my purposes, if the literal-factual dyad cannot be sustained as a baseline reference, the possibility opens up of a different sense of the literal that is not equivalent to, or suggestive of, factuality. I want to understand the literal in a functional and performative sense rather than a descriptive sense. I begin by calling the literal *as written* in place of the descriptive *as is*. But this is not enough. In addition to *what* a text presents, I need to include *how* language and texts are engaged and received. This brings us to certain historical questions and particular remarks in Nietzsche's writings that will help shape what I want to call *mimetic literality*.

Imitation and Identification

The story of the literal-factual dyad cannot be told apart from the complex history of orality and literacy in the Greek world. I will not pursue a detailed examination of this question, except to say that the emergence of philosophical reflection in ancient Greece was intrinsically connected to shifts from an oral mode of culture to one influenced by reading and writing.[8] Oral culture was shaped according to structures of poetic production and audience reception that in retrospect exhibit a nonreflective immediacy: poets were "inspired" vehicles for sacred transmissions (the Muses), and audiences were "enchanted" recipients of entralling poetic performances. The sheer graphics of writing permitted an isolation of texts from such performance milieus, and the fixity of written words permitted a host of reflective operations that greatly altered *how* the linguistic resources of Greek culture would be understood. One way to put this is as follows: both Plato and Aristotle employed visual terms (*eidos, theōria*) to depict intellectual insight (presumably not confined to visual perception). Was it that the sheer difference between "abstract" alphabetic graphics and the embodied immediacy of oral poetic performance opened up a new "look" shaping the now familiar "mind's eye"?[9]

I bring this up only to highlight the "literal" effect of graphic letters in crafting a reflective departure from an *oral* sense of "literalness" that has nothing to do with familiar connotations of rational truth, but rather the *immediate disclosive force* of poetic language in performance. As is well known, Plato critiqued poets and rhetors because they were "out of their minds" when performing their creative and oral functions. Their inspired condition overtook self-control and was incapable of reflective analysis of what they were saying and why they were saying it.[10] What is not always recognized is how this critique of poetic psychology figured in Plato's discussion of imitation (*mimēsis*) in the *Republic*. In addition to Plato's concerns about the content of traditional poetry (particularly its tragic worldview), he also targeted the form of oral performance and its effects on both performers and audiences. The "representational" sense of *mimēsis* (copying a natural object) was not Plato's primary concern (see 603bff.); rather, it was the psychological effects of mimetic identification, wherein performers and audiences would be captured by, and immersed in, oral presentations, thus losing reflective self-control and being enraptured by the "reality" of poetic speech and disclosure.[11] Particularly dangerous for Plato was the mimetic force of empathic identification with the suffering of tragic heroes.[12]

What is important for my analysis here is the notion of mimetic literality, that is to say, the immediate disclosive effects of language, whether oral or written, whether literal or metaphorical, whether factual or fictional. When we render epic or tragic poetry, for instance, simply as "literature," as fiction counterposed to actual reality, we miss the disclosive import and impact of poetry in opening up and sustaining the Greeks' sense of their world and existence. On a less grand level, mimetic literality can show how a metaphorical expression can be taken "literally," in the sense of being irreducible or immediately expressive without further analysis. Consider being told (or reading): "Your mother has passed away," or "Your book proposal is dead." Even technical slips that are fun to expose ("He literally exploded with anger") may in fact harbor a certain truth (the *word* "exploded" can simply *work* with/as immediate force).

Historically, mimetic literality in the context of Greek poetry was *working*, which is why Plato was preoccupied with challenging its cultural status (as opposed to simply venturing a theory of "aesthetics"). Mimetic literality can be called "make believe" in a positive sense, as making belief in the milieu of poetic performance and reception (*poiēsis* in general means to make or create). Poetic speech makes or produces a belief world through the immediate power of words. Mimetic literality can also be understood to operate in the familiar aesthetic phenomenon of "suspension of disbelief." The reception of "fictive truth" requires that we "forget" the fiction, that we conceal the artificial contrivance of, say, a theatrical production so that we can respond to it *as if* it were real; and we *do* so respond when we react emotionally or otherwise to characterizations that are not "really" happening (although actors can mimetically inhabit or become their roles).

There is, however, a certain loaded connotation in suspension of disbelief, wherein "real belief" is the guiding standard. Certainly Greek dramatic performances were understood in a fictive manner: *as* dramatic performances, the plays were not identical with their traditional sources (e.g., the story of Oedipus). But we should not think that mimetic "identification" in dramatic performances was nothing more than an aesthetic zone of experience. The civic and religious functions of tragedy must be kept in mind to comprehend its *world*-disclosive effects and central role in Greek self-understanding.[13] In the case of epic poetry, particularly its oral mode, suspension of disbelief is even more tenuous. The immersion of the poet and audience was more a departure from *everyday* belief in the direction of extraordinary, sacred disclosures that opened up the very meaning of the Greek world. So there is an element of mimetic identification that *produces* belief in a manner different from ordinary experience, reflective analysis, or the discovery of "facts." Art, then, would involve not simply making belief, but a making *special*.[14]

Nietzsche on Mimetic Psychology and Greek Drama

Nietzsche occasionally discusses what I am calling mimetic psychology, especially in his reflections on Greek art. An early essay, "Greek Music Drama," mentions the audience's sympathetic identification with the sufferings of tragic heroes (*KSA* 1, 528). And *The Birth of Tragedy* contains several relevant treatments. Apollonian and Dionysian forces are exhibited in nature herself, *before* the mediation of artistic works (*BT* 2). Forming and deforming powers are intrinsic to nature's very course, and dreams and intoxicated states (both of which exceed conscious control) are preconditions for the more cultivated manifestation of Apollonian and Dionysian powers, particularly those of language and music. Artists are said to "imitate" such primal natural energies, which could not mean representational simulation, but rather the more performative sense of "impersonating" these energies in artistic practices (impersonation being one of the meanings of *mimēsis* in Greek). Singing and dancing, for example, exhibit an enchanted, ecstatic elevation, a quasi-divine transformation where one is not really an artist because one "has become a work of art" (*BT* 1).[15]

In many respects Nietzsche associates the Dionysian with music (*BT* 6, 17), especially its immediate emotional force, which "overwhelms" conscious individuation. The Apollonian is associated with poetic language and theatrical technologies that shape a more individuated world. But since music and language are coordinated in tragic drama (*BT* 21), immediate disclosive force still operates in its performances. Poetic metaphors are not "symbolic," they possess a living power to disclose (*BT* 8). For Greek audiences, dramatic fiction was not a departure from reality, it produced on stage powerful scenes of "a world with the same reality and irreducibility that Olympus with its inhabitants possessed for the believing Hellene" (*BT* 7). Tragic drama produced a Dionysian effect of mimetic identification, originally embodied in choral impersonation, where one acts "as if one had actually entered into another body, another character" (*BT* 8). If we consider the connotations of capacity and power in the word "virtue" (the "virtue" of a tool, the phrase "by virtue of") and the notion of "virtual" indicating an actual effect without formal recognition (a virtual king), we can say that the power of poetry on the Greek stage produced a *virtual reality*.[16]

The problem with Euripidean drama, as Nietzsche saw it, was that it brought the critical "spectator" on stage (*BT* 11). Particularly problematic was the effect of the prologues in Euripides' plays, where the context and course of the drama was laid out in advance for the audience. The effect was to preclude or diminish mimetic identification, so that the audience would no longer "become completely absorbed in the activities and sufferings of the chief characters or feel breathless pity and fear" (*BT* 12). The modern "aesthetic" audience has been thoroughly schooled in the mode of critical reflection, where art is meant to be understood by way of interpretive tools beyond the immediate presentation of the work, beyond the "powerful artistic magic" that should "enrapture the genuine listener" (*BT* 22).

In later texts, Nietzsche reiterates this sense of poetic immediacy. In section 811 of *The Will to Power*, artists are described as intoxicated with an overwhelming force of extreme sensuous acuity, which produces a "contagious" compulsion to discharge images that are "immediately enacted" in bodily energies: "An image, rising up within, immediately turns into a movement of the limbs." Section 84 in *The Gay Science* likewise discusses the origin of poetry in discharges of rhythmic force that compel both body and soul toward disclosive effects. Here musical-poetical effects are also mentioned as functioning in Greek oracular prophecy, which "binds the future" with "literal (*buchstäblich*) and rhythmical precision." Nietzsche then remarks that such effects never disappear entirely, even though philosophy has labored to overcome such "superstitions." Serious philosophers still call on poetry "in order to give their ideas force and credibility." And yet, Nietzsche adds, it is dangerous to enlist poetry in the quest for truth, because the Greeks conceded that the poets are capable of telling lies.

A remarkable section in *Thus Spoke Zarathustra* is relevant for this discussion. In "On Poets" (*Z* II, 17), Zarathustra confesses his ambivalence about poetry: he *is* a poet but he has become weary of poetry's manner of speaking. Poets "lie," of course, owing to the inaccessibility of foundational truth. Yet Zarathustra yearns for something more than poetry, something on the horizon that will overcome past poets' superficiality, "because their thoughts have not penetrated deeply enough." It is clear that Zarathustra's confession marks the ambiguous confluence of poetical and philosophical language throughout the text.

I have highlighted three factors in Nietzsche's thinking that figure in my analysis: (1) Poetical language has immediate disclosive force. (2) Yet such disclosive force cannot be equivalent to factual truth because it "lies" when compared to factual assumptions and its creative, performative "appearances" are in keeping with a baseline flux that cannot give full "reality" to forms. (3) The immediacy and sensuous imagery of poetic language does not suffice for philosophical thinking. These three elements in fact also circulate throughout *The Birth of Tragedy*, especially in remarks about myth.

Myths and Concepts

In *The Birth of Tragedy*, Nietzsche celebrates tragic myth as being more profound than (1) an abstract, rational model of existence (*BT* 23) and (2) a tendency to ossify myths into a kind of "juvenile history" (*BT* 10), what we would call a religious fundamentalism that conflates mythical images with actual realities. Tragic drama undermines this kind of religious "literalism" in two ways: (1) theatrical artifice is recognized as a form of creative appearance; and (2) Dionysian deformation "takes back" all forms through the force of negative fate. The Apollonian-Dionysian confluence in tragic drama at once *displays* and *limits* the formation of cultural meaning. This is why Nietzsche thinks that in tragedy "myth attains its most profound content" (*BT* 10). Tragic myth *presents* a finite world of meaningful appearances that, despite being "apparent," are *not* renounced in favor of transcendence or abnegation. Tragic appearances have a "reality" because they tell us: "Look there! Look closely! This is your life" (*BT* 24). Recalling the association between the Dionysian-Apollonian dyad and the music-language dyad, Nietzsche clearly indicates that Apollonian language and imagery prevent an impulse toward "orgiastic self-annihilation" in sheer Dionysian experience (*BT* 21). Tragedy is the "fraternal union" of these two sacred forces, an indissoluble blend of music and language (*BT* 21) that unfolds "in a strict reciprocal proportion, according to the law of eternal justice" (*BT* 25).[17]

At the same time, Nietzsche admits that "the meaning of tragic myth set forth above never became transparent in conceptual clarity to the Greek poets, not to speak of the Greek philosophers," which is one reason why tragedy did not have the strength to survive (*BT* 17). Again we notice why Nietzsche found favor with Kant and Schopenhauer: they made it possible for *philosophy* to confront tragic limits and thus expand the sense of tragedy beyond its original artistic forms. Indeed, Nietzsche designates the tragic turn in philosophy as "*Dionysian wisdom* apprehended in concepts" (*BT* 19).[18] In this way, *The Birth of Tragedy* prefigures the productive tensions between (1) creative form and abysses, (2) philosophy and poetry, and (3) speaking and singing, tensions that we noticed in Zarathustra's venture toward life affirmation and the thought of eternal recurrence. In gathering these issues, I want to argue that eternal recurrence can be understood as a tragic-mythic-poetic concept, a formation meant to engender a "virtual reality"—a literal, immediate disclosure that yet is not construed as a cosmological fact.

Mythical Truth and Mimetic Identity

There is lasting ambiguity in Nietzsche's approach to truth. One the one hand, traditional confidence in truth is debunked by connecting it with "lies," while on the other hand, such lies are necessary for life and meaning creation (see *WP* 853). The rhetoric of "artistic creation" cuts across both notions and thus has both a negative and positive function: negative as a tactical subversion of foundationalism, positive as the productive source of culture formation. In light of *The Birth of Tragedy*, mythical truth can be selected as a focal phrase for such ambiguity. Tragic drama presented myth *as* a nonfoundational, fictive production. But in historical context, Greek myth was equivalent to the early Greek *world*, its sense of meaning, purpose, and knowledge. In this respect, "myth" is a deeper term than "art," because the latter has taken on a restricted sense that cannot convey the full function of myth in Greek culture. So myth is a world-disclosive fictive truth (in Greek, *muthos* was not equivalent to a "falsehood" because it referred primarily to speech and narrative). In addition, I have tried to incorporate a performative element into the matter of myth and art, in order to take the discussion in different directions, particularly as it pertains to eternal recurrence. Nietzsche recognized that mythic truth involved not only *what* was presented in Greek culture, but also *how* it was presented and received. Greek poetic production had a nonreflective immediacy in both its inspired creative sources and its enthralling effects on audiences. This performative sense of "mimetic literalness" was the real target of Plato's critique of poetry, and it can be said to mark a critical difference between tragic myth and philosophical reflection.

Nietzsche wrestled with all the forces described above, particularly in his attempt to philosophize "in between" poetic disclosure and philosophical concepts. But intrinsic to Nietzsche's medial posture was the central question of meaning, because the Greek mythical tradition exhibited life-affirming elements that were threatened by the rise of philosophical reflection. So the poetry-philosophy dyad in Nietzsche's thought reaches all across his intellectual endeavors, touching on how philosophy is to be written, how it is to be read, and how it tracks the question of life affirmation in a finite world. Eternal recurrence, in my view, gathers all these strands together, especially in the narrative context of *Thus Spoke Zarathustra*.[19]

Eternal recurrence can be taken as a conceptual myth of life affirmation intended to operate with immediate (literal) disclosive force. The notebook reference to eternal recurrence as "imprinting on becoming the character of being" (*WP* 617) is packed with suggestive meanings. In German, *prägen* can refer to written print (and note the possible allusion to written "characters"); also to "coining" in both a literal and figurative sense (producing coins and "coining a phrase"). The connotation of "creative writing" in the "fixing" of flux (the eternalization of finite becoming) is indicated when Zarathustra calls everything permanent or abiding (*unvergänglich*) a *Gleichnis*, or parable (*Z* II, 17). The creative function of eternal recurrence is also suggested in the account of redemption as *re-creating* the "it was" as "thus I willed it" (*Z* II, 20). Since eternal recurrence itself is placed within a textual narrative, a myth-as-story, it can be understood as a philosophical mythic-concept in the following ways: (1) it functions within the story of Zarathustra's quest for life affirmation; (2) it performs a general (philosophical) function of forming a structure of repetition for all possible stories; (3) its formal structure, however, is inseparable from its material effect of drawing out the reader's *own* specific life story by way of its disclosive force. The confluence of these mythical-narrative functions lies behind my suggestion that the conceptual myth of eternal recurrence also draws on the ancient idea of "literal" mimetic identity. I believe that Nietzsche wanted us to take eternal recurrence *as written* and *as read* in an immediate sense, because if it were taken as symbolic of something other than repetition, or even as a hypothetical as-if, it would lack the existential force to draw out a concrete response to the issue of life affirmation. In other words, if the "virtual reality" of eternal recurrence were to be recast as a reducible metaphor, a gesturing away from its direct sense, then its *power* to evoke meaning *by virtue of* its repetition scheme would be lost or weakened.[20]

Despite some reservations expressed about suspension of disbelief, I think this phenomenon of aesthetic reception can help articulate what I mean by mimetic literality. I should mention a passage from *Beyond Good and Evil* that gathers together life affirmation, eternal recurrence, and musical-theatrical references. Nietzsche describes a world-affirming human being "who wants to have *what was and is* repeated into all eternity, shouting insatiably *da capo* [a musical direction: "from the beginning"]—not only to himself but to the whole play and spectacle (*Stücke und Schauspiele*), and not only to a spectacle but at bottom to him who needs precisely this spectacle" (*BGE* 56). Recalling the visual references to eternal recurrence in the gateway passage, can we say that Nietzsche wanted readers of his text to experience a theatrical, mimetic reception of eternal recurrence, "impersonating" and "inhabiting" its disclosive force in the way fictive truth operates in the performance and reception of dramatic performances? I want to say Yes because of the subtle differences between suspension of disbelief and the more reflective senses of metaphor, allegory, thought experiment, or even a hypothetical as-if.[21]

Suspension of disbelief is surely different from a straightforward sense of sheer identity or referential literalness because of its background milieu of theatrical artifice and its periodic, intermittent departure from more "realistic" modes of belief. Nevertheless, in a functional sense it requires *moments* of mimetic identification if it is to work; attention to the artifice or reflection on the performance undermines disclosive effects. This does not mean that reflection is some violation of the dramatic presentation (which is not, after all, an immanent "fact" in a strictly realistic sense); it simply means that reflection is a second-order disposition derived from the momentary, *virtual reality* of mimetic identification. Of course Nietzsche assumed that eternal recurrence would prompt reflection, and he did mean it to have philosophical significance. But I do not think we can say, for instance, that Zarathustra was engaged in a "philosophical analysis" of eternal recurrence; he was responding to its world-disclosive impact directly in terms of his own life and experience of meaning. There is still nothing wrong with standing back from eternal recurrence and reflecting on it (I hope not, otherwise my entire project is ruined). Yet, recalling Nietzsche's complaint about an exclusively "critical audience" with respect to drama, I think Nietzsche would question a philosophical audience that is exclusively critical, that engages recurrence solely in terms of philosophical adjudication rather than existential impact. He would not object to his audience *becoming* critical, but rather *arriving* critically.

Even a philosophical text can be read "literally" in the sense of momentary suspension of disbelief and mimetic identification. We all engage in mimetic reading when responding directly and nonreflectively to written texts. When we do so we suspend *philosophical* disbelief in the immediate disclosive force of language, a disbelief indicated in the long-standing theoretical habit of questioning the relationship between language and reality, words and things (almost as though language itself were a kind of theatrical artifice).[22] With respect to eternal recurrence, would not an *aversive* response (which is different from a skeptical, critical response, and which Nietzsche would not dishonor) stem from a kind of literal, mimetic reading on some level? This is why I think a "hypothetical" reading of recurrence would not do full justice to mimetic identification. *After* experiencing suspension of disbelief, we can easily reflect back and describe the experience hypothetically: we responded "as if" the presentation were real and true. But *during* the experience there is an immediacy that would be lost in a hypothetical stance; in other words, we would have to suspend mimetic *belief.* So a hypothetical as-if, although responsive in a way, would lack the immediate responsive effect that I believe Nietzsche wanted to activate, and that requires a stronger literal sense of as-written and as-read. Subsequent reflection is surely possible and foreseen by

Nietzsche, but not divorced from moments of immersion that generate a direct impact and that provide the material element *for* reflection.

Accordingly I want to call suspension of disbelief *making belief*, which is stronger than "make-believe" (construed as pretending or letting oneself believe in a fiction). Both phrases imply a useful differentiation from cognitive belief—in other words, not believing-that but believing-in; and the latter has relevant connotations of esteeming, valuing, and trusting that would be important to Nietzsche (believing in someone, believing in life). Yet I have mentioned how suspension of disbelief might be loaded in favor of realism, and likewise make-believe might miss the productive immediacy and world-disclosive function of ancient modes of myth making, as well as the "realistic" effects of mimetic identification. According to the *OED*, there is an obsolete form of make-believe derived from the French *faire croire*, which meant to produce belief in people, which captures the stronger sense of making belief that I am proposing: *creation* of belief that is world-disclosive.[23]

In fact Aristotle suggested something along these lines when he ranked poetic *mimēsis* higher than history because it is "more philosophical" (*Poetics* 9). The "factual reality" of history cannot present *universal* meanings that are disclosed through the concrete effects of poetic imagery in drama. So even Aristotle recognized the nonfactual disclosure of important truths in immediate poetic depictions. Nietzsche goes further than Aristotle by not only recognizing a philosophical dimension in poetry (which was recognized in certain respects by Plato too), but by posing a derivational relationship between poetry and philosophy that Aristotle (and Plato) would not espouse. Nietzsche claims that before something is thought (*gedacht*), there must already have been something poeticized (*gedichtet*) in prereflective invention (*WP* 544). In other words, "thinking" is abstracted from an already functioning and living poetic language (which fits the historical situation of the Greek world analyzed in *The Birth of Tragedy*).

One final point in this section. My proposal of the mimetic literalness of eternal recurrence should not be taken to mean primarily some kind of "identification with the self," which at first might seem quite appropriate, especially in terms of existential significance (i.e., in reading eternal recurrence I incorporate it into my self and my life). I resist this idea because it can suggest an "internalization" process in the direction of self-immediacy or self-constituting apprehension (which is how the subjective turn in modern aesthetics would want to put it). For me, the ecstatic element of mimetic identification has more of an *externalizing* immediacy in moments of sheer disclosiveness, which in a way *gives* the self a *world*.[24] Here we might find a clue for understanding a rather strange passage from the first part of *Thus Spoke Zarathustra* ("On Reading and Writing"). Stressing the existential spirit of profound writing, Zarathustra says: "I love only what a man has written with his blood." He complains that the widespread learning of reading corrupts both writing and thinking. Adding in the notion of aphoristic writing, Zarathustra then says: "Whoever writes in blood and aphorisms does not want to be read but to be learned by heart (*auswendig*)." The meaning here is certainly unclear, but it might suggest a complaint about an overly reflective and critical spirit in a predominantly literate culture, which more and more overtakes ancient performances of mimetic disclosure. My reading may surely be a stretch, but I cannot help noticing that the adverb *auswendig* means both "by heart," and "outwardly," which suggests (to me at least) a word-for-word literalness with ecstatic revelatory force.[25] Learning by heart in this sense is not slavish imitation but the overture of thinking fed by textual lifeblood circulating between writers and readers.

Nietzsche's Prophetic Offering

I turn now to the section of *Thus Spoke Zarathustra* named "On the Gift-Giving Virtue." Here Zarathustra first advances the idea of mythic forms to replace strict cognition. All renderings of meaning and value "are parables: they do not describe, they only beckon (*winken*). A fool is he who wants knowledge of them!" (*Z* I, 22, 1). But mythic speech is a virtue, a *capacity* stemming from a compelling power to give meaning to life. "Watch for every hour, my brothers, in which your spirit wants to speak in parables: there lies the origin of your virtue. There your body is elevated and resurrected; with its delight it enraptures the spirit so that it turns creator and esteemer and lover and benefactor of all things" (1).[26]

Creativity here is connected with power and an insatiable need to give. We must note that power as a *virtue* is more than simply a force of overcoming; it is also a capacious potency, the power to create, indeed an overwhelming abundance of creative force. The gift-giving virtue is actually associated with all the central elements extolled in the overall text: love, creating, valuing, power, the meaning of the earth, the *Übermensch*, "recovery" from nihilism, and "unexhausted and undiscovered" paths yet to be walked (2). This section of the text is important for understanding the creative advent of eternal recurrence, particularly in the light of Nietzsche's own account of how the story of Zarathustra arose, which sounds very much like prophetic inspiration, and which therefore provides another link with ancient modes of poetic speech.

In *Ecce Homo* Nietzsche relates the "history" of *Zarathustra* and its "fundamental conception" of eternal recurrence, which "came to" him during a walk through the woods in August 1881 (*EH* III, Z, 1). *Zarathustra* is also described as requiring a *rebirth* of "the art of *hearing*," and as having "invaded" and "overtaken" him. Then Nietzsche offers an account of inspiration that clearly articulates the advent of the text as he experienced it. I quote this important passage in full, with the hope that the reader will see confirmation of several key points I have been addressing.

> Has anyone at the end of the nineteenth century a clear idea of what poets of strong ages have called *inspiration*? If not, I will describe it.—If one had the slightest residue of superstition left in one's system, one

could hardly reject altogether the idea that one is merely incarnation, merely mouthpiece, merely a medium of overpowering forces. The concept of revelation—in the sense that suddenly, with indescribable certainty and subtlety, something becomes *visible*, audible, something that shakes one to the last depths and throws one down—that merely describes the facts. One hears, one does not seek; one accepts, one does not ask who gives; like lightning, a thought flashes up, with necessity, without hesitation regarding its form—I never had any choice. A rapture whose tremendous tension occasionally discharges itself in a flood of tears—now the pace quickens involuntarily, now it becomes slow; one is altogether beside oneself, with the distinct consciousness of sudden shudders and of one's skin creeping down to one's toes; a depth of happiness in which even what is most painful and gloomy does not seem something opposite, but rather conditioned, provoked, a *necessary* color in such a superabundance of light; an instinct for rhythmic relationships that arches over wide spaces of forms—length, the need for a rhythm with wide arches, is almost the measure of the force of inspiration, a kind of compensation for its pressure and tension. Everything happens involuntarily in the highest degree but as in a gale of a feeling of freedom, of absoluteness, of power, of divinity.—The involuntariness of image and parable is strangest of all; one no longer has any notion of what is an image or a parable: everything offers itself as the nearest, most obvious, simplest expression. It actually seems, to allude to something Zarathustra says, as if the things themselves approached and offered themselves as parables ("Here all things come caressingly to your discourse and flatter you; for they want to ride on your back. On every parable you ride to every truth.... Here the words and word-shrines of all being open up before you; here all being wishes to become word, all becoming wishes to learn from you how to speak"). This is *my* experience of inspiration; I do not doubt that one has to go back thousands of years in order to find anyone who could say to me, "it is mine as well." (*EH* III, Z, 3)[27]

The "residue of superstition" mentioned in this passage does not discredit the inspirational moment, but rather rhetorically retrieves something ancient to express the receptive authenticity of Nietzsche's experience. In fact, in another text Nietzsche traces modern conceptions of self-produced thoughts to a kind of superstition:

With regard to the superstitions of logicians, I shall never tire of emphasizing a small terse fact, which these superstitious minds hate to concede—namely that a thought comes when "it" wishes, and not when "I" wish, so that it is a falsification of the facts of the case to say that the subject "I" is the condition of the predicate "think." *It* thinks; but that this "it" is precisely the famous old "ego" is, to put it mildly, only a supposition, an assertion, and assuredly not an "immediate certainty." After all, one has even gone too far with this "it thinks"—even the "it" contains an *interpretation* of the process, and does not belong to the process itself. (*BGE* 17)

Pierre Klossowski has written a brilliant account of eternal recurrence that stresses its ecstatic, revelatory force. For Klossowski, eternal recurrence erupted for Nietzsche out of an inchoate mood and impulse that demanded expression: "Finally, the Eternal Return, at its inception, was not a representation, nor was it, strictly speaking, a postulate; it was a *lived fact*, and as a thought, it was a *sudden* thought. Phantasm or not, the experience of Sils-Maria exercised its strength as an ineluctable necessity. Alternating between dread and elation, Nietzsche's interpretations will be inspired by this moment, by this felt necessity."[28]

If we grant Nietzsche a serious consideration of his remarks on inspiration and the nonsubjective origin of thought, can eternal recurrence be understood as a quasi-religious revelation delivered to an audience through a prophetic voice? In this case the medial position of a prophet who "speaks-for" a god would be speaking for *life*, or perhaps the sacralization of life in the figure of Dionysus. Indeed Nietzsche connects eternal recurrence with Greek mystery religion (*KSA* 10, 340). And both eternal recurrence and will to power are called a "Dionysus world," a "mystery world," which is "without goal, unless the joy of the circle is itself a goal," and "without will, unless a ring feels good will toward itself" (*WP* 1067). The element of mystery suggests that Dionysian will to power cannot be reduced to our creative productions out of it. Creativity *is* will to power, which therefore itself is not "created" (*WP* 1066). Nietzsche seems to be saying in a "religious" sense that there is something behind us or within us that cannot be reduced to human productions. We might be confronted with an *Übermenschlich* life-religion, with Zarathustra/Nietzsche as its prophet. Eternal recurrence is able to express the meta-human-production element by affirming *all* productions *and* their temporal limits.

In a notebook passage, Nietzsche specifically calls eternal recurrence a prophecy (*WP* 1057), which would match the way he describes its inception in his experience as something that "came to" him.[29] We can also think of the prophetic *audience* in terms of how Nietzsche wants eternal recurrence to come to *us*. Religious prophecies have certainly been open to interpretation, but *as* prophecies they have been taken as given, *as* spoken, in other words as an authoritative, sacred emergence delivered through a special, receptive voice. Both for Zarathustra and Nietzsche, eternal recurrence does not arise as a hypothesis or thought experiment, but as a compelling presence with ambiguous bivalence: (1) a powerful surge of life-affirming energy, and (2) a dreadful force that shakes one to the core (in other words, an affirmation pump with highly flammable fuel). Can we say that Nietzsche experienced a revelation that compelled him to speak *to*-us-*for*-life? Did he want to transfer the prophetic identity of his inspirational moment to the mimetic identity of the reading moment?

If there is any truth to this, it matters a great deal *how* we read eternal recurrence (in addition to *what* it reveals). I think that Nietzsche wanted his text to have something of the charge of his original moment, which did not begin with the "thought" of eternal recurrence (a finished conception to be analyzed) but with a powerful experience that gave shape to the conception. What kind of experience can be meant here? I suggest that it can be understood as a reverberation of Greek tragic experience: the concentrated immediacy of the productive fluidity of life, with *nothing outside itself*, a creative flux that is simultaneously self-affirming and self-exceeding, which spawns an Apollonian expression of a Dionysian force. Eternal recurrence *out of* such an experience could be understood accordingly: The image of repetition gives form to the form-exceeding forces of life by *forcing* attention to life formations *in the midst of* form-exceeding conditions—in other words, life unfolding as it is with no exception, remainder, or alteration. Such an experiential milieu would account for all the existential appeals and strategies that energize Nietzsche's texts, especially the poetic, dramatic narrative of *Zarathustra*, so different as it is from a philosophical treatise.

This kind of prophetic immediacy I am suggesting raises an interesting problem concerning the relationship between eternal recurrence and life affirmation. Surely life affirmation is central to the meaning of eternal recurrence, but the prophetic milieu Nietzsche hints at makes me cautious about assuming recurrence to be "based" in life affirmation in some way, in the sense that affirmation was Nietzsche's primary message and recurrence served a kind of instrumental function, to draw out or test affirmative dispositions. This is a widely held view and there is certainly something right about it. But I am not sure Nietzsche was simply searching for devices that could express or serve the kind of life affirmation that marks his thought (recall the distinction between affirmation and life enhancement). I pose the following question: Could we, or even Nietzsche, have imagined his strict sense of life affirmation without or before the presentation of eternal recurrence? I'm not sure. Could it be that absent or prior to the stark sense of eternal recurrence, "affirmative" postures toward life would simply be confined to, or delimited by, affirming various kinds of life *enhancement*, which are not equivalent to Nietzsche's agonistic/holistic conception of affirmation?

At any rate, in Nietzsche's own case we can say that a certain life-affirming impulse and the existential experience of the death of God launched the thought of eternal recurrence, crystallizing and voicing what had been brewing in his thinking up to that point. In this respect perhaps we can understand why Nietzsche considered eternal recurrence a special revelation, even though he recognized previous indications of a similar conception in ancient thought. What was distinctive about Nietzsche's vision was its singular existential force in the wake of the modern eclipse of God—in other words, eternal recurrence was the simultaneous announcement of, and antidote to, modern nihilism. The traumatic force of nihilism and its existential challenge made eternal recurrence come to Nietzsche in a unique manner and with unique implications.

What is important here is the recognition of a nonreflective original base out of which eternal recurrence takes shape. And I am suggesting that Nietzsche aimed to offer his readers the possibility of a comparable nonreflective engagement with recurrence, its immediate disclosive force that might (or might not) tap into a comparable readiness (or nonreadiness) for experiencing the full range of its existential significance. Such has been the gambit of my call for a "literal" reading, which should combine, therefore, three elements: (1) the sense of eternal recurrence *as* written, (2) the effect of recurrence *as* read (which requires a momentary mimetic identification of reader and text, and (3) a background existential capacity (or incapacity) to "hear" the life-affirming force of eternal recurrence.[30]

As I have said, eternal recurrence certainly admits of reflective consideration and interpretation. But I think that for *Nietzsche*, the first-order condition of engaging recurrence should be at the level of mimetic reading and direct impact, rather than theoretical examination of a proposed "worldview" pondered by the gaze of philosophical study. Consequently, of equal importance to what eternal recurrence is presenting would be the way in which we read the text, or better, the way in which the text presents itself to us. The existential element of Nietzsche's thought has long been recognized. Less evident has been the existential force of *reading* Nietzsche in a certain way, which means much more than simply responsive readers; Nietzsche's texts are *charged* by his life and are charged with the power to open up the reader's life.[31]

Nietzsche's Life and Eternal Recurrence

To reiterate the basis of my argument in this study: life affirmation and eternal recurrence represent the core and climax of Nietzsche's thought. These reciprocal notions acutely concentrate the perennial question of the meaning of life in the wake of the death of God—and by force of Nietzsche's naturalistic alternative. In addition, this core reverberates in the consideration of any and all philosophical enterprises. For Nietzsche, all philosophical and cultural matters stem from and turn on existential meanings in a finite world (by either expressing or suppressing tragic finitude). Even scientific causality, for instance, is diagnosed as an expression of the *problem* of order and disorder in life. With the death of God, tragic finitude is the brute given, and all thinking is informed in one way or another by this fateful restriction to worldly conditions. Eternal recurrence forces our attention on this brute restriction and draws out the most basic dispositions toward finitude. With the textual offering of eternal recurrence, we are "sentenced to life" (the ambiguity of which turns on whether we hear the sentence as a blessing or a curse).

The existential character of Nietzsche's thinking is consistently deployed in his texts, with his stylistic tactics, probing questions, and especially his refusal to bracket his own personality when he writes. This creates unique problems for readers, especially philosophical interpreters, and particularly with respect to eternal recurrence. For Nietzsche, all thought is fueled by life drives, instincts, and matters of meaning. Philosophical texts as such are derivative epiphenomena emerging out of life energies that as such can never be reduced to philosophical documents. This is why it is a mistake to read Nietzsche solely in terms of the "propositional content" of his thought, as though he were participating in the professional examination of typical philosophical "problems" (the nature of time, knowledge, truth, the good, etc.) albeit in an imaginative and provocative manner. Such approaches are not false or pointless, but they cannot do full justice to Nietzsche's vision of how philosophy does or should function in human life. Propositional judgments can never capture the deeper issue of *life forces* operating in texts, in writers, and in readers. Nietzsche's texts are deliberately charged with such forces, and they charge readers with the appropriate task of a lived response. I have been arguing that eternal recurrence, above all Nietzsche's offerings, must be addressed in such a manner, especially because the existential task of its appropriation is the dramatic form of its presentation. Moreover, Nietzsche interjects *himself*, without hesitation or apology, into the matter of eternal recurrence in his most personal text, *Ecce Homo*.

Given Nietzsche's insistence on a lived, personal engagement with philosophical questions, *Ecce Homo* may be his most philosophical book. It presents an unusual "autobiography," but one that may indeed be the capstone of his philosophical task: exposing his own journey to us as a signal for how *we* should encounter his philosophy. The book literally sizzles with Nietzsche's persona, and yet in a way that is disclosive of many issues central to his thought, particularly his challenge to traditional expectations for philosophy. Chapters such as "Why I Am So Wise," and "Why I Write Such Good Books" might seem megalomaniacal, yet they may also be deliberate jabs at the obsession with "impersonal objectivity" in philosophy. Or we might agree that he *was* being objective, since he *was* wise and he *did* write great books. In any case, of particular interest for my purposes is the chapter "Why I Am So Wise," as it pertains to eternal recurrence.

The drama of *Zarathustra* portrays eternal recurrence in terms of the existential task of redeeming life, and Nietzsche clearly identifies himself with Zarathustra: "his task—it is mine, too" (*EH* III, Z, 8). Zarathustra's task, as we have seen, also included confronting his own deep resistance to eternal recurrence, and thus to life, because of the specter of meaninglessness in the face of the necessity of what is *other* to one's sense of meaning. Identical repetition compels a confrontation with any and all possible life-denying dispositions in oneself. Nietzsche also discloses to us his own struggles with this challenge, in that his redemptive task passed through, indeed *had* to pass through, experiences of nihilism, pessimism, and decadence.

> I have a subtler sense of smell for the signs of ascent and decline than any other human being before me; I am the teacher *par excellence* for this—I know both, I am both.... Looking from the perspective of the sick toward *healthier* concepts and values and, conversely, looking again from the fullness and self-assurance of a *rich* life down into the secret work of the instinct of decadence—in this I have had the longest training, my truest experience; if in anything, I became master in this. Now I know how, have the know-how, to *reverse perspectives.* (*EH* I, 1)

Nietzsche calls himself a *Doppelgänger*, in the sense of being both a decadent and its opposite (*EH* I, 2–3). He experienced pessimism to its depths and yet overcame it; indeed, the opposite ideal came *out of* such world-denying depths (*EH* I, 2; *BGE* 56).[32] Nietzsche's self-overcoming of life-negating dispositions is expressed positively in *Ecce Homo* as an experience of gratitude (*Dankbarkeit*) toward life and for his own life. Note this recollection that heads the book:

> On this perfect day, when everything is ripening and not only the grape turns brown, the eye of the sun just fell upon my life: I looked back, I looked forward, and I never saw so many and such good things all at once. It was not for nothing that I buried my forty-fourth year today; I had the *right* to bury it; whatever was life in it has been saved, is immortal.... *How should I not be grateful to my whole life?*

Shortly thereafter Nietzsche goes to express gratitude even toward his malefactors and opponents (*EH* I, 5, 7).[33] In fact, his affirmative posture toward opponents is expressed directly in terms of the agonistic structure of will to power, in that affirming one's own meaning must include that which counters and works against it. Every strong nature "needs conditions of resistance; hence it *seeks out* resistance" (*EH* I, 7). Nietzsche even applies this agonistic structure to his "practice of war," in a way that can tell us much about the point of his polemical tactics: "I only attack things (*Sache*) that are victorious—I may even wait until they become victorious" Attacking something "is in my case proof of good will, even gratitude" (*EH* I, 7).

An agonistic dynamic helps us gauge the tenor of Nietzsche's autobiographical reflections. It is evident that Nietzsche came to see his life and philosophical practice—which were anything but trouble-free—in a spirit of gratitude; and he was thankful not despite the troubles, but by way of them. His disposition, then, seems to satisfy the strict existential ground rules entailed by eternal recurrence: that the meaning of life affirmation must pass through the counterforces of one's life and the abyssal force of this encounter.[34]

Accordingly, the relationship between life affirmation and will to power may be reciprocal in a specific and unexpected way. It is not only that affirmation must come to terms "with" will to power as the dynamic energy of life;

life affirmation *itself* is a manifestation of will to power in its encounter with, and overcoming of, life denial. As will to power, affirmation must unfold out of resistance; yet not simply resistance to "external" instances of life denial in culture or world history, but also resistance in *oneself*, owing to the necessity of confronting one's own otherness, that which at first one would naturally want to *deny* as contrary to one's values. The brute force of finitude in life compels a recognition of tensional conflict, and so an authentic task of life affirmation cannot bypass the actual conflicts that tear at our own lives. In this way, affirmation is inseparable from tragic finitude, and life as such exhibits a tragic structure in that the meaning of life and its possible affirmation emerge *by way of life resisting itself*.

Can we generalize from Nietzsche's own biographical account and say that his sense of life affirmation is not possible apart from experiencing nihilism, pessimism, and life-denying propensities? Could it be that "happy" people, those who are not haunted by a deep discontent with life, cannot experience or lay claim to a genuine affirmation of life because they are shielded from the genuine threats to meaning that pervade life? If this is so, then there is a curious fraternal relationship between Nietzsche's ideal of the Yes-sayer and the No-saying ascetic ideal, in that both face up to the dark side of life, both do not or cannot hide from the catastrophic fact of finitude. But what would explain the possibility of Nietzshe's call for a parting of the ways in this dark fraternity? To personalize the matter, what accounts for the very different paths of fraternal twins like Schopenhauer and Nietzsche? With a common worldview, how is it that one said No and the other Yes? There may be an answer to this question that articulates further the foreground rhetoric of weakness and strength (the meaning of which is often ambiguous anyway in Nietzsche's texts). I think an answer can be sketched by recalling Nietzsche's subsumption of individual selfhood under the more primal dynamic of life energies.

Nietzsche often talks about life-affirming and life-denying *instincts*, which undermines any sense of foundational selfhood construed as conscious control or individual agency. Affirmation is often described as a Dionysian release into the larger economy of life. The precedence of life over selfhood may open up a way to distinguish affirmative from pessimistic possibilities in the dark fraternity's common exposure to tragic finitude.

In general terms, Nietzsche describes cultural creativity as the overcoming of discontent, the formation of meaning in the midst of threats to meaning, whether they be resistance, obstruction, or destruction. The ascetic ideal overcomes discontent with life as a whole by finding meaning in life denial, whether it be religious transcendence or Schopenhauerian pessimism. As Nietzsche puts it, the ascetic priest's will to power is not over something *in* life but over life itself (*GM* III, 11). In this way discontent is resolved by magnifying itself into a cosmic condition of "truth" that discerns the meaning of life in crossing over, or crossing out, the conditions of life. Nietzschean affirmation, while likewise experiencing discontent, seems to be predicated on *not* project-ing discontent onto life itself, or put another way, on experiencing discontent as one's own dispositional problem, even though this disposition is a genuine response to the *reality* of tragic finitude. The possibility of affirmation out of discontent seems to require an intimation (whether instinctive or otherwise) that one's own suffering is not the last word on life. In other words, the possi-bility of affirmation would require *radical* discontent, a discontent with discontent, which seems to be lacking in the ascetic ideal. Schopenhauer, for example, forcefully interrogated optimistic attitudes, but never seemed to put a life-aversive disposition into question. What is remarkable about Nietzsche and his dramatic surrogate Zarathustra is the extension of interrogation all the way to self-interrogation. I am suggesting that the difference between affirma-tion and denial turns on the degree to which selfhood has been shaped in rela-tion to self-exceeding life forces. Life denial seems to stem from a dispositional preserve of discrete selfhood, so that psychological discontent, as the horizonal *limit* of experience and meaning, sees no alternative to "objectifying" its content as an insight into life itself. The ascetic self is able to move from "I have no meaning" to "Life has no meaning," a projection that opens the door for transcendent projects or the (more honest) pessimistic project of sheer denial.

The possibility of saying Yes to life would seem to follow from a less perfected individuation, in that discontent is recognized as a limited perspec-tive on life, as something that can be overcome, perhaps following intimations of Dionysian "feelers" into the innocent spontaneity of life energies surging on despite tragic effects. In this way we can see life affirmation in terms of Nietzsche's structural delimitation of selfhood in the midst of self-exceeding forces. Even though all matters of philosophy, for Nietzsche, are psychological in the sense of being founded on questions of meaning, value, and interest, this does not entail a subjectivistic psychologism of any kind. *Life* is the base-line term for Nietzsche, and so life affirmation is more than a human disposi-tional matter; in fact it depends on an *Übermenschlich* reach beyond human selfhood. In a manner of speaking, affirmation "of" life is both a subjective and objective genitive. This would account for Nietzsche's depiction of eternal recurrence as having a "cosmic" dimension, as simultaneously expressing existential meaning and a world-disclosive force.[35]

To close this section, I want to cite a passage from the notebooks, written in 1886 as a sketch for a new Preface to *Human, All Too Human*. It is a good example of Nietzsche's self-reflection on his movement away from pessimistic dispositions by virtue of instinctive intimations brewing in him and leading in a new direction. In the bargain, he mentions reading the "sentence" of his life, which of course perks my interest because of the linguistic tactics of my study. Nietzsche describes a period when a pervasive tone of alienation was beginning to change.

What was actually happening to me then? I did not understand myself, but the impulse was like a command. It seems that we are at the mercy of a distant and remote fate: for a long time we experience nothing but riddles. The choice of events, the grasping and sudden desire, the rejection of what is most agreeable, often the most venerated: This is what terrifies us, as though something arbitrary, wayward, insane, volcanic was arising here and there from deep within us. But this is only the higher sense and circumspection of our future task. Does the long sentence of my life—I was asking myself uneasily—perhaps want to be read *backwards*? Reading it forwards, and here there is no doubt, I found only "words devoid of meaning."

A great and ever greater *detachment*, an arbitrary becoming-foreign, an "alienation," a coldness, a disillusionment—this and this alone was my desire during these years.... Then I examined many things that had hitherto remained foreign to me, with a careful and even loving curiosity. I ... avoided any conclusion in which sickness, or solitude, or fatigue from wandering *could* have played the slightest role. "Onward!" I told myself. "Tomorrow you will be healthy: today it is enough to act healthy." Then I managed to master everything in me that had been "pessimistic," the *will* to health, the theatrical performance (*Schauspielern*) of health was my remedy. (*KSA* 11, 664–65)

The central element in Nietzsche's philosophy is here expressed in autobiographical terms: the examination of life cannot be advanced without self-examination, the performative task of coming to terms with life.

My Life and Eternal Recurrence

Normally philosophy presumes an impersonal stance in the pursuit of truth. Personal interjections are at best a rhetorical flourish and at worst an embarrassing impediment to the enterprise. There has been some relaxation of such a mandate in recent years. Yet engaging the philosophy of Nietzsche would seem to require a complete suspension of the mandate. For Nietzsche, philosophy cannot be grounded in rational argumentation but in the reflective exposure of *interests*. Accordingly, it might be that no interpretation of Nietzsche could be considered serious if it did not mimic Nietzsche's case by interjecting one's own story of motivations and interests. So, here goes. (Fervent impartialists and voyeurs, please skip to the next chapter.)

Why have I been so drawn to Nietzsche and to defending his account of eternal recurrence? On one level I can trace my interest in the doctrine to my generally contrarian character. The fact that eternal recurrence has almost invariably been received as strange, problematic, or dispensable has only enhanced my attraction to it. I like going against the tide.[36] On a deeper level, however, my attraction can best be described as stemming from a therapeutic need.

For as long as I can remember, I have always felt alienated from life—nothing like misery, but a general sense of disengagement, of not being at home in the world, a stranger in a familiar place. The clinical term for my condition is dysthymia, a pervasive, low-grade, functional depression, an incapacity for enjoyment, and a kind of default pessimism. To others who do not know me very well, this would be surprising. Students, for example, commonly praise my enthusiasm and animation in the classroom. It is a strange thing, but I can only say that when I teach, my vitality is real, but pure theater nevertheless. It is the situation that brings out my performance, which recedes when the play is over. My self-perception is that my enthusiasm is only tapped by public contexts of performing; it is a self-regarding "act" arising out a need for approval and admiration. I'll never forget the powerful effect of reading one of Kierkegaard's journal entries: he attended a social gathering where he was the life of the party; he came home (long dash) and wanted to shoot himself.

At the same time, I have not projected my condition onto life; I have seen my bearing as *my* fate, and I have envied enthusiasm for life in whatever form it takes in others (when I read Schopenhauer, it is with a sense of recognition that is nonetheless mixed with disappointment). Yet I have also reveled in my alienation, creating a script for myself of the lost and lonely hero who ventures into dark places that most people cannot abide. When I first read Nietzsche in college I was thunderstruck. On the one hand, his aura of solitude and heroic penchant for darkness were familiar, illuminating, and reinforcing; but on the other hand, his passion for life and call for affirmation admonished me, and I have been haunted ever since. Philosophically, I have been thoroughly persuaded by Nietzsche's naturalism: this life, in all its elements, is all there is; whatever can be thought and experienced can only be on life's terms. I suppose I had a strong readiness to hear Nietzsche's elemental call to life, probably *because* I felt like such an outsider and therefore could appreciate on a deep level, *by contrast*, the import of affirmation as Nietzsche conceived it.

I have never been religious in any formal sense. I was raised as a Catholic and from early on I was rebellious against its teachings and demands. The only genuine spiritual experience I can remember was a powerful feeling of being cleansed one day after a lengthy confession. Leaving the church I felt the world afresh, as though it was welcoming me into its arms. The feeling did not last, of course, and I confess that I also savored in the back of my mind the pleasure of a clean slate that was now cleared for new transgressions. Despite my rebellion from formal religion, my alienation did make me susceptible to the lure of spiritual transcendence. In college, after flirting with Christian versions of spiritual renewal, I became interested in Asian alternatives, particularly the Buddhist and Hindu mystical traditions, which were foreign enough to be exciting and dedicated to direct experience without formal trappings. I practiced Transcendental Meditation for over a decade and tasted what I suppose was the bliss of an ecstatic, formless unity beyond individuated states and freed from the stresses of life.

Nevertheless, the specter Nietzsche kept track of me; again and again I tried to reconcile my mystical interests with a Nietzschean posture toward life. I came to realize that this was an impossible task. When I was honest about my motivation for mystical experience, I could not avoid the conclusion that I was turning away from life, even though the posture of the Transcendental Meditation movement presented itself as worldly in a nonmonastic manner. Chastened by Nietzsche, I came home to myself, even my homeless self, because I could no longer abide what I had to confess was my fugitive disposition. The shift occurred after experiencing my "dark night of the soul" while traveling through Europe after the completion of my master's degree. I had sold everything, broken with friends and family, and was literally rootless. But I did not take well to the abyss, and was on the verge of a breakdown. I sought refuge in Majorca, where a training retreat for Transcendental Meditation teachers was being held. I stayed for a month, meditating daily, and attending lectures with the hope of joining the movement. But I got worse: in part, I think, because of a mandatory vegan diet, but also because of a growing revulsion against the dreamy spiritualism, the cheerful sense of victory over ignorance and *samsara*, the unsexed bodies (everyone's hands looked like nuns' hands to me), and my own presence in this four-star monastery. I left and retreated to my parents' home in New Jersey for some months of recovery (and some meat). I read *Zarathustra* like a bible, and eventually decided to complete my graduate studies, where I wrote my dissertation on eternal recurrence. So I suppose it is clear that my turn to Nietzsche was far from simply an academic exercise.

Nietzsche's philosophy has had an indelible influence on my life, inspiring it, informing it, admonishing it, measuring it. My fascination with eternal recurrence stems from it being an irresistible measure of meaning in my life. Its concentrating effects have been emblematic of the overall impact of Nietzsche's texts as I have experienced them. Even if I could not measure up to the existential test of eternal recurrence, somehow I believe that I ought to measure up. Aside from my personal disposition toward eternal recurrence, I am enormously impressed by the way in which its literal force can open up the task of life affirmation and whatever effects or responses this task might bring forth. In retrospect, for me Nietzsche's myth has had a kind of religious effect—serving as a prophetic inspiration, a revelation, a conscience, and a warning against demons wherever they may lie. And it has proclaimed the "good news" of the possibility of life before death. So I confess that my work on eternal recurrence has surely been driven by a personal subtext, and I trust that my testimony is far from inadmissible to the philosophical case at hand. I think I can say that I know Nietzsche's sentences "by heart."

6
Calling Witnesses:
A Review of the Literature

In this chapter I present a brief sketch of other interpretations of eternal recurrence. It is not an exhaustive account, but selective of various readings organized by five basic headings that are indicative of common trends in the scholarly literature. The headings do not always represent precise descriptions of the included selections because of occasional overlaps and the rich complexity of many notable treatments. I will generally not pursue a detailed examination of the different interpretations or a detailed critique from the standpoint of my analysis, but rather a survey of general orientational differences. I proceed in this way because much of what I would say has already been prepared in previous chapters, and so to avoid repetitiveness the critical differences can, I think, be adequately noted in broad strokes. At times, however, I will zero in on some significant hermeneutical issues and contrasts that can further serve my overall argument or duly attend to important matters of analysis in what continues to be a provocative conversation about a most provocative topic. I organize the various interpretations by way of the following types of reading: cosmological, existential, normative, symbolic, and ontological.

Cosmological Readings

This heading names interpretations that (1) assume eternal recurrence to have been advanced by Nietzsche as primarily a scientific theory about cosmic time, or (2) at least take seriously Nietzsche's interest in a factual sense of cyclic repetition. I have already noted two excellent discussions and critical analyses by Magnus and Small. And I have briefly sketched a general assessment of the cosmological version that several scholars have cogently delivered: that eternal recurrence is intrinsically unverifiable and indemonstrable because there is no extra-cyclic vantage point from which any relationship between cycles (causal or otherwise) could be ascertained; and even if it were possible, cross-cyclic relations would "add" to repeated occurrent events and thus ruin their supposed "identity."[1] For the same reason, any recollection of previous cycles is ruled out because a remembered event would be discernibly different from the event itself. This has moved some readers, such as Ivan Soll, to plausibly wonder what possible difference eternal recurrence could make to us if there is no sense in which the "different" cycles can be a focus of any consideration, and so repetition as such would lack any significance one way or another.[2] Indeed, from a strictly objective standpoint, there is some truth to this criticism. The recurrence of identical cycles adds nothing to the occurrence of a cycle per se, and so repetition would be no different from *one* occurrence. At the same time, it should be said that the recurrence of a cycle of events should be no more strange or unthinkable than one occurrence of a set of possible events (which is another way of saying that eternal recurrence is no more refutable than it is demonstrable). At any rate, an objective model of recurrence, as we have seen, need not be exhaustive or decisive, and an existential perspective can certainly read repetition as "making a difference."[3]

I here mention some notable interpretations that assume Nietzsche to be advancing a cosmological account (and that, unsurprisingly, find the doctrine deficient in different ways). Arthur Danto argues that Nietzsche's case operates under the principle of sufficient reason and causal necessity as warrants for repetition.[4] Yet Nietzsche does not frame his case in this manner, and his peculiar separation of necessity and causality makes this kind of reading suspect. Georg Simmel presumes Nietzsche's cosmological intentions and offers a refutation of his attempted "proof."[5] He aims to demonstrate the possibility of a finite number of states in a certain arrangement that would never repeat itself, even in infinite time: Imagine three wheels on a common axle, each of which is marked at a point on its circumference and lined up precisely with the other wheels at these points. If the wheels are rotated at speeds of n, 2n, and n/π, they can turn eternally without ever returning to the original alignment. Simmel argues that even this contrived example ruins Nietzsche's claim. Soll has critiqued this tactic on the grounds that Simmel's argument depends on a regulated (mathematical) arrangement of recombination patterns, which departs from Nietzsche's insistence on chance, "the great dice game of existence" (*WP* 1066), and it also enacts an intentional scheme at odds with Nietzsche's commitment to spontaneity.[6]

Wolfgang Müller-Lauter believes that the repetition scheme in eternal recurrence issues a contradiction when considering the textual importance of the *Übermensch*.[7] In the course of *Thus Spoke Zarathustra*, the *Übermensch* displays two incompatible standpoints: the "powerful *Übermensch*" affirms all that is as completed in his "dominant" position, while the "wise *Übermensch*" sees his position embedded in all that is and affirms the recurrence of both his dominance and all else in existence (thus neutralizing dominance). As I hope my previous discussions have shown, this would be a contradiction only if the initial posture of affirmation were seen as some completed state, rather than the *beginning* of a journey that shows the meaning of affirmation to be intrinsically linked to engaging otherness, rather than a position of dominance.

Karl Löwith has written an extremely important and well-versed analysis of eternal recurrence.[8] His work stands out not only by taking Nietzsche seriously on recurrence, including its factual sense, but by recognizing its central role in Nietzsche's thought. Unlike interpretations that try to marginalize eternal recurrence, Löwith sees it as the animating core of Nietzsche's entire project. Indeed, we should take Nietzsche's cosmological experiments seriously because eternal recurrence was for him far more than just an existential matter; it gathered Nietzsche's proposal of a *worldview* (94, 121). Yet Löwith also reads the doctrine as having a normative element in prompting a way of life. Because of this conjunction, Löwith detects a contradiction at the heart of Nietzsche's philosophy: that between (1) the cosmological version as a goal-lacking *fact* devoid of meaning, and (2) the "anthropological" *value* of the normative version (83). I have argued, however, against any kind of fact-value polarity in Nietzsche's thinking, and my gambit of a literal reading is meant to avoid the polarizing effects of taking recurrence as either a cosmological fact or a mere human, personal value.

I have conceded that our best evidence suggests that Nietzsche retreated from proposing a cosmological account of eternal recurrence. But this need not mean that Nietzsche "rejected" the account and exchanged it for a nonliteral version that has nothing to do with the repetition of life. I have maintained that repetition is essential for charging the existential element of recurrence (the spirit of the published versions, which preceded the notebook experiments). Even if Nietzsche could pull off a scientific demonstration, it could not supercede the existential base of the doctrine; indeed, as an objective, disengaged analysis, it could not express (it would even suppress) the core significance of life affirmation and its encounter with meaninglessness. Yet the fact that Nietzsche *did* venture a cosmological account at all suggests (to me) that some kind of descriptive sense of recurrence was important to him and operative in his thinking. Even a notebook entry depicting eternal recurrence as a life ideal interjects a surprising dose of objectivity: "My teaching says: Live in such a way that you must *desire* to live again; this is the task—you will live again *in any case!*" (*KSA* 9, 505).

Nonetheless, I have contended that only if one *begins* with the death of God and the existential *problem* of time (akin to the traditional problem of evil) can the force of eternal recurrence (and the default argument in its favor) make sense. If one begins with an objective, cosmological orientation (which Nietzsche did not), the baseline significance of eternal recurrence will get sidetracked. The cosmological account should be seen as derived from, and subordinate to, the existential version; and yet Nietzsche probably thought that the former could play a supplemental or catalytic role in his overall project.[9]

Since Nietzsche held that science (including physics) is, like everything else, an interpretation rather than a factual explanation (*BGE* 14), we should not ask whether or how Nietzsche hoped that recurrence could be "demonstrated" by science, but rather: What interpretive, and specifically *rhetorical*, role could science play in Nietzsche's philosophical enterprise? In section 55 of *The Will to Power*, where eternal recurrence is deemed an (extreme) interpretive alternative to theology, he does call recurrence "the most *scientific* of all possible hypotheses." But as I have noted, the context of this claim does not involve espousing scientific "objectivity," but rather the *nonteleological* character of modern science.[10] I think it is plausible that Nietzsche's cosmological venture was analogous to the tactical role that Kant and Schopenhauer played in *The Birth of Tragedy*, and that scientific perspectives played in the middle period writings: namely the deconstructive self-limitation of reason as a preparation for a tragic worldview that would replace metaphysical, moral, and epistemological optimism. Something along these lines is suggested in section 1057 of *The Will to Power* (where eternal recurrence is called a "prophecy"). There Nietzsche outlines a set of steps leading to the deep cultural challenge posed by cyclic repetition: "(1) Presentation (*Darstellung*, which can also mean "theatrical performance") of the doctrine and its theoretical presuppositions and consequences. (2) Evidence (*Beweis*) of the doctrine. (3) Presumed consequences of its being *believed* (it makes everything *break open*)." Nietzsche follows this with a heading: "Means of enduring it." In another note he elaborates on what "enduring" eternal recurrence would entail, which expresses existential yet nonsubjective features:

> The revaluation of all values. No longer joy in certainty but in uncertainty; no longer "cause and effect" but the continually creative; no longer will to preservation but to power; no longer the humble expression "everything is *merely* subjective," but "it is also *our* work!—Let us be proud of it!" (*WP* 1059).

Existential Readings

Because of the critical and textual problems haunting the cosmological version, many interpreters take the existential version to be primary, as a test or prompt for life affirmation and as an antidote to nihilism and the fugitive tendencies of Western thought. Richard Schacht grants that Nietzsche may have seriously pursued a cosmological proof but considers it a failed thought experiment that can be tossed without affecting Nietzsche's overall endeavor, particularly the live option of the existential version.[11] John Richardson reads eternal recurrence as an affirmation test that selects the *Übermensch* type and weeds out the sickness of nihilism. The "truth" of eternal recurrence is not a cosmological fact but a practical-epistemological willing it to be true, which joins the self with the whole of becoming.[12] Laurence Lampert, Gary Shapiro, and David Allison provide excellent discussions of eternal recurrence by way of careful readings of the narrative drama in *Thus Spoke Zarathustra*.[13]

Tracy Strong takes Nietzsche seriously on eternal recurrence and thinks he was straightforward about its meaning and significance. But he thinks that the cosmological version cannot be sustained and so the doctrine should be aimed at transforming individuals rather than a scheme of cyclic repetition. A transformed individual can be in a "state of eternal return," which is a repeatable capacity for excellence, performing at high levels of life in accordance with the world.[14] Kathleen Marie Higgins offers a provocative reading wherein eternal recurrence is an expression of an attitude toward life rather than a cosmological theory or a practical imperative.[15] The affirmative posture expressed by recurrence is a joyful present-centered attitude likened to the temporal experience of music, where the delight in musical moments cannot be separated from past and future notes in the overall compositional structure.

I have already mentioned Bernd Magnus's fine study of eternal recurrence, which presents a thorough treatment of different approaches and which focuses on life affirmation.[16] For Magnus, the existential version is "indifferent" to the literal truth of recurrence and is emblematic of an *übermenschlich* disposition that overcomes nihilism. Alexander Nehamas has written an important and influential treatment of Nietzshe's thought that emphasizes literary elements, which provide a nonfoundational formation of the "text" of one's life. In an ingenious way, Nehamas reads eternal recurrence as an overarching metaphor for the world as a text to be interpreted. The cyclic image of time expresses a manner of composing an integrated, unified self in the midst of becoming.[17] Finally, Maudemarie Clark provides a thorough analysis of the various perspectives and critical questions concerning eternal recurrence. She stresses the existential version based on life affirmation because the problematic cosmological version adds nothing to this life ideal, for which a belief in repetition is neither necessary nor sufficient.[18]

Since I believe that the existential significance of eternal recurrence is its core concern, I find all the studies noted here to be congenial in one way or another. Yet I have argued that rejecting or limiting the cosmological version can still admit a literal meaning that I think is essential in drawing out the existential disposition of life affirmation. I have also ventured that affirmation—in Nietzsche's strict sense of the term—may not be articulable, or distinguishable from life enhancement, without the concentrating force of cyclic repetition. Recalling an earlier discussion of the relationship between eternal recurrence, affirmation, and the course of Nietzsche's thinking out of an inchoate mood, I can summarize as follows: Nietzsche's thought from the beginning was aiming to embrace the finite life-world and work against life-denying tendencies of all kinds. Nietzsche's mood of discontent with the tradition (and with himself?), together with intimations of affirmation and its call, brought him to a revelatory moment that gathered the force of his disposition into a Dionysian experience of self-exceeding concentration on finite life—with nothing *other* than this life. Eternal recurrence can be understood as an Apollonian formation that shaped and articulated this Dionysian experience, and that (like tragedy) would "speak back" to the Dionysian impulse by catalyzing, prompting, or rendering the ongoing *possibility* of its force. Here we notice Dionysian experience and the articulated script of eternal recurrence in a reciprocal relation of "crossing" effects.

There is also a reciprocal crossing effect between (1) the self-exceeding whole of life, (2) the productive, self-constituting character of this whole (the meaning of any moment is caught up with all other moments), and (3) the inescapable experience of life in concrete personal terms, which means that I can only affirm life as *my*-life-in-the-midst-of-the-whole. All these relationships intrinsic to eternal recurrence present the possibility of an *articulated and specific* affirmation of life, which would be more robust than either of the following options: some kind of visceral, mystical, primal affirmative mood that cannot be ascertained, communicated, measured, or tested, and a merely reflective, abstract, "armchair affirmation" that bypasses (or flees) an engagement with the tensional, passional, material character of life *as lived*. Recalling Zarathustra's confession, this kind of affirmation would love life "far away" but fear it "close by."

Such an analysis avoids what I think is the misleading idea that eternal recurrence is nothing more than a test for affirmation, as though the latter took full precedence and the former performed only an instrumental function. In addition, my approach has the advantage of fitting better Nietzsche's own depiction of how eternal recurrence came to him, which can be understood as having revelatory, disclosive power (not simply a test), born out a long-brewing disposition that finally took shape with a kind of "inspired" immediacy. Nietzsche's *writing* can then be perceived as a charged confluence of Dionysian and Apollonian forces that he offers to readers as a potential energy/thought system meant to tap into the very movements Nietzsche experienced, and prompt all the existential and intellectual effects that bear on this complex engagement.

I concede a possible objection that could call into question my entire enterprise: even if I am right that eternal recurrence should be understood in terms of a mimetic reading analogous to Nietzsche's genetic experience, is such a reading *possible* for us? Is reflection perhaps so intrinsic to philosophical reading that we cannot break through from a hypothetical as-if rendition to what I call mimetic identification? Perhaps. Nevertheless, my approach presents itself as an analysis that might be more faithful to *Nietzsche's* understanding of eternal recurrence than other interpretations, and that at least can deploy this contrast for a host of philosophical discussions.

Normative Readings

A number of writers have depicted eternal recurrence as a kind of ethical imperative that presents a Nietzschean spin on the Kantian categorical imperative.[19] The inspiration for such a reading is found primarily in the notable passage from *The Gay Science*: "The question in each and every thing 'Do you want this again and innumerable times again?' would lie upon your actions as the greatest weight!" (*GS* 341). The idea is that the prospect of eternal recurrence can serve as a measure for action in terms of whether one would want a certain action repeated eternally. Unlike a Kantian test of universality and rational consistency, the concentrating effect of repetition can simply generate a powerful focus on an individual's choices and possibilities; it can thus prompt a reflective posture that overcomes careless or thoughtless behavior because of the psychological impact of considering the eternally repeated "record" of a certain course of action.

I think it is entirely plausible to deploy eternal recurrence in this manner, but I do not think it can suffice as a reading of what Nietzsche had in mind.[20] I say this not because of what would seem to be the obvious objection: that Nietzsche was a vigorous critic of morality. I have argued elsewhere that Nietzsche's philosophy is critical of *certain ways* morality has been conceived and that a robust approach to ethics can indeed be drawn from his texts.[21] My objection is that a normative account of eternal recurrence at the very least covers up the central issue of life affirmation and the nonreflective, immediate force of experience I have been trying to highlight. I do not think the texts support a reflective stance wherein possible actions are gauged by way of repetition as a measure for decisions. Section 341 is not presented as a subjunctive hypothetical ("would you want …"), but simply *willst du* ("do you want …"); nor as a test to "weigh" the value of action, but simply a great weight (*Schwergewicht*, as stress or emphasis) that marks one's capacity to *affirm* life in whatever way it unfolds. The passage continues with a disjunction: "Or how well disposed would you have to become to yourself and to life to *desire nothing more* than this ultimate eternal confirmation and seal?" The "or" seems to call for some caution in reading this passage as a type of imperative. The disjunction could be separating the two surrounding passages in such a way that the former is a kind of oppressive gravity and the latter is a welcoming affirmation—both passages being reactions to the announcement of eternal recurrence.[22] Even more, could the "or" signal an exchange of affirmation for the entire interrogative posture of the former passage? In any case, the phrase "confirmation and seal" in the latter passage suggests a kind of celebratory denotation rather than the outcome of a normative test.

In general terms a moral interpretation of eternal recurrence runs counter to its global inclusiveness, which for one thing has tragic implications that sit uneasily with ethical formats.[23] Eternal recurrence is a meta-conception about the value of all forms of life and would not itself, therefore, serve as an ethical procedure for measuring specific forms of life. Moreover, Nietzsche maintains that the *global* purposeless "necessity" of life (an essential element of eternal recurrence) is incompatible with moral principles and ideals, which can only reflect *local* projections (*BGE* 9). Finally, the following notebook passage is straightforward: "To *endure* the idea of eternal recurrence one needs: freedom from morality; … the *enjoyment* of all kinds of uncertainty, experimentalism, as a counterweight to this extreme fatalism" (*WP* 1060).

An important and influential reading has been advanced by Gilles Deleuze, who discounts global repetition and argues for a Kantian-style imperative that provides *selective* practical guidance in promoting "active" over "reactive" forces of becoming.[24] According to Deleuze, eternal recurrence affirms the "being" of becoming, which provides a kind of philosophical stability; but as such it must involve a "selective ontology," stemming from Nietzsche's remark about recurrence being a "selective principle" (*WP* 1058). Since becoming-active is the only authentic affirmation of becoming, it would be inconsistent to propose the return of nihilistic modes of becoming-reactive, which on Nietzsche's terms would have no true being. The problem with this account is that it misreads "selection" in ontological rather than dispositional terms. For Nietzsche, eternal recurrence is selective "in the service of strength" (*WP* 1058), in differentiating affirmative from nihilistic *bearings* toward life. Moreover, Deleuze must sidestep clear indications in the texts that recurrence includes otherness, including affirmation's Other, because of the agonistic structure of becoming and value. Indeed, in a notebook discussion of recurrence, Nietzsche specifically mentions the repetition of even nihilism (*WP* 55).

In some ways I think that normative readings have been motivated, consciously or otherwise, by an interest in neutralizing or overcoming an obvious effect that repetition can spark, namely moral repugnance. I will have more to say on this important matter in the next chapter, but it is clear that one crucial burden of eternal recurrence is the call to affirm the repetition of any and all conditions that one could presume to be morally deficient, if not monstrous. This subject is essential and unavoidable because it echoes Zarathustra's nausea in coming to terms with eternal recurrence. I only say here that normative or selective interpretations cannot resolve this problem and cannot avoid departures from Nietzsche's texts.[25] Rather than trying to dodge or resolve the problem of moral repugnance by finding an ethical (per-)version of eternal recurrence, it would be preferable to confront the problem honestly in the terms of the texts, with the option of repudiating Nietzsche rather than converting him.

I conclude by quoting in full the notebook passage that seems to advance a hypothetical test but adds the decidedly fatalistic check that repetition will occur "in any case." The passage goes on to display multiple possibilities of life projects, to an extent that would undermine any kind of selective normative measure. Furthermore, each possibility must embrace the full range of conditions (including the fearful) that constitute its possibility.

> My teaching says: Live in such a way that you must *desire* to live again; this is the task—you will live again *in any case*! He for whom striving gives the highest feeling, let him strive; he for whom rest gives the highest feeling, let him rest; he for whom ordering, following, and obeying gives the highest feeling, let him obey. Only *provided* that he *becomes aware* of *what* gives him the highest feeling and that *no means* toward it are avoided or feared. *Eternity* is at stake! (*KSA* 9, 505).

Symbolic Readings

I use the term "symbolic" here loosely to designate interpretations that redescribe the literal sense of eternal recurrence in other terms having nothing to do with the repetition of life. Presumably these readings are sympathetic to Nietzsche in trying to rescue the doctrine from all the problems adhering to its literal depiction. Given that Nietzsche celebrated a nonfoundational, open approach to language, symbolic readings can have much to recommend them and in fact can display important interpretive insights. Moreover, the close connection between eternal recurrence and other basic concepts in Nietzsche's thought make it plausible to recast recurrence in terms of one or more of these concepts, a notable example being will to power.[26] My argument is not that there is no value in such approaches, but that the reductive redescription of eternal recurrence is not faithful enough to the texts, that the literal meaning need not be sacrificed to make better sense of Nietzsche, and that, perhaps, symbolic modifications might be complicit with the very fugitive disposition targeted by Nietzsche when he advanced repetition as a "final exam" for life.

A notable representative example of symbolic readings is offered by Joan Stambaugh in an honest, inventive, and stimulating work. Stambaugh admits to going beyond Nietzsche's account in the texts but thinks it necessary so as to resolve the many problems associated with eternal recurrence, particularly what she takes to be its nihilistic implications if understood literally.[27] She wants to understand recurrence not as repeated cycles of time but as the occurrence of time itself. If we forego thinking of time as durational stretches (whether cyclic or linear), recurrence can be taken as a metaphor for the unfolding of occurrences in an instant, every instant (105). Eternity can be construed as the ending of each moment out of itself into its temporal process. In this way eternal recurrence can be likened to a Buddhist "enlightened ending" (116) in that the world is "finished" in every moment. An openness to the "end" of each moment can sustain Nietzsche's idea of eternal value without having to posit cyclic repetition. There is much to admire in this analysis, but I think it misses what I have suggested is the essential role of repetition in the task of life affirmation. Exchanging repetition for a formal analysis of "momentary occurrence" bypasses the *material* element so important to Nietzsche: *this* and *these* moments as lived. And the assumption that repetition is nihilistic stops halfway in Zarathustra's journey of passing *through* meaninglessness to *finite* meaning informed by this passage. For this reason I press for a literal meaning of recurrence, and in so doing I (no doubt presumptuously) disagree with Stambaugh (and surely many others) when she says that eternal recurrence is an elusive enigma, a "doctrine still to be fathomed" (115).

Another provocative account is presented by Robert Gooding-Williams. He does not discount the cosmological and existential aspects, but he thinks it profitable to redescribe recurrence in terms of the central role of creativity in Nietzsche's philosophy. Eternal recurrence is then read away from the repetition motif toward its function in Zarathustra's task of opening the possibility of creating new values. Recurrence, then, is the repetition of the possibility of a future that interrupts present and past productions; repetition is a Dionysian process of deploying "uncreated passions" to create a future different from the past.[28] Once again this is an ingenious interpretation that folds eternal recurrence into elemental forces in Nietzsche's project. Yet again I question why recurrence must be redescribed in this and other ways. Given the obvious challenges and difficulties surrounding eternal recurrence, I recognize in these readings the laudable attempt to give Nietzsche a philosophical "assist," but I suppose my point is that Nietzsche may be able to score on his own (in a game that many of us perhaps should confess to having a hard time watching, much less playing).

Ontological Readings

This heading overlaps somewhat with symbolic readings, in that the repetition scheme is exchanged for something else hidden within the surface depiction. Ontological readings are marked by an appreciation of eternal recurrence as the core of Nietzsche's thinking, and so these interpretations aim to uncover a general, overarching philosophical content implied by the doctrine. For example, Jaspers reads eternal recurrence as the philosophical response to the death of God, a worldly replacement for traditional constructs and an antidote to the nihilism following God's demise.[29] For Deleuze, as we have seen, eternal recurrence accomplishes an ontologizing of becoming; repetition symbolizes the attribution of "being" to becoming and therefore marks becoming as a philosophical primum that must inform all thinking.[30]

Surely the most important reading in this category is that of Martin Heidegger.[31] I cannot do any justice to Heidegger's brilliant and influential interpretation in such a brief sketch, and I only mean to mark it off from my approach by placing it among ontological redescriptions of eternal recurrence. The gist of Heidegger's account is that eternal recurrence shows Nietzsche's philosophy of becoming to be still caught up in metaphysical constructs of "being," in that repetition fixes conditions of becoming with eternal significance. For Heidegger, metaphysics entails any ascription of a positive foundation to the whole of beings. Even though Nietzsche was the firm opponent of being-constructions, his "reversal" of being into becoming was still enmeshed in positive metaphysics (becoming as the constructed, polarized *Other* of being). Since Heidegger's alternative to metaphysics requires a step back from all such constructions, he sees Nietzsche as the consummation of metaphysics rather than its overcoming. Eternal recurrence and its redemptive departure from Western "revenge" against time depict a deep philosophical discovery rather than mere psychological or dispositional features. Since Heidegger diagnoses modern metaphysics as grounded in human subjectivity (at the expense of being), Nietzsche's affirmation of the will in eternal recurrence (the will willing the repetition of its willing) amounts to a climax of modern metaphysics. For all of Nietzsche's worthy assaults against the tradition, his reversal could not escape its opponent and sustained the modern danger of reducing the meaning of being to human assertions and projects.

Heidegger's profound analysis does find some traction in some of Nietzsche's rhetorical moments of polarization, but I hope that earlier discussions (and some to come) can disrupt Heidegger's reading. Nietzsche's philosophy of agonistic becoming entails a continual "crossing" dynamic that cannot rest in any "position" (even "becoming"). And the animating spirit of Nietzsche's call for life affirmation, culminating in eternal recurrence, departs from and calls into question any foundation in the "human," or the "subject," or even the "will" as a discrete concept apart from the dynamic of life forces and world-disclosure.

This concludes my sketch of other readings, all of which in one way or another miss what I think is Nietzsche's direct commitment to eternal recurrence as written. Opponents and proponents alike, while offering important and even plausible discussions, seem united by the conviction that Nietzsche could not or should not have meant what he wrote. The posture of my book is to call this consensus into question and attempt to write ably about what Nietzsche himself wrote.

7

The Trouble with Repetition: Confronting Critical Questions

This last chapter will confront a number of critical problems that arise if eternal recurrence is granted any kind of validity. The discussion will engage four questions: (1) Does eternal recurrence entail a deterministic denial of freedom? (2) Does eternal recurrence subvert Nietzsche's promotion of creativity? (3) Does the charge of moral repugnance make eternal recurrence intolerable? (4) How can eternal recurrence admit of truth in any worthy sense?

The Question of Freedom

Nietzsche rejects both the notion of a free will and an unfree will (*BGE* 21). Yet he also champions an idea that seems clearly at odds with freedom, namely necessity. It is important to begin with an analysis of this idea in order to address critical assessments of eternal recurrence and to fathom how freedom can function in Nietzsche's thought. As we have seen, Nietzsche specifically associates eternal recurrence with necessity, and the repetition scheme seems to imply a rigid determinism, because any event that happens, has happened, or will happen cannot admit of any alternatives. Whatever I do next has happened an infinite number of times in the same way, and so there is only one possible future. Surely this sounds like determinism and a denial of freely chosen acts in any sense, since choice implies real alternative possibilities.[1] My argument is as follows: Nietzschean necessity does rule out classic conceptions of free will, but it does not fit classic conceptions of determinism either. Nietzsche advances an unusual sense of necessity that echoes the ancient Greek understanding of fate, most especially the force of tragic fate.

For Nietzsche, the necessity of an event does rule out alternatives, but simply from the standpoint of the "self-evidence" of the immediate event as such, with nothing *other* or outside it, whether that be a causal chain or a self-originating "will" or "substance." This is why Nietzsche says that "occurrence (*Geschehen*) and necessary occurrence is a *tautology*" (*WP* 639). Necessity is counterposed not only to free alternatives but to any sense of mechanism,

127

causality, or law: "Let us beware of saying that there are laws in nature. There are only necessities" (GS 109).[2] We have previously seen that one connotation of necessity follows from the absence of global purposes, an absence that makes the idea of an "accident" senseless (GS 109). But necessity is also different from logical or causal necessity. Nietzsche dismisses any radical sense of causality or law. The reason he denies both a free and an unfree will is that each is a false attribution of causality: freedom as self-causation and unfreedom as external causation (BGE 21). Necessity does not follow from the force of law but from the *absence* of law (BGE 22); it cannot mean some fixed relation between successive states (which violates the primacy of radical becoming) but simply that a state is what it is rather than something else (WP 552, 631). Necessity indicates that an occurrence "cannot be otherwise" *simply* by force of its immediate emergence, independent of any sense of causality—whether the self-causality of freedom, the final causality of teleology, or the efficient causality of determinism—since causality always looks *away* from an occurrence as such and in one way or another relies on the possibility of alternatives. Teleology looks "ahead" for intelligibility, mechanism looks "before" and "after" for causal regulation, and freedom looks "within" for a spontaneous agent. Alternativeness, of course, is essential to freedom, but it operates in teleology too ("straying" from telic movement—an accident— helps define proper movement), and in scientific causality as well (current causal findings depend on positing future repetitions and alternative results under different causal conditions).

Nietzsche does not deny the possibility of causal thinking, only its primal posture as "explanation." Causality is an *interpretation* of experience that is useful for "designation and communication" (BGE 21–22). Necessity names the primal immediacy of events-in-becoming *as such*, for which in each case an "alternative" would not be "another event" but *no event* (see WP 567). It is important to note that the "immediacy" of occurrence should not be taken as an isolated state or a pure "present," because all occurrences are temporally structured. An occurrence is an extended span of movement that can be acknowledged in Nietzsche's conception of necessity. Any occurrence, even a locally purposeful one, can be taken *as is* (as it becomes) independent of a global teleological account or a scientific causal account.

Necessity is intrinsically linked with the affirmation task animating eternal recurrence, which forces attention on events *as they occur*, as opposed to the nihilistic implications of wanting life to be otherwise, or even of regulating intransigent forces by way of causal explanations. What is important for Nietzsche is that necessity is charged with existential meaning.[3] And the meaning of necessity is not something entertained by intellectual analysis or adjudication, but rather the dispositional response to the desirability of life as it is in just the way it is. An affirmative response is not simply recognition or acceptance, but the *love* of necessity (*amor fati*). In this way Nietzsche points back to (and intensifies) the early Greek notion of fate as a *religious* phenomenon, that is to say, a *reverence* for the power of tragic finitude. Recall that Nietzsche works with a literal rendering of necessity (*Not-wendigkeit*) as the "reversal of distress" (distress over the force of becoming).

In early Greek thought, fate (*moira*) was described in both personal terms (the gods) and impersonal terms (usually associated with death and destruction), the latter being a power that even the gods could not control.[4] In any case, fate was a force that could not be avoided, controlled, or comprehended by mortals. Fate was also variously linked with the words *anankē* and *chreōn*, both often translated as "necessity" and carrying meanings of compulsion, constraint (specifically enslavement) and inevitability. Another link was with the word *tuchē*, or chance, which was frequently referred to as a sacred power.[5] In philosophy necessity took on altered meanings of strict rationality, but this was still an analogical extension of older meanings. Moreover, Plato and Aristotle recognized and even employed the association of necessity and chance.[6] Zarathustra, when speaking of affirmation, celebrates chance as something ancient, and as something that brings a kind of freedom construed as a liberation from purpose and rational constriction:

> Verily, it is a blessing and not a blasphemy when I teach: "Over all things stand the heaven Accident, the heaven Innocence, the heaven Chance, the heaven Prankishness." "By chance"—that is the most ancient nobility of the world, and this I restored to all things: I delivered them from their bondage under purpose. This freedom and heavenly cheer I have placed over all things like an azure bell when I taught that over them and through them no "eternal will" wills. This prankish folly I have put in the place of that will when I taught: "In everything one thing is impossible: rationality." A *little* reason to be sure, … a little wisdom is possible indeed; but this blessed certainty I found in all things: that they would rather *dance* on the feet of chance. (*Z* III, 4)

Necessity and chance, therefore, name the power of sheer manifestation apart from causal explanations and global purposes (both of which are implicated in nihilism). Determinism cannot be the proper depiction of this peculiar conception of necessity, which accordingly cannot be ascertained as a "refutation" of any sense of freedom. Indeed, the affirmative disposition intrinsic to necessity implies something different from deterministic control or fatalistic resignation. The *love* of fate is not the same as "being fated," and its joyous participatory element can indicate traces of freedom.[7]

We have seen that Nietzsche objected to the idea of free will because of its false attribution of causality and its complicity in promoting the slavish conception of moral responsibility. But since he also rejects an unfree will by disrupting causal and teleological governance, a modified sense of freedom can be drawn from the texts and coordinated with eternal recurrence in a number of ways. Causal and teleological thinking came to redefine necessity—beyond the early Greek notion of a revered, inexplicable, uncontrollable force—as a rationalized explanation that in different ways mandates a closed future (either the predictable future of causal legislation or the consummated future of teleological completion). But *by contrast*, Nietzschean necessity—the tautological immediacy of occurrence—entails an *open* future. Moreover, the open-ended character of striving (always ahead of itself and irreducible to fixed conditions) will always be closed off or nullified by causal or telic "results" (*WP* 688, 787). Such irreducible openness allows for a kind of "default" freedom that is different from metaphysical models taken as *self*-causation.

Another way to understand freedom emerges from the correlation of necessity and chance in Nietzsche's analysis. Chance is incompatible with the idea of controlled production, the execution of a plan. In this way chance is "free" from both teleological direction and the mix of scientific findings with telic direction in modern technology (the regime of prediction and control in the service of human projects made possible by causal accounts of nature). Moreover, modern conceptions of freedom have been counterposed to scientific determinism on behalf of a "self-caused" alternative that is likewise motivated by control—*self*-control. Modern freedom and determinism, therefore, are both animated by control, whether active (self-control) or passive (control by external causes). The kind of freedom possible in Nietzsche's analysis is not the opposite of causal determinism, but simply the radical *openness* of the as-is necessity of occurrence ungoverned by any explanatory trace (whether to natural laws or a self that exceeds nature).

Yet is not the fact that eternal recurrence entails only one possible future a foreclosure of freedom in any meaningful sense? Only if the future were determinable from a present position *within* the cycle of possible events (recall that "retrieving" anything from past cycles is ruled out). To my knowledge nothing in the texts indicates any such thing, and so the necessity of eternal recurrence can fit the previous discussion of the openness of necessity. Whenever the affirmation of life by way of eternal recurrence is specifically portrayed in terms of discernible events, the reference is to present and past events, not the future. We have noted that Zarathustra celebrates seafaring and its venturing toward undiscovered horizons (e.g., *Z* III, 16, 5); and he calls on his followers to "work on the future" (*Z* III, 12, 3). Although cycles as such are identical repetitions, *within* a cycle there are no repeated identities (*KSA* 9, 523); and as I suggested, the extent of variations within a cycle can be so vast as to be open enough to dampen the repulsion over a restricted set of possibilities (for all but the greediest variety-enthusiasts). Thus freedom and necessity can coexist in Nietzsche's account, as indicated (albeit cryptically) in Zarathustra's remark about time as "a happy mockery of moments," wherein necessity is joined with freedom in "playing happily with the goading (*Stachel*) of freedom" (*Z* III, 12, 2).

Freedom, for Nietzsche, is nothing like a substantive faculty or power possessed by a "subject," but rather a relational term in line with the agonistic structure of will to power. Even the "free spirit" cannot be understood apart from the context of diverging from cultural conventions and expectations (*HAH* I, 225). The human sense of freedom arises from the delight in overcoming obstacles (*BGE* 19); indeed the measure of freedom can only be gauged "according to the resistance that must be overcome" (*TI* 9, 38). This helps in comprehending Nietzsche's supplement to his dismissal of a free and unfree will: he adds that there are only strong and weak wills (*BGE* 21), according to their capacity or incapacity for agonistic practice and experimentation.[8] There is also help in understanding Nietzsche's dictum, "Become what you are" (*GS* 270, 335), which is clearly ambiguous with respect to necessity and freedom. For one thing it denies a radically open tabula rasa, but it also requires a movement of becoming not governed by external causes or purposes. And since there is no systematic order of becoming, different lines of force confront each other in radically agonistic relations. Therefore one may not be free to be other than what one is, but one can be free in relation to *other* force lines aiming to control or impede one's path. Self-affirmation would then entail saying Yes to what one is together with all the tensional relations involved in becoming what one is. Such an account matches (1) the outcome in eternal recurrence of willing to be what one has always been, and (2) the denial of the idea that what one is stems from a self-sufficient, self-originating agency.

One way to separate Nietzschean freedom from the modern binary of determinism and indeterminism is to designate action as a "middle voice" construction (a grammatical form more common in ancient Greek than in modern languages). The middle voice is neither active nor passive in a strict sense because the agent participates in an enactment wider than the agent's initiative or control. Middle voice action happens "to" or "within" an agent, but still "through" the agent: for instance, sneezing, awakening from sleep, being educated, falling into enemy hands.[9] Nietzsche presents such a construction when he says that in willing, "we are at the same time the commanding *and* the obeying parties" (*BGE* 19). Once again we witness a retrieval of the Greek perspective on human life. In early Greek culture, fate was an effective force that could not be predicted, controlled, or comprehended by humans, a force that was also regarded with a receptive bearing. Yet this bearing was nothing like fatalistic resignation because Greek myth displayed multiple lines of competing sacred parties, and it also celebrated heroic achievement in the midst of (and sometimes at odds with) fate. A telling climax of this outlook was the figure of Oedipus, the worthy hero whose own enactment brought about his fated downfall; indeed his *resistance* to fate was both the agency of fate and the precondition for all of his estimable social achievements (the benefits of his intelligence and leadership) that arose from his path of action.[10]

Another way to grasp the middle voice conception of freedom comes from Nietzsche's references to play as a nonfoundational mode of becoming and production not bound by causality or purpose: for example, the image of the child as the "play of creation" (*Z* I, 1); and the comment about Heraclitus, who put forth "the teaching of *the law in becoming and the play in necessity*," and in doing so "raised the curtain on this greatest of plays (*Schauspiel*)" (*KSA* 1, 835). Playing in a game, for example, obviously involves agency, but performance is both governed by preestablished rules that players agree to follow, and constrained by the competitive actions of other players.[11] And Nietzsche's reference to dramatic performance indicates a similar blend of agency and constraint. Actors contribute their own behaviors and inflections to the drama, but shaped by the script and relations with other actors. Greek tragedy in particular, in its thematic content, can be said to portray a "theatrical world," wherein the heroic character's life plays out within limits set by the tragic narrative.[12]

Nietzsche proclaims: "One is necessary, one is a piece of fatefulness, one belongs to the whole, one is in the whole"(*TI* 6, 8). But the "whole" is not a systematic order but the field of all possible relations and counterrelations (adding up globally to a "chaos"). And since "there is nothing besides the whole," neither the totality nor anything in it can be ultimately judged or measured, which leaves us with the "great liberation" of the "innocence of becoming" (*TI* 6, 8). In this same text Nietzsche concludes that nothing is "responsible" for man being the way he is, including *himself*. Again we notice the powerful ambiguity of selfhood necessarily embedded in a larger network of forces and yet *not* governed, compelled, or explained by anything "external" to the immediacy of active becoming.

The ambiguity of middle voice action, along with the affirmative posture intrinsic to the necessity of eternal recurrence, allows Nietzsche to distinguish his sense of *amor fati* from any kind of fatalistic resignation. With no "external" force in the field of action, a "passive" response to fate would be far from mandated, because such an outlook presumes a false dichotomy. This point is underlined in Nietzsche's account of "Mohammedan fatalism."

> Mohammedan fatalism embodies the fundamental error of setting man and fate against one another as two separate things: man, it says, can resist fate and seek to frustrate it, but in the end it always carries off the victory; so that the most reasonable thing to do is to resign oneself or to live just as one pleases. In reality every man is himself a piece of fate; when he thinks to resist fate in the way suggested, it is precisely fate that is here fulfilling itself; the struggle is imaginary, but so is the proposed resignation to fate; all these imaginings are enclosed within fate.—The fear most people feel in the face of the theory of the unfreedom of the will is fear in the face of Mohammedan fatalism: they think that man will stand before the future feeble, resigned and with hands clasped because he is incapable of effecting any change in it: or that he will give free reign to all his impulses and caprices because these too cannot make any worse what has already been determined. The follies of mankind are just so many pieces of fate as are its acts of intelligence: that fear in the face of a belief in fate is also fate. (*WS* 61).[13]

Nietzsche's argument seems to be that something like fate or necessity has no bearing at all on how we are to understand human action *in practice*. Even if scientific determinism were demonstrably true, the openness of the future and introspective convictions about having real choices are phenomenological facts that cannot be explained away. Indeed, the determinist faces the puzzle that a belief in freedom must also be determined, and so people are determined to think that determinism is false.[14] Necessity and fate, for Nietzsche, do not play an explanatory role; rather, they prompt (by force of eternal recurrence) the deeper existential questions of the meaning of life, and they diagnose the presence of fugitive dispositions in all manner of philosophical theories, including those promoting free will or determinism.

The Question of Creativity

The charge that eternal recurrence subverts Nietzsche's interest in freedom is undermined by his consistent rejection of traditional conceptions of freedom, construed as self-sufficient agency: "Nothing is self-sufficient, neither ourselves nor things" (*KSA* 12, 307). Yet the issue of creativity is different because of Nietzsche's enduring advocacy of creative production as the source of cultural becoming, as the subversion of timeless truths, and as the adventure of innovation over against herd conformity and mediocrity. If eternal recurrence dictates the identical repetition of events, then a "creative" act is anything but new and unprecedented from the standpoint of the eternal span of time. In this respect even a current conforming mentality (an individuated perpetuation of a generalized belief) is more distinctive and various than the repeated clones of supposed innovations across cycles. If there is a way to meet this objection and resolve the problem of creativity, it begins by pointing out the confusion between intra-cyclic and cross-cyclic standpoints in the objection. If we grant the impossibility of a cross-cyclic viewpoint, then a consideration of creativity can follow the lines of Nietzsche's approach to freedom (and he does consider creativity to be likewise implicated with necessity, chance, and acausal immediacy). The problem of creativity in light of eternal recurrence is a worthy question. But as in the case of freedom, Nietzsche's response will involve not only the possible coexistence of recurrence and creativity, but also a revision of the very meaning of creativity in general terms.

For Nietzsche, creativity is not an absolute or purely formal concept, but a relative, contextual phenomenon in (agonistic) relation to existing forces and conditions: "A new creation ... needs enemies more than friends: in opposition alone does it *feel* itself necessary, in opposition alone does it *become* necessary" (*TI* 5, 3). Assuming the constraint of an intra-cyclic viewpoint (which, as we have seen, presumes no identical repetition within the set of possible events), creative acts are clearly plausible; and yet they are not de novo singularities, but necessarily constituted by tensional relations with existing states. Regarding eternal recurrence, just as events in general must be affirmed as structurally dependent on opposing conditions—and not merely in formal but *material* terms—creative events can be understood in the same way. This may help in deciphering a remark by Zarathustra that is far from clear. In discussing affirmation and recurrence, Zarathustra says of his followers: "I taught them to work on (*schaffen*) the future, and to redeem through creation (*schaffend*) all that *has been*" (Z III, 12, 3). What can this mean? Simply the affirmation of past creative tokens in prior cycles? More plausible, I think, is the affirmation of past conditions as requisite for a creative departure from their propriety.

Creation in the setting of eternal recurrence is related to Nietzsche's frequent association of creativity with necessity. In one sense Nietzsche is retrieving the early Greek notion of poetic production. Poets were certainly innovative in bringing forth from concealment a language that could reveal for the community culture-shaping narratives. But poets were not perceived in the modern Romantic mode of individual geniuses drawing from out of their depths autonomous creations. Poets were inspired recipients of sacred forces beyond the conscious control of the human mind. We have seen how Nietzsche described the advent of eternal recurrence as an inspired process rather than a deliberative act. Nietzsche even calls himself a "disciple and initiate of the god Dionysus," the "tempter/experimenter god (*Versucher-Gott*)" who comes to him and teaches him (*BGE* 295). We have also noted how Nietzsche depicted artistic types generally as vessels of surplus energy that breaks forth as a compelling impetus. We must always keep in mind that Nietzsche gives pride of place, not to human selves, but to life. With creative acts, it is life as a whole that advances *through* such acts (*TI* 9, 33).

Considering Nietzsche's typological approach to human possibilities, artistic types are creative in their *relation* to herd types; but in relation to the wider economy of life forces in which they operate, artistic types are *not* creative in the sense of being a discrete "origin" of their activity. Artistic types in a way cannot help but be creative and their work is not fully under conscious control. This is why Nietzsche will extend his concept of necessity to creative acts. Again, necessity is not a causal process but the immediacy of active becoming. The artist as a causal "creator" is rejected for the same reasons that Nietzsche dismisses the "subject" as the cause of thinking. The matter of creativity has particular resonance for Nietzsche's general critique of causality. Creative experience is by nature disruptive and unfamiliar; and Nietzsche suggests that the very impulse to find causal regularities and to trace events to causal origins stems from "fear of the unfamiliar and the attempt to discover something familiar in it" (*WP* 551).

The immediacy of necessity as an emergence *not* explicable in causal or teleological terms allows Nietzsche to connect it with the inexplicable and uncontrollable character of creative experience. Of most thinkers and scholars, Nietzsche says:

They picture every necessity as a kind of need, as a painstaking having-to-follow and being compelled. And thinking itself they consider something slow and hesitant, almost as toil, … not in the least as something light, divine, closely related to dancing and high spirits…. Artists seem to have more sensitive noses in these matters, knowing only too well that precisely when they no longer do anything "voluntarily" but do everything of necessity, their feeling of freedom, subtlety, full power, of creative placing, disposing and forming reaches its peak—in short, that necessity and "freedom of the will" then become one in them. (*BGE* 213)

In one of the texts where Nietzsche promotes scientific nonteleology against moralistic judgments and teleological purposes, the immediacy of creativity is joined with this departure from normative constraints:

Sitting in moral judgment should offend our taste. Let us leave such chatter and such bad taste to those who have nothing else to do but drag the past a few steps further through time and who never live in the present…. We, however, *want to become what we are*—human beings who are new, unique, incomparable, who give themselves laws, who create themselves. To that end we must become the best learners and discoverers of everything that is lawful and necessary in the world: we must become *physicists* in order to be able to be *creators* in this sense. (*GS* 335)[15]

Nietzsche even connects creativity with fatalism in his discussion of Goethe, whose creative "freedom" stems from a faith in the "whole," an affirmative, *übermenschlich* integration that overcomes world-negating divisions and separations from the necessity of enveloping forces.

Such a spirit who has *become free* stands amid the cosmos with a joyous and trusting fatalism, in the *faith* that only the particular is loathsome, and that all is redeemed and affirmed in the whole—*he does not negate anymore*. Such a faith, however, is the highest of all possible faiths: I have baptized it with the name of *Dionysus*. (*TI* 9, 49)[16]

To close this section, there are some tangential points about creativity that do not bear directly on eternal recurrence but that are worth mentioning because they chasten assumptions about Nietzschean creativity that have more to do with a generalized emancipatory rhetoric and hyperbolic openness than with Nietzsche's complex position on creation. First of all, Nietzsche is an elitist about cultural creativity; freedom from norms and constraints is not for everyone but only the able few who have the strength and talent for innovation.[17] Furthermore, the freedom of the creative type does not do away with structures and constraint. Creativity breaks the hold of existing structures in order to shape new ones. Creativity is a complicated relationship between openness and form. Certain "fetters" (*Fesseln*) are required to prepare cultural overcomings of purely natural states (*HAH* I, 221), and to provide a comprehensible shape to new cultural forms (*WS* 140). Creative freedom, therefore, is not the opposite of normalization, discipline, or constraint; it is a disruption of structure that yet needs structure to both prepare and consummate departures from the norm (see *GS* 295 and *BGE* 188). For Nietzsche, creativity is a kind of "dancing in chains" (*WS* 140).[18]

In general terms, this perspective on creativity reiterates Nietzsche's reflections on Apollonian and Dionysian forces in Greek tragedy. Dionysian energy *alone* is not "creative" in the sense of culture-formation; it supplies the underlying power of becoming in life, but without the Apollonian, such becoming would be more chaotic than creative. But because creativity is intrinsically a blend of forming and de-forming powers, Dionysian excess will have to be given a certain emphasis because of its bad press in the tradition. That is why Nietzsche continually gives voice to underreported forces in life—exuberance, boundary crossing, competitiveness, adventure, discontent, power, and so forth—since such forces provide the fuel for creative departures from the given. Furthermore, try as some readers might to say otherwise, Nietzsche does not advocate a generalized promotion of creativity for all human beings. First of all, Nietzsche's interest in creativity is at the level of culture formation and great talent. Secondly, it takes special strength to confront and endure the de-forming forces fueling creative dispositions. Nietzsche's selective elitism stems from his conviction that most people are incapable of sustaining, or unwilling to adopt, the courage and strength required for inhabiting the medial position between form and creative openness, between being and becoming.

The nexus of becoming and being, of openness and form, can also be located in Nietzsche's thoughts on the relation between immediate experience and language. Experience, for Nietzsche, is literally "extemporaneous," out of and from temporal becoming; as such it is without external or transcendent governance, whether in causal or teleological terms. Language and writing bring to experience an articulated "text," a con-text in the manner of a "weaving" of words to organize experience. Although Nietzsche sometimes does describe language and form as "fictions," we should take this as rhetorical hyperbole rather than a substantive judgment. Nietzsche's philosophy continually addresses (and performs) the reciprocal "crossing" of experience and language, of extemporaneous and textual forces, where the latter are ineradicable sources of meaning creation and world formation. It is the polarized reduction to language forms (apart from extemporaneous energies) that distorts the reciprocal nexus by turning to fixed structures, causal relations, or teleological completion. Eternal recurrence, of course, is a text, but one that explicitly embraces the extemporaneity of life and all possible world-formations *in the same breath*. How does eternal recurrence not become the ultimate "fixation" by way of its repetition scheme? By fixing *everything* it fixes *nothing*, because recurrence includes all possible conditions, which include counterforces, modifications, innovations, and so on—and thus the full set of positive and negative conditions that cannot admit of any fixed position in its overall economy.

Finally, I want to note a number of ways creativity and repetition need not be taken as incompatible. In an early note, Nietzsche draws a connection between eternal recurrence and the human desire to experience artworks over and over again (*KSA* 9, 505). The enjoyment of repeat performances of the same text is surely different from exact repetition, but it points to some evidence for the attraction of repetition in human experience.[19] In addition, we should consider the poetic effects of repetition in rhythm, rhyme, and word/phrase reiteration. Such techniques are creative in relation to the normal absence of such patterns in ordinary language. These patterns are temporally structured recurrences that interrupt the familiar directional passage and ongoing business of speech by "re-calling" elements of the passage in different ways: metrics and rhymes infuse temporal passage with rhythmic and sonic attractions; repetition of words or phrases gives them unusual emphasis or retrieves them from temporal passage so as to spotlight something normally hidden by familiarity: their sheer happening *as such*. A poetic "refrain," therefore, is anything but tedious repetition. The word "refrain" comes from the French *refraindre* (to resound) and the Latin *refringere* (to break up or to check). A poetic refrain refrains language in the following way: it is a formal temporal structure that restrains the ordinary material business of linguistic passage; and in doing so, a refrain creates a heightened accentuation of the sheer disclosive force of language. We should note Nietzsche's extended use of refrain in Zarathustra's speech in "The Seven Seals," especially the repeated phrase "For I love you, O eternity!" In this regard, could eternal recurrence be heard as a global poetic refrain?

The Question of Moral Repugnance

The challenge of eternal recurrence to morality is fundamental in the following sense: it would seem that the moral point of view in different ways is animated by the belief or hope that what is deemed immoral ought not to be, and can be eliminated, overcome, modified, transformed, replaced, or punished. The identical repetition of immoral conditions or acts would seem to render any such moral response ultimately impossible or futile. Western philosophy and religion have issued various projects meant to counter a tragic sense of finitude that dictates intrinsic limits to moral rectification. Yet eternal recurrence apparently adds insult to injury by extending the tragic beyond moral limitation to the affirmation of the exact repetition of all transgressions—from the banal to the monstrous—thus mandating no relief (not even a finale in nothingness) from the material presence of specific offenses. It is one thing, say, to know that a friend's murder could not be helped or will go unpunished; quite another that this very scenario will and must occur again and again in the same way.

The charge of moral repugnance is to my mind the most authentic critical response to eternal recurrence, and the one most entitled to repudiate Nietzsche because it squarely engages the core existential significance of cyclic repetition.[20] Moreover, the force of moral repugnance is inevitable for *any* authentic encounter with eternal recurrence because here we identify its genuine "ethical" significance: not that recurrence can serve as a measure for moral action, but that it crystallizes the existential problem of meaning and value. Repetition dictates that everything I value must include everything that limits, opposes, or negates my values; and this surely can cause me to recoil at the prospect of eternally certifying everything that for me diminishes life. Zarathustra's nausea over the return of the small man is precisely this kind of moral repugnance. We can say, then, that eternal recurrence is meant to be and should be repellent to one's value estimations. If it is not experienced in this way, its full material significance is surely missed or evaded. And the only way such significance can be truly gauged is to confront what is *most* offensive to one's values and sense of meaning.[21] Thus it is entirely appropriate to raise examples such as the Holocaust in discussions of eternal recurrence.

It seems to me that finding eternal recurrence morally repellent need not be a sign of life-denial in the manner of overt projects of transcendence, perfection, or annihilation prosecuted by Nietzsche. If moral repugnance were the same as life-denial, there would be nothing to distinguish Zarathustra's resistance from slavish resentment.[22] Can I not affirm life in some kind of Nietzschean way without willing a return of the Holocaust? Would such an omission necessarily indicate a fugitive disposition? Can I not accept and even affirm the existence of an evil without my nose being rubbed in it by endless repetition?

Even though it is possible to chart "grades" of life affirmation by the degree to which one can measure up to the test of eternal recurrence—I presume Schopenhauer would receive (and not contest) an F, but could I maybe get a B?—nevertheless Nietzsche takes a hard line (pass-fail) by insisting that true affirmation demands *amor fati* and saying Yes to the recurrence of the same (recall the default argument). Accordingly he speaks against any moralistic dismissal of one's alter-value. But apart from the charge against moral repugnance of latent nihilism—which seems excessive and even inert against a heartfelt decision to repudiate eternal recurrence—is there any way in which Nietzsche can respond to this critical problem in a positive manner analogous to previous discussions of freedom and creativity?

I think a way stems from the agonistic structure of will to power and Nietzsche's special sense of life affirmation. We know that life affirmation, as distinct from life enhancement, celebrates the necessity of opposing conditions because of their constitutive and productive role in any meaning formation. Accordingly, anything of value absent countervailing forces would not *be* (or become) a value. Eternal recurrence amounts to an intensive magnification of the agonistic structure of values and indeed (for Nietzsche) the only true "preservation" of worldly value when measured against all other possible models that in one way or another turn away from radical agonistics and thus obviate the very nature of values as such—thereby positing meaninglessness under the guise of positive constructs.

Nietzschean agonistics must be distinguished from certain strategies in traditional theodicies meant to resolve the problem of evil, wherein God can permit the existence of evil as a necessary precondition for establishing the good. For instance, one could plausibly ask if the high achievements of Greek culture would have been possible apart from the leisure afforded by a slave economy; or if the establishment of the state of Israel would have occurred if the Holocaust had not happened. There are, of course, intrinsic problems haunting any such theodicy: (1) victims conceived as instrumental means toward a good end; (2) seemingly excessive degrees of evil conditions (would a million less victims of the Holocaust have been insufficient?); (3) mixed effects of the good (Palestinians might balk at such a providential justification of the Holocaust). What makes eternal recurrence different from theodicy is the effect of repetition on teleological hopes and the essentially tragic script that includes inescapable limitations on any perceived good. In particular, Nietzsche's worldview contains no a priori conception of intrinsic goodness or worth that would render instrumental rectifications of evil problematic; and no overarching script of benevolence or perfection that would create the "problem" of evil in the first place or that would make any perceived extent of evil conditions seem excessive as instruments for the good. For Nietzsche, there *is* no problem of evil, only the "problem of the good," of how the binary opposition of good and evil has made life itself problematic and subject to denial masked by rectification.

How *can* a belief in eternal recurrence respond to the question of moral repugnance? An answer is implied in Zarathustra's own passage *through* such repulsion as a necessary stage in the path of life affirmation, which for Nietzsche must be understood in agonistic terms. If Zarathustra affirms the recurrence of the small man, this does not mean that he now abandons his opposition to mediocrity and life denial. Affirmation can be understood as a twofold response that characterizes Nietzsche's agonistic pluralism: first, that creativity is not for everyone, that herd values are appropriate for certain types; second, that will to power must include resistance and opposition, so that any value *requires* countervalues to become what it is—an overcoming. The crucial point is that affirmation does not mean *approving* of everything, but rather affirming the necessity of otherness for the emergence of one's values, which means that affirmation retains *opposition* to countervalues, retains the space of one's Yes and No. Confirmation of this idea can be found in Zarathustra's objection to indiscriminate approval, which he calls "omni-satisfaction" (*Allgenügsamkeit*):

> Verily, I also do not like those who consider everything good and this world the best. Such men I call the omnisatisfied. Omnisatisfaction, which knows how to taste everything, that is not the best taste. I honor the recalcitrant choosy tongues and stomachs, which have learned to say "I" and "yes" and "no." (Z III, 11, 2)

Eternal recurrence, therefore, cannot entail the approval of everything that returns. If I will the return of something I find heinous, I also will the return of my opposition to it. *Amor fati* cannot mean the indiscriminate love of all things but rather the love of the agonistic necessity that intertwines everything I value with otherness. This does not necessarily dilute or neutralize the moral repulsion that eternal recurrence can generate, but at least there is a way to disarm a charge such as Magnus's that recurrence calls on us to love the extermination camps unconditionally.[23]

Nietzsche's philosophy is all about moral evaluations, in that will to power implies judgments and preferences for living one way over and against other ways. Indeed, "all experiences are moral experiences, even in the realm of sense perception" (GS 114). Nietzsche's fight against the slavish binary of good and evil is itself an evaluation; and he clearly states that "beyond good and evil" does not mean beyond "good and bad" (GM I, 17). The former is an eliminative project while the latter is an agonistic overcoming that requires the existence and persistence of that which is overcome. So Nietzsche's "immoralism" is a rhetorical move against a particular (and dominant) conception of morality in the Western tradition, not an amoral or antimoral posture in strict terms.

Moreover, Nietzsche's perspectivism does not recommend anything like radical skepticism or a facile relativism (see BGE 207–208), but rather the task of finding one's own meaning and living it out *at odds with* differing meanings.[24] Although perspectivism disallows one's own morality being binding on all, to conclude from a plurality of values that no morality is binding or worthy of commitment (*Unverbindlichkeit aller Moral*) would be childish (GS 345). In the midst of different moral possibilities, what matters is "a brave and rigorous attempt (*Versuche*) to *live* in this or that morality" (D 195). Living in such a way requires that one contend with other perspectives, that one believe one's own perspective to be the *better* option. This is why something like equanimity would be inappropriate, indeed ruinous, for Nietzsche's agonistic perspectivism, and why eternal recurrence must include one's stance against other perspectives.

Nietzsche believes in the necessity of having "enemies," which distinguishes his unique form of affirmation from traditional projects of the good that are betrayed by their eliminative tyranny. Consider this fascinating passage on the "spiritualization of hostility (*Feindschaft*)," which is discussed in both external and internal terms:

Another triumph is our spiritualization of *hostility*. It consists in the profound appreciation of having enemies: in short it means acting and thinking in the opposite way from that which has become the rule. The church always wanted the destruction of its enemies; we, we immoralists and Antichristians, find our advantage in this, that the church exists. In the political realm too, hostility has become more spiritual.... Almost every party understands how it is in the interest of its self-preservation that the opposition should not lose all strength.... Our attitude toward the "internal enemy" is no different: here too we have spiritualized hostility; here too we have come to appreciate its value. The price of fruitfulness is to be rich in internal opposition; one remains young only as long as the soul does not stretch itself and desire peace. (*TI* 5, 3)[25]

As in the drama of Zarathustra, Nietzsche specifically connects affirmation with saying Yes even to the presence of priestly decadence (*TI* 5, 5–6). Even the joy associated with eternal recurrence must be correlated with tragic limits: "All eternal joy wants itself, hence it also wants heartbreak (*Herzeleid*)" (*Z* IV, 19).

The central implication of eternal recurrence is that nothing can be ruled out or wished away when it comes to understanding the significance of any and all human outlooks. Contrary to exclusionary binaries or alternative worlds, recurrence mandates that *everything is in play.* Even binary opposition is necessary, not only as a conceptual set up for the mutual constitution of agonistic parties, but also as the spur for Nietzsche's alternative notion of reciprocal crossing. The *field* of play is the given background of becoming, within which all possibilities of form unfold. None of these possibilities by themselves can be definitive of "reality," to which only the whole field of play can lay claim. Eternal recurrence amounts to the *tangible* presentation of this reality field: neither an abstract generality of "all forms" nor an (equally abstract) amorphous flux, but the concrete fluid totality of all specific conditions and counterconditions, a field that calls for its existential "realization" through affirmation.

The "ethics" of eternal recurrence, therefore, concerns its maximal concentration on the agonistic structure of values. One way to articulate this matter is to examine the counterideal of self-sufficiency that has been pervasive in the Western tradition. Consider an interesting moment in Aristotle's *Nicomachean Ethics*. For Aristotle, human ethical life is marked by limits, lacks, and needs, which is why virtue involves the balancing act of *phronēsis*, the negotiation between competing forces at work in the desires of fragile, embodied beings. Accordingly, Aristotle denies that the gods exhibit moral virtue, since they are completely self-sufficient, and thus they need or lack nothing (1178b10–16). The life and activity of the gods are identified with contemplation (*theōria*), which is completely self-referential and needs nothing outside itself (1178b20ff.). An illuminating gloss on Aristotle is provided by Plotinus (*Enneads*

VI.8.5): No truly virtuous person would *want* to have the opportunity to act courageously or generously (which presuppose the existence of danger and need). If these virtues were *essential* to well-being and fulfillment, we should *wish* that there be things like war and poverty.[26] What is useful here from a Nietzschean standpoint is the clarification of a certain self-consuming character in traditional ethical conceptions: that virtue is intrinsically related to finitude and that a preference for the "divine" perfection of self-sufficiency implies the deconstruction of finite ethical life.[27] Nietzsche's question resounds: What would affirmation of life truly entail? For Nietzsche, it would have to reject any project of overcoming the limits of finitude. Is there not a certain nihilistic implication in the aforementioned position on virtue in relation to divine perfection? Would it not also explain why Christian writers found such Greek philosophical models congenial? Put it this way: Given the analysis of Aristotle and Plotinus, what would be left in human life if the ideal of self-sufficiency were to be fully realized, if limits on desire, knowledge, and achievement were lifted? With regard to life as we know it, *nothing* would be left. So at least it can be said that the force of life affirmation in eternal recurrence implies a *defense* of an immanent ethics of finite life.

In addition to the direct significance of eternal recurrence for the topic of moral evaluation, two tangential considerations deserve mention. The first has to do with action theory. The absence of a ground for moral action will strike some as a threat to moral commitment, but Nietzsche would diagnose this worry as a weakness in the face of the only possible condition for any kind of commitment: a willingness to stand for something that is *not* guaranteed (a "commitment" to 2 + 2 = 4 would be odd). The absence of a warrant need not prevent, and has not prevented, people from fighting for beliefs in the midst of opposition. In fact, I think that one of the most profound elements in Nietzsche's conceptions of agonistic will to power and eternal recurrence can be stated as follows: To act in the world cannot help but be action in the face of obstacles and resistances. To dream of action without agonistic alterity is actually an unwitting annulment of action. Any assertion of a stable, essential "being" would be "the expression of a world *without* action and reaction" (*WP* 567).[28] To affirm otherness as constitutive of one's action is not only to affirm the full field of action (which is the sense of eternal recurrence), but also to affirm action *as* action, that is to say, an actual move in life amidst actual resistances. An agonistic model of action is advanced to counter the fantasy of self-sufficient, fully free, uncontested movement born in Western conceptions of divine perfection and sustained in various philosophical models of demonstrative certainty, theoretical governance, and self-originating agency.[29] The advantage of Nietzsche's agonistic model of action is twofold: first, rather than inhibit action it can spur it toward the existential environment of its enactment (as opposed to the passivity of waiting for warrants or deferring to external governance); second, it can avoid the latent tyranny of closed models of agency, wherein presumed standards of regulated action can underwrite the exclusion, silencing, or destruction of agents that stray from or contest the proper form of life.

The second tangential point has to do with certain normative implications of an agonistic worldview. It seems to me that a dedication to tensional will to power would be inconsistent with a number of commonly purported moral transgressions. As was noted earlier in this study, a *radical* agonistics would rule out violence to the extent that it aims to *eliminate* conflict by incapacitating a contending party. The same can be said for destroying, dominating, excluding, or silencing a cultural opponent. If any such eliminative project were to succeed, the force of resistance intrinsic to will to power would come undone; indeed, in Nietzsche's terms, the fulfillment of any such project would no longer *be* will to power (a tensional overcoming sustained by resistance).

Many serious readers of Nietzsche believe that he would not have been a supporter of National Socialism—for a host of reasons, including his objections to antisemitism and nationalism. It can also be said that for all the (misplaced) deployment of a Nietzschean rhetoric in Nazi ideology, its eliminative racism was more a sign of what Nietzsche would call weakness rather than strength, if weakness is defined as the inability to abide the presence of otherness and strength is the capacity for power *in the presence* of differing forces. Nietzsche insists on *wanting* "enemies" to persist and have strength, since power is *measured* by the character of resistance. In short, the affirmation of agonistic power (and the repetition of all possible results of power by way of eternal recurrence) implies a certain "measure" of life that is neither peace nor destruction, neither passivity nor domination, neither harmony nor chaos—but rather a medial posture of striving *with and amidst* alterity for the achievement of fragile advances.

The Question of Truth

If we concede that eternal recurrence was held by Nietzsche to be essential for his philosophical project, how can it lay claim to any viable sense of truth, especially given his apparent dismissal of traditional epistemological standards? My analysis has already attempted to address this question in discussions of mythical truth and nonfactual literalness. It will be useful, however, to articulate further the complex topic of truth in Nietzsche's thinking and how it bears on eternal recurrence. The gist of my argument is as follows. Despite Nietzsche's critique of traditional truth standards, he nevertheless deploys the concept of truth in two basic senses: the tragic truth of becoming and a pluralized array of truth perspectives. Eternal recurrence can bear a kind of truth that amounts to a mythical, meaning-laden responsiveness to the tragic truth of becoming. Moreover, in a certain manner, eternal recurrence can be *about* truth, both tragic truth and the more positive sense of how truth perspectives unfold and operate.

Nietzsche's perspectivism issues a complicated posture on the question of truth.[30] Naturally this posture subverts the traditional notion of an absolute, uniform, stable truth. There is no free-standing truth or purely objective, disinterested knowledge; there are only perspectives of different and conflicting instances of will to power.

> Henceforth, my dear philosophers, let us be on guard against the dangerous old conceptual fiction that posited a "pure, will-less, painless, timeless knowing subject"; let us guard against the snares of such contradictory concepts as "pure reason," "absolute spirituality," "knowledge in itself": these always demand that we should think of an eye that is completely unthinkable, an eye turned in no particular direction, in which the active and interpretive forces, through which alone seeing becomes seeing *something*, are supposed to be lacking; these always demand of an eye an absurdity and a nonsense. There is *only* a perspective seeing, *only* a perspective "knowing." (*GM* III, 12)

Accordingly, motifs of knowledge and truth are better rendered as an open field of interpretations (*GS* 374). In Nietzsche's texts, appearance, perspective, interpretation, will to power, and meaning-creation all circulate as indications of an agonistic process of becoming, which rules out traditional convictions about being and truth.[31] It is important to note, however, that Nietzsche does not equate perspectivism with subjectivism. Usually when he is discussing different perspectives, it is not in terms of different *individual* takes on the world, but different *settings* for how the world can be understood—in art, science, history, and so on. Also significant is Nietzsche's frequent use of the first-person plural (we, our) in the depiction of knowledge.[32] Certainly individual creativity is essential for Nietzsche, but primarily in the service of culture-formation rather than mere self-creation. And, as we have seen, creativity involves nonconscious forces that cannot be traceable to individual "subjectivity." Since interpretation as will to power is a process of becoming, one cannot even ask "Who interprets?" because even "the subject" is an interpreted creation meant to simplify and "define" the process (*WP* 556).[33] How far Nietzsche is from basing interpretation in human subjectivity can be gleaned from his claim that all events in the organic world—even "all that exists"—are constituted by interpretation and will to power (*GM* II, 12).[34]

Contrary to some readings of Nietzsche (and some of his own rhetoric), I think it is clear that he accepts and employs certain motifs of truth, as long as they are purged of metaphysical foundationalism and restricted to a more modest, pluralized, contingent perspectivism. Even if knowledge is variable, historical, and born out of human interests, that does not render it false, arbitrary, or uncritical.[35] Nietzsche's many judgments against life-denial in favor of life-affirming perspectives would seem to rule out a crude relativism or radical skepticism and suggest something like a "life realism."[36]

There are also provocative passages where Nietzsche hints at a pluralized "objectivity," wherein the more perspectives one can adopt, the more adequate one's view of the world will be.

> The *more* affects we allow to speak about one thing, the *more* eyes, different eyes, we can use to observe one thing, the more complete will our "concept" of this thing, our "objectivity" be. (*GM* III, 12)

> It may be necessary for the education of a genuine philosopher that … he himself must have been critic and skeptic and dogmatist and historian and also poet and collector and traveler and solver of riddles and moralist and seer and "free spirit" and *almost everything* [my emphasis] in order to pass through the whole range of human values and value feelings and to be *able* to see with many different eyes and consciences. (*BGE* 211)

We can make headway in the discussion of truth by way of the following distinctions: (1) Nietzsche affirms a global negative truth of becoming; (2) he denies the possibility of a positive foundational standard of truth; (3) he strikes a balance between these negative and positive poles by advancing a pluralized field of perspectival truths. A brief elaboration follows.

(1) Throughout his writings Nietzsche affirms a dark, tragic truth of becoming, in the sense that flux must be recognized as a primal force that renders all forms and structures ultimately groundless (see, for example, *BT* 21–22; *TI* 3, 2 and 6; *WP* 708). Various passages speak of a difficult, fearsome truth that must be faced to counter our myopic fixation on life-enhancing beliefs (*BGE* 39; *GM* I, 1).

> A thinker is now that being in whom the impulse for truth and those life-preserving errors clash for their first fight…. The ultimate question about the conditions of life has been posed here, and we confront the first attempt to answer this question by experiment. To what extent can truth endure incorporation? That is the question; that is the experiment. (*GS* 110)

In this way Nietzsche is exploring a negative truth that so far has been forbidden (*EH* P, 3). Indeed, faith in traditional belief systems has meant "not *wanting* to know what is true" (*A* 52).

(2) Because of Nietzsche's commitment to the tragic truth of becoming, positive doctrines of truth that presuppose foundational conditions of "being" are denied and often designated as "appearances" or "errors" (*OTL*; *WP* 616, 708). Our knowledge structures stem from a filtering process, which screens out strange and unusual elements that disturb our need for stability (*GS* 355). Although such structures are life-enhancing, they must still be unmasked as a reliance on the falsification of experience (*BGE* 24).

(3) Despite the ammunition becoming provides for Nietzsche's charge that traditional truth conditions are appearances and errors, he does notice the trap in sustaining the binary discourse of reality-appearance and truth-error. Falsification is the flip side of verification. Undermining "truth" also destabilizes any designation of "error," because error has always been measured by some governing truth standard.

> The true world—we have abolished. What world has remained? The apparent (*scheinbare*) one perhaps? But no! *With the true world we have also abolished the apparent one.* (*TI* 4, 6)

Appearance can be given the positive sense of temporal emergence and showing forth ("She appeared from behind the curtain"), which certainly fits Nietzsche's outlook. Indeed, in the notebooks, Nietzsche describes appearance as a nonmetaphysical *reality*, which makes possible the constructed forms of meaning that, while ultimately groundless, are necessary for life.

> "Appearance" itself belongs to reality (*Realität*): it is a form of its being; i.e., in a world where there is no being, a certain world of *identical* cases must first be created through *appearance*: a tempo at which observation and comparison are possible, etc. Appearance is an arranged and simplified world, at which our *practical* instincts have been at work; for *us* it is perfectly real (*recht*); that is to say, we live, we are able to live in it: *proof* of its truth for *us*...: the world, apart from our condition of living in it ... does *not* exist as a world "in itself," it is essentially a world of relations: possibly it has a different aspect from every point: its being (*Sein*) is essentially otherwise (*anders*) from every point: it presses upon every point, every point resists it—and the sum of these is in every case entirely *incongruent*. (*WP* 568)

> The world of "phenomena" is the adapted world that *we perceive to be real*.... The antithesis of this phenomenal world is *not* "the true world," but the formless unformulable world of the chaos of sensations—thus *another kind* of phenomenal world, one "unknowable" for us. (*WP* 569)

Here Nietzsche posits two levels of appearance: the primal, formless flux of becoming, and the subsequent gathering of this flux into livable forms. Since both are designated as appearance, there is no other "reality" against which either one could be called "apparent" in a deficient sense. So we can locate in this discussion two levels of truth: the tragic truth of becoming and the livable truth of meaning perspectives. When it comes to truth, we do not have to confine ourselves to the choice between sheer flux and sheer being. In different ways, Nietzsche provides avenues for discerning a modified, contingent, pluralized array of truths that are neither utterly unhinged nor fixed: "There are many kinds of eyes ... and consequently there are many kinds of "truths," and consequently there is no truth." (*WP* 540).

I will briefly catalog a number of motifs in Nietzsche's texts that indicate a sense of truth that is world-disclosive yet open and nonreductive: *Pragmatic efficacy*. Enhancement of life interests (power) is a fundamental theme in assessing beliefs" (*BGE* 4). Against the view that strength of belief cannot be a sufficient criterion for truth, Nietzsche asks: "But what is truth? Perhaps a kind of belief that has become a condition of life? In that case, to be sure, strength could be a criterion" (*WP* 532). Indeed, "the criterion of truth resides in the enhancement of the feeling of power" (*WP* 534). *Art*. Creative art has great metaphorical value for Nietzsche because it presents meaning without the pretense of fixed truth, a lack which makes art more "truthful" than traditional belief systems (*OTL*, 96–97). Moreover, the cultural meanings disclosed by art are what give human existence its bearings amidst the tragic truth of becoming: "We possess *art* lest we *perish of the truth*" (*WP* 822; see also *WP* 853 and *GS* 107). Nietzsche even allows that truth can be redescribed as an open-ended process of creative formings that can never itself become fixed or closed (*WP* 552). *Perspectival interpretation*. A radical perspectivism can still permit appropriately modified conceptions of knowledge and truth: "In so far as the word "knowledge" has any meaning, the world is knowable; but it is *interpretable* otherwise, it has no meaning behind it, but countless meanings.—'Perspectivism'" (*WP* 481; see also *BGE* 43). *Experimentalism*. Nietzsche connects an experimental disposition with truthfulness (*GS* 51), and he names his new philosophers *Versucher*, "attempters" or "experimenters" (*BGE* 42). He does not espouse unbridled thought or an abandonment of intellectual discipline, but rather continual self-assessment through experiments (*GS* 319). *Criticism*. In view of experimentalism, Nietzsche does not dismiss critical reason, interrogation, or giving reasons for beliefs; he opposes only a reductive and impersonal rationalism (*GS* 2, 191, 209, 307).

Even granting the plausibility of Nietzsche's perspectival approach to truth, the specter of the self-reference problem looms for any such project and challenges everything from Nietzsche's judgments against life-denial to the very posture of perspectivism itself. If Nietzsche is right that thought is an unregulated swarm of perspectives, why should we put any stock in his many critical judgments or his theory of perspectivism? His judgments and his perspectivism would themselves only amount to a certain perspective. Is not Nietzsche guilty of what Habermas calls a performative contradiction in simultaneously advancing his philosophy and denying a foundation for philosophical validity?[37]

I want to argue that Nietzsche's judgments and his perspectivism can be advanced without self-referential inconsistency. I begin with a passage in which Nietzsche seems to embrace the fact that a perspectival approach can be thrown back at itself as a threat to its objective validity. After challenging the proposal of a law-governed world with the counterproposal of an unregulated, interpretive field of power relations, Nietzsche closes with this remark: "Supposing that this also is only interpretation—and you will be eager enough to make this objection?—well, all the better" (*BGE* 22). Rather than retreat or evasion in the face of such a charge, Nietzsche says "all the *better.*" In other words, it would be *worse* if his proposal were not self-referentially limited. The force of the inconsistency charge is completely disarmed by this surprising response, by in effect *wanting* to be "only" a perspective. The questions at hand are: How and why does Nietzsche regard his general perspectivism and his critical judgments as themselves only perspectives? Why would he prefer that this be the case?

Although Nietzsche speaks against fugitive perspectives in favor of life-affirming perspectives, he also concedes that, because all such outlooks stem from perspectival interests, any *overall* evaluation of life cannot be given veridical status: "The total value of the world cannot be evaluated" (*WP* 708). Evaluations of life, then, are local estimations that serve particular interests but that cannot stand as a global measure to rule out other estimations. And Nietzsche's texts are not inconsistent with this delimitation. Although he strenuously fights against "weak" forms of life, he nevertheless affirms the necessity and authenticity of these perspectives.[38] Life-denying perspectives serve the interests of certain types of life, who have thus been able to cultivate their own forms of power that have had an enormous effect on history. The coherence of Nietzsche's position can be noticed by reiterating my distinction between life enhancement and life affirmation. Even life-denying perspectives are life-enhancing because they further the needs of weaker forms of life. The "strength" of life affirmation denotes the capacity to embrace the full agonistic field of all life forces—*as* an unresolvable, tragic limit on all forms of meaning.

I think that the complex question of Nietzsche's perspectivism can be sorted out. On the one hand, in my reading Nietzsche *does* advance a global philosophical position, summed up as an *agonistic, existential perspectivism,* which has the following basic features: (1) existential meaning, and not a disinterested objectivity, is the first-order description and origin of any belief system; (2) the life-world is a field of differing meaning-perspectives that emerge by way of a reciprocal process of tensional relations; (3) the overall process-field is radically agonistic and therefore incapable of coalescing around, or reducing to, any particular meaning-perspective. Nietzsche is ready and willing to declare this philosophical position and contend with all comers—not with a view toward refutation and justification, but rather capacious performance in an ongoing competition.

On the other hand, within this global perspectivism, Nietzsche advances his *own* perspective in the field of play: namely the *affirmation* of the perspectival whole, of all the finite forces of life without exception—and thus the necessity of all life conditions dramatically portrayed in eternal recurrence. Here Nietzsche opposes other perspectives that cannot affirm the agonistic whole, that seek conditions of being as a resolution of tragic becoming. From the standpoint of his global perspectivism, however, Nietzsche allows that these fugitive perspectives are at least affirming their own interests (life enhancement). What they cannot affirm is the agonistic whole—and this is Nietzsche's particular battle to wage in the perspectival field. What is distinctive about Nietzsche's posture becomes clear: he grants that both his global perspectivism and his affirmation project are themselves perspectives, that neither can claim any warrant beyond their presentation as a philosophical contender offered by Friedrich Nietzsche.

> "This—is then *my* way—where is yours?" Thus I answered those who asked me about "the way." For *the* way—that does not exist! (*Z* III, 11)

The consistency of Nietzsche's posture can be articulated further by recalling the previous discussion about the agonistic nature of action. Philosophy too is a mode of action, a radically agonistic, interrogative, addressive *practice*. The fantasy of philosophy as foundational governance, as the achievement of a fixed warrant (a dream fostered by traditional models of a divine mind) would not *be* philosophy but a nihilistic divorce from its field of enactment. Nietzsche will simply take a stand for his position without aiming to erase opposing views. Even perspectivism need its opposition, something to be overcome. Since any life condition is constituted by tensional alterity, the erasure of otherness would also be self-erasure. That is why it is *better* that perspectivism be a perspective in the midst of other perspectives.

Another angle on this matter has to do with philosophy as a mode of will to power. Philosophical beliefs can be understood as *powers*, as capacious *possibilities*, as potencies that cannot be reduced to completed actualities. Belief construed as an irreducible capacity can only be exercised as energy in the midst of countercapacities, and thus can only be performed in relation to competing energies that cannot be eradicated without incapacitating a belief's own energy *as* a power.

I conclude that the charge of self-referential inconsistency assumes something that Nietzsche does not accept, namely that a global philosophical position must amount to a "panoptical scan" of the field of knowledge, measuring the entire territory and correcting all the different regions by way of its overarching vision—and if its own content can be placed in its scan and be subject to the same correction, it confronts the dilemma of self-reference. Nietzsche, however, rejects the possibility of a panoptical scan (whether it be called something nonperspectival or metaperspectival), and so the self-reference problem cannot get off the ground. For Nietzsche, philosophy can never surpass the *immanent* address of perspectival agonistics, wherein we must simply take up our positions in context and in contest with others, never to achieve panoptical heights. Nietzsche's account of philosophy presents a "virtuous circularity" in the following way: (1) life is a tensional process of movement; (2) philosophical reflection is itself a form of life; (3) philosophy is a reflection *on* the process of life that cannot help but be a participant *in* the process of life.

It seems that critics advancing the self-reference charge assume that philosophy cannot or should not be perspectival, that global statements are *meant* to be panoptical. Nietzsche simply disagrees and offers up his philosophical gambit for response. One thing in Nietzsche's favor is that committing to philosophy as an agonistic field without resolution can be taken as the more "realistic" option, as a phenomenology of intellectual practice (at least so far), rather than the fantasy of "completion" that has governed the traditional analysis of such practice.

In sum, Nietzsche's perspectivism—which includes all perspectives and their reciprocal relations in agonistic practice—allows him the following: an end-run around the self-reference problem, an inclusive permission of all perspectives, and a commitment to his own perspective against others. Accordingly, Nietzsche can offer judgments about better and worse beliefs without a project of refutation or erasure. In particular, he can contest certain beliefs on the grounds of life affirmation but include them on the grounds of life enhancement and agonistic relations. Life-denying perspectives are necessary to enhance certain forms of life and to forestall practical nihilism; they are even necessary as a competitive partner in Nietzsche's own project of life affirmation. If I am a perspectivist, I *need* antiperspectivism, otherwise the dynamic tension of my will to power evaporates. I must *want* to be "only" a perspective, I must want my Other, I must will its presence. Such is the deepest animate meaning of eternal recurrence. Willing the repetition of life is the fullest expression of my capacity to affirm the finite conditions of existence—but not in the abstract, since the true test emerges when faced with willing the repetition of my *own* antagonists. Yet willing recurrence does not mandate resignation, universal approval, or the enjoyment of all possibilities. My antagonists will be eternally *opposed*, I affirm them *as* opponents in a global agonistic field, so that I also will a commitment to my own perspective over others.[39] That is why being "only" a perspective requires scare quotes. It must be kept in mind that an agonistic structure does not entail a relativistic equanimity, but rather a capacious contest for persuasive success (even a presumption of superiority). An agonistic perspectivism thus allows an interest in winning the contest, but without the mandate of "total victory" presumed by traditional contests armed with metaphysical warrants.

Obviously eternal recurrence itself can be offered by Nietzsche "only" as an interpretive perspective and not as a demonstrated truth, for all the reasons discussed in this investigation. But beyond this it is possible to see in eternal recurrence a special claim to truth in the light of certain textual passages that bear on life affirmation and other relevant topics. In pursuing such a path I am going beyond earlier discussions of mythical truth and nonfactual literalness to explore other ways eternal recurrence and truth might coincide in Nietzsche's thought.

Nietzsche tells us that Dionysian affirmation means "saying Yes to reality" and as such it is a form of *knowledge* (*EH* III, BT 2). In this same passage he says that overcoming nihilism demands strength and courage, and that "precisely as far as courage may venture forward, precisely according to that measure of strength one approaches truth." Furthermore, a plurality of interpretations is a sign of strength (*WP* 600). And the "elevation of humanity" comes from overcoming "narrower" perspectives (*WP* 616). If we add the passage cited earlier concerning how "objectivity" might be measured by a greater accumulation of different perspectives, can we say summarily that the maximal inclusiveness of eternal recurrence expresses not only an affirmative strength but also the most extensive attainment of "objective truth" in this special sense? Can we also say that eternal recurrence presents a kind of global "realism," the farthest thing possible from skepticism or any other gambit of radical contingency? With the cyclic compression of repetition, there is nothing else beyond actual events (not even nothingness) against which the world could be compared or measured. In this respect, from a global standpoint does the world present itself as *self-evident*?

Finally, we should consider the way in which eternal recurrence can be called "true to life." First of all, it arises out of an existential "truthfulness" that Nietzsche insists upon: facing up to the tragedy of life. In a certain manner even pessimism and optimism are truthful in *not* ignoring the baseline issue of existential meaning (even though they cannot abide tragic wisdom). Being "untruthful" would involve ignoring, forgetting, or suppressing the deepest and most pressing issues of the meaning of life (for example, indifference or a positivistic objectivity). Eternal recurrence takes existential truthfulness to the extreme extent of affirming any and all elements of tragic existence; and in thus purging any conceivable fugitive disposition, one's "marriage" to life is consummated with the utmost fidelity. Such was Zarathustra's charge to be "faithful" (*treu*) to the earth and to life.

Nietzsche's Default Phenomenology

In this chapter I have tried to show how Nietzsche's philosophy can sustain itself in the face of significant criticisms of eternal recurrence. To gather the different discussions, I want to suggest that the force of Nietzsche's "positions" on necessity, chance, fate, freedom, creativity, and truth can be called a "default phenomenology," in a manner not unrelated to my proposal of a default argument for eternal recurrence. There are obviously complex ambiguities attaching to Nietzsche's "bait and switch" deployment of familiar philosophical terms: necessity that is not causal regulation or logical entailment; chance that is not random or inconsequential; fate that is not compulsion or predestination; freedom that is not autonomy or self-directed agency; creativity that is not self-origination or sheer novelty; truth that is and is not an appearance that is and is not reality.

Such deployments create a vexing burden for philosophical comprehension. Yet there may be no decisive resolutions possible in these matters, because the ambiguity stems from Nietzsche's insistence that the philosophical

tradition itself, in *its* deployment of these terms, carved out polarized conceptual divisions that are not faithful to the actual complexity of experience and
that are symptomatic of fugitive aversions to this complexity. Nietzsche's alternative is to enact a reciprocal crossing effect that is more faithful to experience.
For this reason, it may be that the habit of philosophical concept formation
cannot help but be divisional in some way, and thus cannot avoid the vexation
of sensing its own limits in relation to lived experience.

Nevertheless one could render this situation in somewhat more positive
terms by designating Nietzschean concepts of necessity, freedom, fate, creativity, and truth as default phenomena, which is to say: *not* philosophical posits
with a strictly positive content, or proven to be true, or commanding assent,
but rather the *surviving senses* of such terms after Nietzsche's diagnostic
critique has destabilized binary opposites and given pride of place to existential meaning and finite performance. In this respect Nietzschean concepts can
point to or show the living milieu of their enactment; but because of the
primacy of this milieu, such concepts cannot be "posited" as philosophical
"findings," unless they are *found* in experience (see *BGE* 213). In the bargain, a
default phenomenology is perfectly consistent with the self-limiting
Nietzschean guidelines of perspectivism, interpretation, appearance, and will
to power (especially if this last concept is taken as capacious performance).

What becomes clear in the notion of default phenomena is that Nietzsche's
concepts are intrinsically caught up with the philosophical frameworks he
diagnoses as unfaithful to life; but this is consonant with the agonistic structure of will to power. Nietzsche's phenomenal offerings are *overcomings* in this
tensional mix. Also relevant is Nietzsche's concession that early Greek mythopoetic culture was lacking in conceptual clarity and philosophical articulation.
Historically speaking we might say that the advent of philosophy was a necessary ingredient in the *self*-overcoming of philosophical concepts accomplished
by Nietzsche—which, all told, amounts to an *improvement* over prephilosophical myth. A kind of historical dialectic seems to be operating here: an affirmative tragic culture—overcome by a philosophical culture averse to tragic
life—overcome by a tragic philosophy that retrieves tragic myth, but *by way of*
philosophy's self-transforming critique of its initial flight from tragic cultural
sources. We have seen that Nietzsche embraces poetic language (for more than
simply stylistic reasons) but that poetry is not sufficient for his project.
Philosophical concepts are necessary for the extensive articulation of the deepest cultural matters (and such concept formation may have required an initial
differentiation of experience into polarized divisions for the sake of articulated
clarity).

So Nietzsche's thought does indeed fit in with the familiar agenda of philosophical topics; he does advance positions on knowledge, truth, selfhood,
freedom, and so on. Yet Nietzsche is a rare bird in philosophy and he cannot
be pressed into standard formats, methods, and preconceptions. Nietzschean
concepts, as default phenomena, can perform a critical function and exhibit

philosophical power, but not as ends in themselves; rather, they are signposts on the journey of engaging fundamental problems of existential meaning. Nietzsche's *writings*, as textual artifacts (which is most of the appeal for most philosophers), offer concepts that can best be called residual ambiguities surviving the deconstruction of traditional philosophical methods and results. And as my text has attempted to show, the most telling and far-reaching default phenomenon in Nietzsche's writings is the tragic, reflective drama of eternal recurrence.

Thus concludes my exegetical case for eternal recurrence as the core and climax of Nietzsche's thought, and as plausibly sustainable in the face of various puzzles, problems, and criticisms usually thought to be toxic by Nietzsche's friends and foes alike. Yet of course a question remains: Even if my analysis succeeds as exegesis, what about us? Can one not follow Nietzsche's existential naturalism and even his call for life affirmation without having to commit to eternal recurrence? Wouldn't it be enough (in the words of George Costanza) to simply "Live, damn it, live!"?

Even more, might one question Nietzsche's evident obsession with life affirmation?[40] Why does life have to be given such a "confirmation and seal"? How messianic of Nietzsche to pose as life's redeemer! Perhaps his passion is more symptomatic of his own neurosis, or disaffection, or—Dionysus forbid—resentment. I hesitate to think this way. For one thing, Nietzsche would not deny the psychological role of denial in the task of affirmation. Moreover, Nietzsche has persuaded me that even though the ultimate global meaning of life is unthinkable, the *local* task of engaging the meaning of life from one's perspective is far from optional because human existence at its core is a field of meaning-bearing dispositions. Engaging the meaning of life is, of course, optional for any particular person; but taking up this option in terms of Nietzsche's parameters of affirmation and denial should not be seen as a matter of sheer discretion, but as the *appropriate* full extension of the primal bearings of human life.

From my perspective, I confess to being haunted by eternal recurrence, by its power to evoke the question of meaning with an electric clarity. At the very least, with eternal recurrence Nietzsche conducts an ingenious prosecutorial interrogation: Are the basic trends of Western thought guilty of harboring overt or covert ascetic tendencies, even in the most life-enhancing projects? How telling was Socrates' description in the *Phaedo* of philosophy as a readiness for death? Was Schopenhauer indeed the surprise witness testifying that philosophical wisdom expresses, or should express, nothing less than a death wish? In the course of Western culture, how many death sentences have been written that only eternal recurrence can expose and commute? For me, Nietzsche's question still excites a disturbing wonder: Why not repeat performances of the longest running play ever created?

Epilogue
Laughter and Truth:
Nietzsche's Philosophical Satyr Play

A significant problem persists in scholarly interpretations of *Thus Spoke Zarathustra*: the status of Part 4 in relation to the preceding three parts. The gist of the problem concerns the apparent completion in Part 3 of Zarathustra's narrative journey toward life affirmation animated by eternal recurrence. The first published version of the text in 1884 ended at Part 3; Part 4 was written in 1885. Part 4 seems to shift in style and focus, particularly with respect to the difficulties in the transmission of Zarathustra's teachings and the questionable capabilities of so-called higher men, and a pervasive tone of satire and parody. Accordingly, some scholars argue that Part 4 is an unfortunate afterthought that should be taken as extrinsic to the narrative whole of Parts 1 through 3. Others have argued that Part 4 is intrinsic to the text, but in the manner of an ironic distancing from the supposed doctrines advanced in the preceding text.[1] Naturally, the latter approach can underwrite a dismissal of the literal sense of eternal recurrence, and of course I want to resist any such interpretation. I am persuaded that Part 4 can be seen as both a break in the text and an intrinsically connected destabilization of the text, along the lines of a satyr play following a tragic trilogy.[2]

The notion of a satyr play serves to highlight a central element in the meaning of eternal recurrence and life affirmation: the force of comic laughter in Nietzsche's thought. In this regard, another binary opposition overcome by Nietzsche needs to be added to those listed at the beginning of this investigation—the opposition between the serious and the comical. In what follows I sketch the way laughter fits within the full scope of Nietzsche's philosophy.[3]

In the history of philosophy, laughter has been one of the most marginal of phenomena. Philosophers have written about laughter as a subject of study, but simply as one among other human capacities calling for explanation or analysis. Moreover, the affective force and disruptive effects of laughter have generally earned it low esteem in the "serious business" of philosophy's pursuit of truth. One distinctive feature of Nietzsche's thought is a demarginalization of laughter unmatched in the history of philosophy: he elevates laughter to a level of importance so pronounced that it becomes joined with truth.

> To laugh at oneself as one would have to laugh in order to laugh *out of the whole truth*—to do that even the best so far lacked sufficient sense for the truth, and the most gifted had too little genius for that. Even laughter may yet have a future. (*GS* 1)

What can it mean that laughter is expressive of truth? An answer emerges in the light of Nietzsche's negative sense of truth and his retrieval of the role of drama in early Greek culture. We have seen that truth, for Nietzsche, must always be a matter of existential meaning in a finite world of becoming. Since Nietzsche rules out a baseline being, the only "ultimate" truth is a negative truth of becoming, a primal flux that renders all positive forms and structures in the end groundless. As an existential matter, the truth of becoming is not simply a function of cognition; it is experienced as something dark, fearsome, and difficult. And this is why tragic drama was an abiding interest in Nietzsche's thinking. In *The Birth of Tragedy,* Nietzsche does not give much attention to the "other side" of Greek drama, namely comedy; but in subsequent writings, laughter becomes a major motif in his texts, to the point where the comic is given a status at least equal to the tragic.

The tragic and the comic involve two fundamental existential dispositions: the tragic is a response to the inevitable dissolution of human life and meaning; the comic is an exuberant expression of laughter in a host of sociocultural situations, where a joyous vocal discharge erupts and disables the normal function of serious regard. Usually the tragic and the comic are thought to denote a contrary pair of negative and positive dispositions. But Nietzsche's approach to these phenomena indicates a deep ambiguity in this purported oppositional relation: both the tragic and the comic express an affirmative posture toward life, and they both exhibit a disruption of "being." I argue that tragic pathos and comic laughter present a primal existential bivalence in the human experience of negative limits, and that for Nietzsche, both phenomena depict an *affirmative negation*, which avoids both a pessimistic denial of life and an optimistic fantasy that negative limits can be overcome or resolved in some way. Nietzsche often deploys motifs of tragedy and comedy to name the general character of life, and such motifs do not contradict each other. In fact, Nietzsche comes to emphasize comic laughter as an especially positive response to the tragic, a response that does not overcome or cancel tragic negativity. To understand the ambiguity in Nietzsche's outlook, we need to supplement our treatment of tragedy with a look at comic drama in early Greek culture.

Tragedy and comedy in ancient Greece were distinct phenomena, yet both shared a common origin in the worship of the god Dionysus.[4] And if we can grant that Greek religious belief was a serious engagement with the sacred (rather than mere fanciful stories or conventional props), then tragedy and comedy were more than merely "artistic" works; they portrayed deep cultural meanings with world-disclosive significance. We have noted that tragic drama had its origins in the dithyramb and satyr play, both of which were associated with Dionysian religion. We have also seen how Nietzsche stressed Dionysian religion and artistic energies to uncover the life-affirming character of Greek tragedy. The positive force of Greek drama that attracted Nietzsche can be further explored by detailing the Dionysian connection between tragedy and comedy. Dionysian rites—in the two forms of joyous erotic feasts and somber violent frenzy—were a reenactment of the Dionysian mythos of dismemberment and restoration, thus sanctifying the subversion of individuated form and everyday social norms. The Dionysian roots of comedy display comparable settings of de-formation that indicate overlapping relations with tragic manifestations of Dionysian religion.[5] We can make some headway by considering two cultural phenomena that can be traced to Dionysus: the *komos* and the satyr.

The *komos* was a swarming band of drunken men who engaged in dancing, laughter, obscenity, and mocking language, and who generally dispensed with social conventions and inhibitions.[6] The *komos* represented a more accessible and less severe form of Dionysian self-abandonment (compared with the feminine cult), and a more public "dismemberment" of human norms and hierarchies. The *komodoi*, or "singers in the *komos*," can be called a forerunner of comic drama, not simply on etymological grounds, but in terms of the religious sanctioning of a "reversed world" that came to characterize comedy's public space allowing the mocking subversion of social, political, and divine authorities.[7]

The two-dimensional character of Dionysian religion prepared a common background for the development of dramatic genres of tragedy and comedy. The somber ecstasy of the violent rites involved participation in actual forces of destruction, which tragedy portrayed in the fatal ruination of a noble hero. The frolicking ecstasy of the *komos* and erotic feasts involved revels of disinhibition and the comparatively harmless (and temporary) "destruction" of conventional propriety and cultural roles, which comedy portrayed in its celebration of obscenity, mockery, and debunking tactics. Both dimensions displayed in their way a singular Dionsyian insight: formed conditions (whether natural or cultural) are not fixed or permanent, and a sacred meaning can emerge through the annihilating power of Dionysian ecstasy, which dissolves a fixation on form and opens the self to the self-exceeding truth of natural life energies.

The element of negation in tragedy is clear with respect to how the fate of human life is portrayed. Yet the Dionysian connection allows us to understand how a de-forming function also operates in comedy. While tragic negation is more cosmic in dimension and complete in depicting a ruinous downfall, comedic negation is more a social matter and it depicts the disabling of roles, conventions, and authoritative postures *without* complete destruction—a "safe zone" that simply unmasks, surprises, or mocks in the context of laughable, rather than pitiable, losses. Aristotle confirms this when he claims that comedy portrays human deficiencies but without pain or injury (*Poetics* 1449a34ff.).[8]

Although tragedy and comedy became separate art forms in Greek theater, earlier stages of drama showed a close, even intrinsic relationship between comic and tragic cultural forms. Tragedy evolved from the satyr play, and even mature dramatic performances for a time took the form of tetralogies, a set of three tragic works followed by a satyr play. A discussion of the Greek satyr figure will give our analysis some depth and focus in articulating the following points: (1) the comic-tragic correlation in early Greek culture; (2) Nietzsche's declared interest in satyr motifs; and (3) the satyr construed as a vivid and telling cultural expression of *marginal* forces, in particular of crossing the limits between humanity and animality, between culture and nature.

> I am a disciple of the philosopher Dionysus; I should prefer to be even a satyr to being a saint. (*EH* P 2)

> I estimate the value of men, of races, according to the necessity by which they cannot conceive the god apart from the satyr. (*EH*, II, 4)

With these references to the satyr in his last published work, Nietzsche retrieved an image that had figured significantly in his first published text, *The Birth of Tragedy*. The satyr was an ancient Greek mythical form displaying a combination of animal and human features, and thus representing an ambiguous confluence of nature and culture. This ambiguity characteristic of early Greek culture inspired Nietzsche and it can be seen to mark a fundamental task of his work: how to think human culture and the forces of animal nature as an indivisible blend, which departs from the Western conception of carnal nature as something to be transcended, mastered, or reformed. Nietzsche's cultural naturalism can serve as a backdrop for considering the significance of the satyr figure.

In *The Birth of Tragedy*, the satyr is an important image in Nietzsche's project of demonstrating the Dionysian sources of Greek tragedy. Nietzsche takes the satyr as a synthesis of god and goat (the goat being associated with Dionysus) and as a symbol of Dionysian enthusiasm, a "primal humanity" that experiences the healthy ecstasies of divine madness (*BT* "Attempt at Self-Criticism," 4). The satyr is an expression of the Greek "longing for what is original and natural," an *Urbild* of nature unmediated by knowledge and reflection, of an ecstatic release into the sexual omnipotence of nature driven by the force of the god (*BT* 8). The satyr represents a more dark and wild phenomenon than the modern "idyllic shepherd" and it exposes the delusion of culture taken as the only reality (*BT* 8). The satyr-Dionysus connection, however, is in Nietzsche's estimation a more cultivated dynamic than the "barbaric" expressions of the Dionysian given over to more brutish and licentious forces (*BT* 2).[9]

The satyr chorus and dithyramb in honor of Dionysus are seen by Nietzsche as forerunners of tragic drama. The phenomenon of "drama" (literally an action) and dramatic impersonation are born in the mimetic enchantment of Dionysian enthusiasts who identify with the satyr-celebrants who have identified with Dionysus through ecstatic transformation (*BT* 8). So for Nietzsche, tragedy begins with the satyr, representing a Dionysian experience of exuberant life forces beneath the Apollonian veil of civilization (*BT* 7). And the Dionysian life force behind passing manifestations evokes the positive, celebratory mood that Nietzsche insists be recognized in any account of the Greek phenomenon of tragedy.

What can classical scholarship tell us about Nietzsche's account of the satyr? Nietzsche has been quite influential in opening up concealed or underdeveloped elements in early Greek culture and tragic drama. Nietzsche was roughly right about tragedy deriving from the satyr chorus and Dionysian worship; and he was prescient in overcoming more prudish scholarship by stressing connections between tragedy, Dionysian passion, and the sexual energy of the satyr.[10] What do we know about the satyr? Satyrs were a race of their own, a hybrid of animal and human traits, depicted as a human form with a horse's tail and ears, sometimes with hooves. Satyrs were usually associated with negative moral traits such as laziness and licentiousness. The relationship between satyrs and other animals was not one of hunting or domesticating but of play, dancing, erotics, and role exchanges. The anatomy, dress, and behavior of the satyr suggest an ambiguous human-animality and an oscillation between barbarian and civilized traits.[11]

The association between the satyr and Dionysus may not be primeval, but there are clear connections in the sixth century. Dionysus's entourage did not include males, but rather women, nymphs, and satyrs.[12] The behavior of satyrs as companions of Dionysus included drinking, flute playing, dancing, acrobatics, and erotic gestures directed toward maenads and nymphs, all usually presented with comic effects.[13] The leaping and gamboling of the satyrs expressed the joyful delirium of those who follow Dionysus, who call into question established norms, who undo divisions between social roles, sexes, age groups, animals and humans, humans and gods.[14]

Satyrs were on the margins of the human world, but not isolated from it. As servants of Dionysus, who appeared among humans, satyrs performed roles such as artisans, sculptors, and cooks. Yet they were also depicted as wanton drunkards, thieves, and gluttons, beings who could not control or still their desires. At the same time they were shown as "inventing," or better, *discovering* many elements of human culture, usually exhibiting expressions of amazement, astonishment, or an eager gaze. One can surmise that the wildness and marginality of the satyr were given to represent a primal uncovering or renewal of the human world. The "negative" posture, burlesque, and fringe realm of the satyrs can be said to have functioned as an inversion/deforming of human norms that brought both a comic and an exploratory effect. The satyr, then, was an experimentation with alterity that evoked a heightened attention to human culture by exceeding its normalcy and familiarity.[15]

Visual representations of satyrs usually depicted human mimetic performances of these sacred mythical beings in religious rituals and proto-dramas, typically dancing and cavorting around the god Dionysus.[16] They were shown as masked figures with attached animal ears, tail, and phallus. Such a mimetic, masking mode was typical of *thiasoi*, or cult associations where humans achieved identification through imitation of sacred prototypes. In the case of the satyrs, the mimetic identification was with Dionysian ecstasy and latent animality.[17]

Such mimetic performances set the stage for dramatic arts, especially the role of satyr plays in tragic drama.[18] The dithyramb was a mode of poetry sung and danced in honor of Dionysus by choruses of fifty men or boys. Such practices were continued in the satyr play, a short fourth play following a trilogy of tragic dramas. The Dionysian connection was clear to the audience, and they knew during tragic performances that a satyr play was meant to conclude the presentation. In addition, the same performers acted the parts in all four plays. Accordingly, the satyr play was intrinsic to tragedy's cultural function, and the audience *anticipation* of the satyr play should be kept in mind when trying to understand the effect of tragic drama (for Nietzsche on the satyr play, see *KSA* 7, 42–43).

The satyr play involved a chorus of singers and dancers—part human, part animal—who engaged in playful, violent, sensual burlesque, very dissimilar in style and tone from the tragic chorus. Here the heroes and sacred figures of the tragedies were presented in a different, far from somber register, and yet the link with tragedy was evident, since the same performers were involved and the vocabulary and metrics of the characters were carried over.

What can we make of the satyr effect in tragedy? The satyr was an antitype (especially compared with male citizens) found on the fringes of the human world. Satyr plays presented exotic locales with fantastic characterizations, often with themes of the discovery or invention of something in the human world (wine, music, fire, metallurgy, the first woman). Satyrs, then, represented an inversion/distancing effect creating a scene of surprise and rediscovery of familiar cultural meanings, but always in the setting of a human-animal-nature convergence. With the tragedies portraying somber confrontations with fate, death, the gods, and limits, the satyr effect "played" with culture by way of a disorientation-reorientation structure.

If we recall the Dionysian as both a negative and productive force—given over to both ecstatic abandonment and erotic energies, together symbolizing the cycle of death and regeneration in nature—the tragic trilogies and satyr play can be understood as a confrontation with limit situations in two registers, one a "serious" expression of loss, the other a "playful" expression of comic juxtapositions, celebration, rediscovery, and reorientation. The intrinsic function of the satyr play in tragic performance lends much credence to Nietzsche's insistence that Greek tragedy was at bottom a life-affirming cultural force, understood by way of the dual nature of Dionysian worship.

The function of the satyr was to give presence to the ambiguous commixture in life of the animal and human, of nature and culture, and to celebrate this ambiguity with a playful modulation of tragic alterity. And Nietzsche would stress the cultural juxtaposition of satyric and tragic drama in distinct performances as an ongoing exchange, and as an implicit Greek recognition of the productive tension between the two forms, which would be weakened if the two forms were somehow blended together and lost if one form were to overcome or replace the other.

The duality of Dionysian experience can also apply to the historical links between tragedy and comedy, and thus to a correlation between pathos and laughter. The buffoonery displayed in satyr plays signals an intermediate genre between tragedy and comedy, with closer affinities to comedy.[19] Clearly the satyr figure stands as a gathering point for the multiform boundary-crossing dynamic of Dionysian religion—with an edge given to restorative comic forces—that so impressed Nietzsche and that in many ways marked his thought and manner of writing.

Nietzsche often refers to the relation between philosophy, comedy, and tragedy, including references to the satyr figure. In an 1888 letter to Ferdinand Avenarius, he says the following:

> … this year, where a monstrous task, the reevaluation of all values, lies upon me and I literally have to bear the fate of humanity, it belongs to my proof of strength to be something of a buffoon, a satyr, or if you prefer, a 'Feuilletonist.'… That the deepest spirit must also be the most frivolous, this is almost the formula for my philosophy: it could be that I, above all other "greats," have indeed become cheerful in an unlikely manner.[20]

In *Beyond Good and Evil*, Nietzsche warns against the solemnity of truth and a moral indignation that can ruin one's "philosophical sense of humor." To be a martyr for the truth is a degenerative excess. In fact, philosophy is called a kind of tragedy, but the "fall" of the philosopher is better taken in the spirit of a satyr play, an "epilogue farce" that is the true *end* of any tragedy (25). And a great tragedian shows greatness most in the satyr play, "when he knows how to *laugh* at himself" (*GM* III, 3). This is why a good case can be made that Part 4 of *Thus Spoke Zarathustra*—where the figures and import of the first three parts seem to degenerate into lampoonery—can be read as a satyr play concluding the tragic trilogy of the preceding parts.[21] This helps us make sense out of Nietzsche's reference to *Zarathustra* as both a tragedy and a parody (see *GS* 342 and the first section of the preface).

In sum, the human-animality of the satyr can stand as a symbol for Nietzsche's exuberant naturalism, his affirmation of a finite, carnal existence. For Nietzsche, human culture is not a transcendence of animal nature but a "sublimation" of natural energies that modulates, but never surpasses, its base. Indeed, Nietzsche refers to another hybrid figure in defining the "genius of culture," calling it a "centaur, half beast, half man" (*HAH* I, 241). The satyr embodies this ambiguous animal-human hybrid who lives on the fringes of the human world, and who exhibits astonishment at the unfolding of that world, and whose transgressions and crossings are experienced as comical—which is to say *not* repulsive but pleasurable, interesting, revelatory, and rejuvenating.

The key to Nietzsche's interest in tragedy and comedy is their overlapping expression of a deformation of being. If tragedy and comedy each present an affirmative response to negative limits, it would not be puzzling that a boundary line between them is often hard to draw. We have noticed a distinction between "harmful" and "harmless" negation, each evoking pathos and laughter respectively. But humans can also laugh when suffering from terrible conditions. Though rare, "tragic laughter" would be analogous to comic laughter in being a visceral affirmative response to a destructive limit. This special form of laughter was one of Nietzsche's preoccupations, as indicated in the shepherd scene in *Zarathustra* and its expression of an *übermenschlich* laughter. For Nietzsche, laughter can be, among other things, a most positive, vibrant form of tragic affirmation, a healthy incorporation of the negative limits of being. In this respect, Nietzsche saw himself inheriting the "cheerful fatalism" of the Greeks:

> … the short tragedy always gave way again and returned to the eternal comedy of existence; and "the waves of uncontrollable laughter"—to cite Aeschylus—must in the end overwhelm even the greatest of these tragedians. (*GS* 1)

At another level, laughter can be called a virtue when it is self-directed. The ability to laugh at oneself can manifest an enjoyment of one's own limits in social life, as opposed to the posture of overly "serious" people, who seem defensively fixated on their roles, beliefs, or causes. The virtue of self-directed laughter exhibits the freedom to sacrifice formality, to enjoy a lapse of identity, and to embody a nondogmatic disposition about oneself and one's convictions.

It may be difficult to construct a theoretical explanation of the nature of laughter and why we laugh (which would have to be serious, of course), but a phenomenology of laughter may suffice. *When* we laugh, something special about the human condition is revealed: the peculiar human capacity to appropriate limits in a positive manner; in the laugh, something deep and instinctive in us recognizes and *enjoys* the disruption of structure and being. It is no wonder, then, that Nietzsche, the champion of becoming, would find laughter so important: "Laughter at something is the first sign of a higher psychic life."[22]

It may be clearer now why Nietzsche associates laughter with a "sufficient sense for the truth." The "truth" expressed in a laugh is the visceral deconstruction of a fixed truth. Nietzsche's celebration of laughter goes beyond psychological questions to include his critique of foundational truth. The "seriousness" of Western philosophy and religion has manifested a struggle for, and fixation on, truth and certainty in an unstable world. Truth and salvation have been no laughing matter; frivolity has been scolded because in the end there is "something at which it is absolutely forbidden henceforth to laugh" (*GS* 1). Nietzschean laughter abandons certainty and embraces limits in knowledge and life—and *enjoys* such delimitation.[23] Moreover, when it comes to confronting instances of philosophical seriousness, laughter and humor could be an appropriate form of "critique." As Zarathustra puts it, the spirit of gravity is killed "not by wrath … but by laughter" (*Z* I, 7). Indeed, the ascetic ideal—at bottom a belief in foundational truth of any sort, even in science—is susceptible to only *one* enemy capable of harming it: "comedians of this ideal" (*GM* III, 27).

The substantive role of laughter as a Dionysian supplement to the tragic subversion of truth can help illuminate a prominent motif in *Thus Spoke Zarathustra*. In Part 1 of the text, "The Three Metamorphoses" presents images of spiritual development in the figures of the camel, the lion, and the child. The camel is the beast of burden symbolizing obedience and cultural conformity. The lion is a powerful force of No-saying, the denial of stable conditions, which lets loose the freedom that makes possible the creation of new values. But the creation of new values only comes with the Yes-saying innocence of the child. Later in the text, the free lion and the creative child are joined with the spirit of laughter. When Zarathustra anticipates the replacement of old tablets with new writings, he says he is waiting for a "laughing lion" (*Z* III, 12, 1).[24] Near the end of the text, Zarathustra again anticipates the arrival of laughing lions, and he calls them his "children" (*Z* IV, 11). In the last section of the text, the children are near, signaled by a laughing lion (*Z* IV, 20). In this way, creative innocence is connected with lionine negativity by way of laughter, a "disabling" force that does not destroy but rather *enables* creative activity. Moreover, a poetic interlude in the text joins laughter and poetry as counterposed to truth; indeed, an echo of Dionysian dismemberment, a "tearing to pieces," is modified by a comic supplement to tragic disintegration—a joyful "*laughing* while tearing" (*Z* IV, 14, 3).

The exuberant joy of laughter delimits without destroying, and Nietzsche seems to follow the Greeks in recognizing the reciprocal relation of tragedy and comedy, especially the restorative value of comic laughter, given the potential for pessimism looming in the dark truth of tragedy. Nietzsche even highlights this reciprocal relation with regard to his own writing. After having "slain all gods," he asks: "From where am I to take the tragic solution?—Should I begin to think about a comic solution?" (*GS* 153).

The question of Nietzsche's style is quite relevant here. In addition to using techniques not typical of philosophical writing—aphorism, literary narrative, metaphor, ad hominem invective, hyperbole—Nietzsche may have deployed many of his most radical inversions (e.g., immoralism) in the manner of "black comedy," a satirical negation not bent on elimination. Indeed, for Nietzsche, "attack is in my case a proof of good will, sometimes even of gratitude" (*EH* I, 7). In addition, this disabling-while-preserving structure of comic negation is also self-directed in Nietzsche's writings. Zarathustra's "ape" on the surface sounds very much like Nietzsche's supposed fearsome persona, yet he is repudiated in part for being overly serious and vengeful (*Z* III, 7). Nietzsche hints that *Zarathustra* itself is a parody (*GS* P, 1; *EH* III, Z). It is clearly a parody of religious narratives and prophetic revelation. Yet, as we have noted, Part 4 may be a self-parody in the manner of a satyr play, meant as a warning about the contingent character of Zarathustra's message and against taking the message too seriously and doing wrong with it—or constructing a new "doctrine" to replace old ideologies.

> I *want* no "believers"; I am much too malicious to believe in myself.... I have a terrible fear that one day I will be pronounced *holy*.... I do not want to be a holy man; sooner even a buffoon.—Perhaps I am a buffoon.—Yet in spite of that—or rather *not* in spite of it, because so far no one has been more mendacious than holy men.—But my truth is *terrible*. (*EH* IV, 1)

Once again, here Nietzsche associates comedy with a terrible truth. It is evident that a tragicomic intersection should be a guidepost for reading Nietzsche, from the standpoint of both style and substance. Laughter can no longer be located on the margins of philosophy: "You higher men, ... *learn* to laugh away over yourselves! ... Laughter have I pronounced holy" (*Z* IV, 13, 20). Of course, Nietzsche was a serious thinker dealing with the most serious issues. But the way Nietzsche expressed these issues distinguishes him significantly from other philosophers; and his manner of writing is not separable from the content of his thought. The deployment of comic laughter is Nietzsche's retrieval of Dionysian *wisdom* about life, which "cannot conceive the god apart from the satyr" (*EH* II, 4). Laughter, then, is an essential part of knowledge. Rather than being contrary to serious, indeed tragic matters, comic laughter can be seen as an overture to, and then a consummation of, deeply serious questions. Nietzsche gives us:

> the ideal of a human-overhuman (*menschlich-übermenschlich*) well-being and benevolence that will often appear *inhuman*—for example, when it confronts all earthly seriousness ... as if it were [its] most incarnate and involuntary parody—and in spite of all this, it is perhaps only with this that *great seriousness* really begins, the real question mark is posed for the first time, that the destiny of the soul changes, the hand moves forward, the tragedy *begins*. (*EH* III, Z, 2)
>
> For cheerfulness—or in my own language *gay science*—is a reward: the reward of a long, brave, industrious, and subterranean seriousness, of which, to be sure, not everyone is capable. But on the day we say with

all our hearts, "Onwards! Our old morality too is part *of the comedy!*" we shall have discovered a new complication and possibility for the Dionysian drama of "The Destiny of the Soul"—and one can wager that the grand old eternal comic poet of our existence will be quick to make use of it! (*GM* P, 7)

In dramatic fashion, Nietzsche repositions laughter in an unprecedented way (compared to other philosophers). Through the voice of Zarathustra, Nietzsche tells us that "we should call every truth false that [is] not accompanied by at least one laugh" (*Z* III, 12, 23).

It is plausible, I think, that much of Nietzsche's work—especially its transgressive style and unsettling attacks upon cherished cultural norms by way of startling antipodes—can be seen in the light of a satyr play, in the manner of a comic-noire experiment with inversions and crossovers on the fringe, meant not so much to destroy as to renew human culture by evoking astonishment before its emergence out of animality, and by mocking the gravitas that has marked the West's conception of culture as an overcoming of nature. What kind of laughter might we look for in Nietzsche's menacing iconoclasm?

My concluding discussion of comic laughter serves two purposes: (1) to articulate an essential ingredient in Nietzsche's philosophy of limits and life affirmation; and (2) to intercept the idea that a comic ending of *Zarathustra* functions as a rhetorical "retraction" of the literal sense of eternal recurrence depicted earlier in the text. Since the comic and the tragic, for Nietzsche, are correlative forces of truth, the comic by itself would not possess any special function for "self-consumption." Moreover, Part 4 does not seem to display any specific parody of eternal recurrence: the penultimate section of the text (*Z* IV, 19) voices a powerful exhortation of the climactic importance of recurrence very much in line with the conclusion of Part 3.[25]

Rather than a recoil at the prospect of life repetition, Part 4 can be read as performing a "critique" of eternal recurrence when it is confined to an externalized philosophical "doctrine" apart from its authentic appropriation "in person," in the lived experience of each individual (see *BGE* 213). Or: as a satyr play, Part 4 can remain *part* of the preceding tragedy, as a desettlement without destruction, as a subversion of "serious" dispositions that tend toward reification. In any case, a de-formation effect need not mean that eternal recurrence is radically questionable and thus retractable. Rather, the task of life affirmation intrinsic to recurrence would seem to *require* that the text exhibit an unconsummated character—as a living challenge for each reader. So the unsettling conclusion of the text should not be taken as self-consuming, but as self-*tasking*.

I close by considering the connection between the visceral force of laughter and another carnal phenomenon celebrated by Nietzsche: dance. Dancing has important metaphorical power because of its eclipse of cognitive paradigms in the direction of physical musicality, of rhythmic gestures of life and limb, wherein the tempos of venturing bodies leap into buoyant traversals of space. The measured vitality of the dance continued to inspire Nietzsche's vision of intellectual work: "I would not know what the spirit of a philosopher might wish more to be than a good dancer" (*GS* 381).

In *Thus Spoke Zarathustra*, dancing plays a prominent role in expressing the text's core themes. In the setting of Dionysian life affirmation, "Zarathustra is a dancer" (*EH* III, Z, 6). And dancing is intrinsically related to laughter and *übermenschlich* overcoming, specifically regarding the spirit of gravity—"*over* which one dances and dances away" (*Z* III, 12, 1–3). Finally, in the context of eternal recurrence, with language described as a "beautiful prank," it is through the power of words and sounds that humanity "dances across all things" (*Z* III, 13, 2).

The visceral exuberance of laughter and dancing seems to bear special significance in Nietzsche's call for life affirmation animated by eternal recurrence. With laughter breaking up our words into joyous inarticulation, with dance presenting a primal articulation of wordless expression—Nietzsche senses in these forms of life a capacity to exceed (without dismissing) the form of words that speak of affirmation. In this regard, a remarkable moment in Greek drama occurs at the end of Aristophanes' comedy, *Wasps* (1515ff.): The old man Procleon joins with "crab dancers" in a whirling, frenetic dance meant to express his indomitable spirit of life. The last stanza reads:

> But now it is time to finish our play,
> With an ending that's never been done this way.
> I'm sure this theater has seen every outrage
> Except a chorus dance right off the stage![26]

We do not know if performances of this play had the actors literally dancing off the stage into the audience and beyond the theater site, but the image is a striking reflexive gesture that crosses the boundary between dramatic artifice and cultural reality (which would be fitting for the performative context of Greek theater as part of religious and civic festivals). In any case, I find this scenario to be evocative of an irresistible image I have of Nietzsche's writings and their effects: the mimetic reception of a textual artifice in performance—with Nietzsche's sentences dancing off the page into the reader's life.

The Dancer

We had a pact.
The survivor would dance on the other's grave.
We have a winner! Ah,
the agony of victory.
Should I feel lucky to be the one
to carry out the covenant?—I remember that scene we loved from
Coming Home: the sign on the market doorway: LUCKY
OUT

OK, I'm here to do the dance—
a perfect case of our beloved irreverence
behind a pose of impropriety—our
affectionate burlesque.

No one else could likely tell
where all our nonsense came from,
the depth of its intention,
the darkness of its depth,
its technologies of survival.

What dance will I do?
It really should have been you who survived—
so much the better dancer
in every way.

You were my Zorba,
and for others of us, so many others.
Goddam, the church that day—packed
to the rafters with lovers from everywhere,
shoulder to shoulder in heartbroken joy
at the fact of you; acres of faces
assembling sorrow and shelters of remembrance.
How could one person give birth to all that?
How could one bear it?
What were we missing that day?
Good grief!

I will miss that day,
that achingly electric day—
except for the priest who went too far
comparing you with Jesus Christ.
How could he utter such blasphemy?
You were so much funnier than Jesus Christ!
(Notwithstanding that "turn the other cheek" routine.)
On his zaniest day he didn't have a particle
Of your divine shenanigans.

That crowd in the church—a dance
ensemble less its director.
You and your marriage and family,
a choreography that moved me—
yet sadly, since I mainly lack the moves.
In your vicinity my steps would come sometimes—
my rare near-life experiences.
What do I do now?

Now, here I stand—like
Pozzo I once played—a man
astride a grave. Alone
with Jeanette I ask:
What dance will I do?
The boogaloo, the twist, electric slide, temptation walk?
To you in the earth I promised some steps.
I think I'll wing it; and promise as well
that it won't be my last performance.

You once said death
is just another journey.
So where the hell are you?
Are you dancing?
When darkness comes
do I feel your footsteps
in the night?

Notes

Introduction

1. *The World as Will and Representation,* vol. 1, trans. E. F. J. Payne (New York: Dover, 1969), 324.
2. I owe the Kant reference and the previous reference as well to Eric Oger's article, "The Eternal Return as Crucial Test," *Journal of Nietzsche Studies* 14 (Autumn 1997), 14.
3. See *The City of God,* trans. Marcus Dods (New York: Random House, 1950), book 12, chs. 13, 17, 18, 20.
4. Although I will be referring to translated notes under the title *The Will to Power,* it is important to recognize this as a "nonbook," because it was compiled not by Nietzsche but his sister. The status of this "book," despite Nietzsche's initial aims for it, is undermined by alterations in later notes and by Nietzsche's apparent suspension of plans to publish such a text. For important discussions of this matter, see Bernd Magnus, "Nietzsche's Philosophy in 1888: *The Will to Power* and the *Übermensch,*" *Journal of the History of Philosophy* 24/1 (January 1986), 79–98, and the discussion between Peter Heller, R. J. Hollingdale, Bernd Magnus, and Richard Schacht in *International Studies in Philosophy* 22/2 (1990), 35–66.
5. It should be added that the notebook experiments were begun in 1885, *after* the published existential versions. So at least we can surmise that Nietzsche was *interested* in scientific approaches to recurrence *in addition to* the existential perspective.

Chapter 1

1. I borrow the term "crossing" from John Sallis's *Crossings: Nietzsche and the Space of Tragedy* (Chicago: University of Chicago Press, 1991).
2. Even the idea of sheer becoming cannot be maintained, according to Nietzsche. Discernment of such becoming can only arise once an imaginary counter-world of being is placed against it (*KSA* 9, 503–4).
3. This matter is relevant to the charge that Nietzsche's writing exhibits contradictory positions across different texts (even within texts). Assuming, however, that Nietzsche knew what he was doing, we can say that such incidents portray his warning against oppositional thinking by deliberately modifying fixed positions through the insertion of counterpositions. Moreover, his hyperbolic attacks can be seen as a rhetorical strategy to disturb thinking and reveal things otherwise concealed by commonplace assumptions; and the insertion of counterpositions modifies the hyperbole in order to work against reverse concealments.
4. See Babette Babich, "A Note on *Chaos Sive Natura*: On Theogony, Genesis, and Playing Stars," *New Nietzsche Studies* 5, 3/4 and 6, 1/2 (Winter 2003/Spring 2004), 48–70. For an insightful treatment of Nietzsche's naturalism, see Christoph Cox, *Nietzsche: Naturalism and Interpretation* (Berkeley: University of California Press, 1999).
5. See my discussion in *Myth and Philosophy: A Contest of Truths* (Chicago: Open Court, 1990), chs. 2–6.
6. For an important study of the agonistic nature of will to power, see Wolfgang Müller-Lauter, *Nietzsche: His Philosophy of Contradictions and the Contradictions of His Philosophy,* trans. David J. Parent (Urbana, IL: University of Illinois Press, 1999). The stress on contradiction, however (which influences Müller-Lauter's interpretation of eternal recurrence), is caught up in discrete conditions of opposite states, which misses Nietzsche's critique of opposition on behalf of a crossing dynamic.
7. For important discussions of this idea, see two articles in the *Journal of Nietzsche Studies* 24 (Fall 2002): Paul van Tongeren, "Nietzsche's Greek Measure," 5–24, and H. W. Siemens, "Agonal Communities of Taste: Law and Community in Nietzsche's Philosophy of Transval-

uation," 83–112. See also Christa Davis Acampora, "Of Dangerous Games and Dastardly Deeds: A Typology of Nietzsche's Contests," *International Studies in Philosophy* 34/3 (Fall 2002), 135–151.

8. See my discussion in *A Nietzschean Defense of Democracy: An Experiment in Postmodern Politics* (Chicago: Open Court, 1995), ch. 2.

9. Philosophy, for Nietzsche, is at bottom *ad hominem*, but not in a deficient sense. See Thomas H. Brobjer, "Nietzsche's Affirmative Morality: An Ethics of Virtue," *Journal of Nietzsche Studies* 26 (Autumn 2003), 64–78.

10. For an important study, see Alan D. Schrift, *Nietzsche and the Question of Interpretation: Between Hermeneutics and Deconstruction* (New York: Routledge, 1990).

11. In this passage Nietzsche also asks that readers engage his texts carefully and diligently, and not in isolation from his other texts.

12. See Bernard Reginster, "Nihilism and the Affirmation of Life," *International Studies in Philosophy* 34/3 (2002), 55–68.

13. See Ivan Soll, "Attitudes toward Life: Nietzsche's Existentialist Project," *International Studies in Philosophy* 34/3 (2002), 69–81. Reading Nietzsche is more like being "propositioned" by a seducer.

14. Concerning modern positivism and its rejection of metaphysics, one could say that metaphysics "confesses" its anxiety in the face of finite becoming, while positivism *suppresses* anxiety.

15. Nietzsche does liken life affirmation to a theodicy, but in terms of world conditions that traditional theology had always devalued (*WP* 1019). The "divine," for Nietzsche, was best expressed in pagan religion (*WP* 1052). For a discussion of Nietzschean affirmation as a response to the problem of evil, see Alan Watt, "Nietzsche's Theodicy," *New Nietzsche Studies* 4, 3/4 (2000–2001), 45–54. On a broader level, see Susan Neiman, *Evil in Modern Thought: An Alternative History of Philosophy* (Princeton, NJ: Princeton University Press, 2002). Neiman argues that the problem of evil was at the core of modern philosophy, not simply from a theological standpoint, but in secular, moral, and epistemological concerns about the ability of reason to provide intelligibility in the face of limit conditions.

Chapter 2

1. See John Sallis's important work, *Crossings: Nietzsche and the Space of Tragedy.*

2. Some of the following material is drawn from my essay, "Apollo and Dionysus: Nietzschean Expressions of the Sacred," in *Nietzsche and the Gods*, ed. Weaver Santaniello (Albany, NY: SUNY Press, 2001), 45–56.

3. See my extensive discussion in *Myth and Philosophy*, ch. 2. See also Walter Burkert, *Greek Religion*, trans. John Raffan (Cambridge, MA: Harvard University Press, 1985).

4. The early conception of Hades is not like later conceptions that promise some kind of positive afterlife. Rather, it is a shadow world that held no attraction and can best be called simply an image "locating" the meaning of nonexistence. For a discussion with references, see *Myth and Philosophy*, 51–52.

5. See *Myth and Philosophy*, ch. 5.

6. For studies on the religious meaning of tragedy, see Christiane Sourvinou-Inwood, *Tragedy and Athenian Religion* (Lanham, MD: Lexington Books, 2003), and John J. Winkler and Froma I. Zeitlin, eds., *Nothing to Do with Dionysos? Athenian Drama in Its Social Context* (Princeton, NJ: Princeton University Press, 1990). See also Carl Kerenyi, *Dionysos*, trans. Ralph Manheim (Princeton, NJ: Princeton University Press, 1976)

7. For extensive treatments of the god's nature and his religious following, see Walter F. Otto, *Dionysus: Myth and Cult*, trans. Robert B. Palmer (Bloomington: Indiana University Press, 1965).

8. See Jean-Pierre Vernant and Pierre Vidal-Naquet, *Myth and Tragedy in Ancient Greece*, trans. Janet Lloyd (Atlantic Highlands, NJ: Humanities Press, 1981), 387–88.

9. It is important to note that Nietzsche came to recognize the misleading way in which *BT* employed the term "appearance" (*Schein, Erscheinung*), namely in a seeming metaphysical sense contrasted with an underlying "reality" (thus as "mere" appearance). In his "Attempt at Self-Criticism" (1886), he not only regretted the overheated rhetoric of *BT*, he also rejected the use of Kantian and Schopenhauerian terminology because he was all along attempting "new valuations" that were utterly at odds with the philosophies of Kant and Schopenhauer (*BT* ASC, 6). The primal force of Dionysus prompted an association of Apollonian form with "dreams" and "appearances." But it cannot be said that appearance in

BT was ever meant to suggest something "deficient" because it saves life by giving meaning and shaping culture. Indeed, one sense of *Schein* that Nietzsche stressed is the radiant shining of Apollonian shapes. On this see John Sallis, "Shining Apollo," in *Nietzsche and the Gods*, 57–72. Nietzsche's strongest position against a "deficient" sense of appearance: "The true world—we have abolished. What world has remained? The apparent one perhaps? But no! *With the true world we have also abolished the apparent one*" (TI 4, 6).

10. Early poetic indications of a primal negativity at the heart of the world: In the *Iliad* 14, 300–311, *Okeanus* is a "deep-flowing" origin of the gods located at the "limits" of "allnourishing earth." In *Theogony* 736ff, an "empty gulf" (*chasma*), which has no direction or bearing, is described as the "spring and limit of all things."

11. The Greek world exhibits, with apologies to Wittgenstein, a sense of "family resistances."

12. In addition to works already cited, for descriptions of Dionysian rites see E. R. Dodds, *The Greeks and the Irrational* (Berkeley: University of California Press, 1968), 270–282; W. K. C. Guthrie, *The Greeks and Their Gods* (Boston: Beacon Press, 1950), 147–152; and J. G. Frazer, *The Golden Bough* (New York: Macmillan), 448–456.

13. Kerenyi (*Dionysos*, 213–14, 231–32) points to various historical and mythical references indicating that the Greeks saw Dionysus and Apollo as connected to each other in certain ways, which lends support to Nietzsche's suggestions about a fraternal relationship.

14. Walter Kaufmann, *Nietzsche: Philosopher, Psychologist, Antichrist* (Princeton, NJ: Princeton University Press, 1974), 128ff. In *TI* 9, 10, Nietzsche again links the Dionysian and the Apollonian. And in section 49, Goethe is called a Dionysian spirit, which surely could not indicate the absence of Apollonian formative powers.

15. In *Oedipus the King* (1329ff.), Oedipus affirms both Apollo and himself as causes of his downfall.

16. See *BT* 24, where tragic appearances are said to possess an immediate "reality" in their cultural role. The irreducibility of tragic appearances will figure in my later argument about the literal, though not factual, meaning of eternal recurrence.

17. See Burkert, *Greek Religion*, 148.

18. See Christa Davis Acampora, "Nietzsche Contra Homer, Socrates, and Paul," *Journal of Nietzsche Studies* 24 (Fall 2002), 25–53.

19. Nietzsche cites Heraclitus as a possible exception to his claim of originality.

20. I owe this insight to Matthew Meyer's "Human All Too Human and the Socrates Who Plays Music," *International Studies in Philosophy*, forthcoming.

21. This might help make sense of the following remark in the notebooks: "My task is the dehumanization of nature and then the naturalization of humanity once it has attained the pure concept of 'nature'" (*KSA* 9, 525). Evidence that *Human, All Too Human* was a preparation for tragic philosophy can be found in *KSA* 14, 125.

Chapter 3

1. Some of what follows is drawn from *A Nietzschean Defense of Democracy*, ch. 2.

2. See Jürgen Habermas, *The Philosophical Discourse of Modernity*, trans. Frederick G. Lawrence (Cambridge, MA: MIT Press, 1987), 125–26.

3. We can see why it is wrong to say that Nietzsche's thought is amoral or antimoral; he is in fact preoccupied with how we "value" things. It is a particular system of evaluation that Nietzsche is challenging, and I suppose it is its historical *victory* that prompts him to oppose "morality" and to adopt the rhetoric of "immoralism." Note as well "dependents of every degree" in the cited passage. So "slavery" should be read as rhetorical shorthand for various kinds of submission.

4. Nietzsche uses the French term *ressentiment*, probably because German lacks an effective equivalent. See Kaufmann's discussion in *Basic Writings*, 441–46.

5. See also *GS* 290 and *BGE* 219.

6. Nietzsche suggests in *HAH* I, 101 that slavery is no longer just.

7. See my discussion in *A Nietzschean Defense of Democracy*, ch. 2.

8. Two textual instances of these terms: enhancement (*Erhöhung*) in *BGE* 257, and affirmation (*Bejahung*) in *EH* III, Z, 1.

9. See also *GM* II, 18–19 and *BGE* 51.

10. It might be said that the original masters were more like contemporary action heroes or professional wrestlers. As Nietzsche says, if Homer had been an Achilles, he would not have created an Achilles (*GM* III, 4).

11. *The World as Will and Representation*, vol. 1, 398–402.

12. Moreover, within life-enhancement Nietzsche tends to distinguish *healthier* forms (e.g., the Greeks, the Renaissance) from *sicker* forms (e.g., Christianity). The former are closer to Nietzsche's sense of life-affirmation, but not necessarily up to its full demands.

13. Simon May, in *Nietzsche's Ethics and his War on Morality* (Oxford: Clarendon Press, 1999), conflates Nietzsche's usage of life-affirmation and life-enhancement, and then finds a problem in Nietzsche because the two terms should not be conflated (120). But I maintain that Nietzsche all along does not conflate the two, although I concede that he does not offer a precise, formal distinction along my lines in his texts. The distinction, however, is clearly implied in the texts.

14. See Richard Schacht, "Nietzsche and Nihilism," in *Nietzsche: A Collection of Critical Essays* (Garden City, NY: Achor Books, 1973), 58–82.

15. Nietzsche calls Schopenhauer a nihilist and an "heir of the Christian interpretation" (*TI* 9, 21).

16. See *GS* 377; *BGE* 38, 201, 203, 212; *GM* I, 16, II, 2, 11; *TI* 9, 37–38; *A* 43; *WP* 861–62.

17. Commentators have tended to read the sovereign individual as the model for the creative type and/or as having applications to liberal politics. See the following: Mark Warren, *Nietzsche and Political Thought* (Cambridge, MA: MIT Press, 1988); David Owen, "Equality, Democracy, and Self-Respect: Reflections on Nietzsche's Agonal Perfectionism," *The Journal of Nietzsche Studies* 24 (Fall 2002); Keith Ansell-Pearson, "Nietzsche: A Radical Challenge to Political Theory?" *Radical Philosophy* 54 (Spring 1990); Bonnie Honig, *Political Theory and the Displacement of Politics* (Ithaca, NY: Cornell University Press, 1993), 47–49; and Richard White, *Nietzsche and the Problem of Sovereignty* (Urbana, IL: University of Illinois Press, 1997).

18. I seem to be alone in questioning these interpretations, but help is on the way. See Christa Davis Acampora, "On Sovereignty and Overhumanity: Why It Matters How We Read Nietzsche's *Genealogy* II, 2," forthcoming in *International Studies in Philosophy*.

19. The term Nietzsche generally uses for "morality" is *Moral*, not *Sittlichkeit*.

20. See *HAH* I, 618 for another use of *Individuum* that refers to a nonpluralized, rigid singularity, and section 57, where the self is called a *Dividuum*. Also, *GS* 23 describes individuals as "incalculable," which does not square with the background of the *GM* passage. The sole context of Nietzsche's discussion in *GM* II, 1–3 involves the emergence of responsibility, conscience, and the "right to make promises." Acampora has pointed out that this last phrase *das versprechen darf* is better translated as "one who is permitted to promise" in the social arena because of having developed a *power* over the natural tendency to forget. "Forgetting," it should be added, is something Nietzsche calls "a form of *robust* health" (*GM* II, 1).

21. Determinism is another modernist outcome; consider Kant's affirmation of both freedom and determinism in his differentiation of theoretical and practical standpoints.

Chapter 4

1. My sketch cannot help but be inadequate for understanding this complex question. For an insightful analysis and collection of sources, see Charles M. Sherover, *The Human Experience of Time: The Development of its Philosophical Meaning* (New York: New York University Press, 1975).

2. David Grene and Richmond Lattimore, eds., *The Complete Greek Tragedies* (Chicago: University of Chicago Press, 1959).

3. G. S. Kirk. J. E. Raven, and M. Schofeld, *The Presocratic Philosophers*, 2nd ed. (New York: Cambridge University Press, 1983), fragment 101A.

4. Kathleen Freeman, *Ancilla to the Presocratic Philosophers* (Cambridge, MA: Harvard University Press, 1966), fragment 52.

5. See remarks on the Stoics by Nemesius and Alexander in *The Hellenistic Philosophers*, vol. 2, eds. Long and Sedley (Cambridge: Cambridge University Press, 1987), sections 52c and f. For a discussion, see A. A. Long, "The Stoics on World-Conflagration and Everlasting Recurrence," *Southern Journal of Philosophy* 23 (Supplement 1985).

6. Augustine, *The Confessions*, trans. F. J. Sheed (New York: Sheed and Ward, 1943).

7. Augustine, *The City of God*.

8. For an overview of modern approaches to time, see Mike Sandbothe, *The Temporalization of Time*, trans. Andrew Inkpin (Lanham, MD: Rowman & Littlefield, 2001).

9. The linear path of causal relations in modern science is indifferent to "direction," unlike a teleological line. On a causal line, past and future are "interchangeable coordinates which

can be calculated equally well from an arbitrarily chosen point" (Sandbothe, *The Temporalization of Time*, 11ff.).

10. Nietzsche celebrated Spinoza as a "precursor" in a postcard to Overbeck (see *The Portable Nietzsche*, 92).

11. See Bernd Magnus, *Nietzsche's Existential Imperative* (Bloomington: Indiana University Press, 1978), xiv: For Nietzsche, "to eternalize something is to prize and praise it."

12. See Alexander Nehamas, *Nietzsche: Life as Literature* (Cambridge, MA: Harvard University Press, 1985), 142–43: No empirical standpoint could address a "relation" between cycles, because that would "add" something to the cycles and thus ruin "identity."

13. The word *Schwergewicht* connotes both weight and stress (in the sense of emphasis). Both connotations operate in Nietzsche's deployment of this term here and in later texts.

14. Noted by Eric Oger, "The Eternal Return as Crucial Test," *Journal of Nietzsche Studies* 14 (Autumn 1997), 9.

15. Particular acts of revenge can be understood as motivated by a moralistic drive to undo or reverse the past.

16. Among those who think that Zarathustra's rebuke of the dwarf implies a dismissal of a circular model of time: Martin Heidegger, *Nietzsche*, vol. 2, trans. David Farrell Krell (New York: Harper and Row, 1984), 41–43; Joan Stambaugh, *Nietzsche's Thought of Eternal Return* (Baltimore, MD: Johns Hopkins University Press, 1972), 38–39; and Robin Small, "Zarathustra's Gateway," *History of Philosophy Quarterly* 15/1 (1998), 86–91.

17. See, for example: Georg Simmel, *Schopenhauer and Nietzsche*, trans. H. Loiskandle, D. Weinstein, and M. Weinstein (Amherst, MA: University of Massachusetts Press, 1986); Ivan Soll, "Reflections on Recurrence," in *Nietzsche: A Collection of Critical Essays*; and Bernd Magnus, *Nietzsche's Existential Imperative*, 66–68, 98–110.

18. See Magnus, *Nietzsche's Existential Imperative*, 67–68, 98ff.

19. On this question, see Robin Small, *Nietzsche in Context* (Burlington, VT: Ashgate, 2001), ch. 2.

20. I owe some of what follows to Gary Shapiro's important essay, "Nietzsche's Story of the Eye: Hyphenating the *Augen-Blick*," *Journal of Nietzsche Studies* 22 (Autumn 2001), 17–35.

21. Time, for Nietzsche, is therefore not an "absolute" formal concept independent of material events, but "relative" to the content of events and especially their creative, productive effects. For a critique of readings that attribute absolute time to Nietzsche, see Paul S. Loeb, "Death and Eternal Recurrence in Nietzsche's Zarathustra: A World-Historic Agon With Plato's Socrates," *New Nietzsche Studies*, forthcoming.

22. The notion of "writing my will on my tablets" is curious. Does it refer to further philosophical attempts to explore the potentials opened up by Nietzsche's texts? Also, "perfection" (*Vollendung*) can be misleading here. It cannot connote traditional ideals of de-finitized perfection. Note the comparative (*voller Vollendung*); and that *voll* can refer to something "round," and that *vollenden* can refer to death as a "completed" life.

23. This same image of the sun was advanced in the opening section of the book.

24. For example, see Heidegger, *Nietzsche*, vol. 2, 54; Magnus, *Nietzsche's Existential Imperative*, 172ff., and David B. Allison, *Reading the New Nietzsche*, (Lanham, MD: Rowman & Littlefield, 2001), 124. Laurence Lampert, in *Nietzsche's Teaching: An Interpretation of* Thus Spoke Zarathustra (New Haven, CT: Yale University Press, 1986), 214–18, shares my view that the rebuke of the animals only turns on their missing the necessary confrontation with meaninglessness. Yet he also separates the "literal" aspect of the animals' account from Zarathustra's encounter with existential "horror" (220–23). I argue against such a separation.

25. Although language, for Nietzsche, is problematic compared with temporal experience, nevertheless language is essential for shaping any sense of a world (as in the case of tragedy). Indeed, Nietzsche claims that language, and specifically words, are the very origin of thought: "We think *only* in the form of language" (*WP* 522); "we have at each moment only the thought for which we have at hand the words" (*D* 257). This gives a special ring to Nietzsche's idea of the "text" of *homo natura*, and of "translating" man back into nature (*BGE* 230).

26. Lampert argues persuasively that Zarathustra's whisper is about eternal recurrence: *Nietzsche's Teaching*, 238–39.

27. In German, *geschieden* can mean "divorced," and *aus dem Leben scheiden* means "to depart from this life."

28. In *WP* 692, Nietzsche warns against the concept "will" as an empty generalization, because such an abstraction subtracts from its "content" (*Inhalt*) and its "where to" (*Wohin*).

29. We will return to this interesting passage in a later discussion, particularly with respect to "imprinting" and the creative sense of *prägen* (as in "coining a phrase").
30. Nietzsche does allude to eternal recurrence as "a corrective to a great host of world hypotheses" (*WP* 1066).
31. One might also mention Asian models of reincarnation and cosmic periods. In such cases there seem to be no suggestions of identical cycles, which perhaps can be explained by the salvational element in Hinduism and Buddhism. Although salvation here is not grounded in personal immortality or perfection, it is still conceived as a release from *samsara* (the wheel of time). This explains why Nietzsche occasionally associated Western pessimism with Buddhism, in terms of a nonteleological impulse toward escape. Since I am concentrating on the West (and my knowledge of Asian thought is limited), I will not address Nietzsche's misconceptions of Buddhism (he was not alone in this). Elements of Mahayana Buddhism, especially in the Zen tradition, undermine the binary opposition between *nirvana* and *samsara*. For an interesting collection of essays, see Graham Parkes, ed., *Nietzsche and Asian Thought* (Chicago: University of Chicago Press, 1991).
32. *The World as Will and Representation* I, 352.
33. *The World as Will and Representation* I, 324.
34. It is interesting to note that Descartes insisted on a voluntaristic account of creation to preserve God's freedom. Creation is "indifferent" in not being governed by any prior conception, including goodness and purpose. It seems that there was another motive behind Descartes thinking: to shore up the "indifferent" nonteleological character of mechanical physics. See Blake D. Dutton, "Indifference, Necessity, and Descartes' Derivation of the Laws of Motion," *Journal of the History of Philosophy* 34/2 (April 1996), 193–212.
35. A similar point against "infinite worlds" is found in *Z* III, 10, 1.
36. See Robin Small, *Nietzsche in Context*, especially chapters 1–8, and Magnus, *Nietzsche's Existential Imperative*, especially chapter 4.

Chapter 5

1. For a rich discussion, see Johannes Schwitalla, "Nietzsche's Use of Metaphors: Semantic Processes and Textual Procedures," *Journal of Nietzsche Studies* 22 (Autumn 2001), 64–87. See also Sarah Kofman, *Nietzsche and Metaphor*, trans. Duncan Large (Stanford, CA: Stanford University Press, 1993).
2. And consider this passage: "*Being profound and seeming profound.* — Those who know that they are profound strive for clarity. Those who would like to seem profound to the crowd strive for obscurity. For the crowd believes that if it cannot see to the bottom of something it must be profound. It is so timid and dislikes going into the water" (*GS* 173).
3. Note the ironic departure from *factum*, in that scientific facts require reflection and sophisticated vocabularies, rather than mere actions and deeds.
4. See "White Mythology," in *Margins of Philosophy*, trans. Alan Bass (Chicago: University of Chicago Press, 1982).
5. Aristotle dismissed metaphor from reasoning and definition (*Posterior Analytics* 97b37ff.).
6. See Stephen Halliwell, *Aristotle's Poetics* (Chicago: University of Chicago Press, 1998), 349.
7. On this matter see Wayne Klein, *Nietzsche and the Promise of Philosophy* (Albany, NY: SUNY Press, 1997).
8. See two works by Eric A. Havelock, *Preface to Plato* (Cambridge, MA: Harvard University Press, 1963) and *The Muse Learns to Write* (New Haven, CT: Yale University Press, 1986); see also Kevin Robb, *Literacy and Paideia in Ancient Greece* (New York: Oxford University Press, 1994); and Walter J. Ong, *Orality and Literacy* (New York: Routledge, 2002).
9. See Havelock, *The Muse Learns to Write*, 111.
10. See the *Ion* and the *Phaedrus*.
11. References for this performative sense of *mimēsis* can be found in *Ion* 533ff., *Republic* 603, and *Sophist* 267. Indeed, Aristotle associates *mimēsis* with feeling the reality of dramatic performances (*Poetics* 1462a15–17). For an important discussion of the immediate disclosive effects of spoken/heard poetry, see Raymond A. Prier, *Thauma Idesthai* (Gainesville: Florida State University Press, 1989), 169–79. Prier also extends this discussion to something that accords with my intentions: a phenomenology of reading comparable to oral reception. In this regard, we should take notice of Nietzsche's interesting construction of "hearing with the eyes" (*Z* P, 5).
12. See *Republic* 605; see also Aristotle's *Poetics* 1453b.

13. See Christiane Sourvinou-Inwood, *Tragedy and Athenian Religion*. In the *Poetics*, Aristotle refers to tragic mythical characters as "historical persons" (ch. 9), and he seems to affirm the necessity of traditional stories in tragedy (ch. 14).
14. See Ellen Dissanayake, *What Is Art For?* (Seattle: University of Washington Press, 1988).
15. It is important to stress the Dionysian force of impersonation. Theater is not only a play for audiences but also for actors who play their parts by inhabiting a role, a fictive truth that is *lived out* on stage. See William Storm, *After Dionysus: A Theory of the Tragic* (Ithaca, NY: Cornell University Press, 1998).
16. For an insightful discussion of Greek *mimēsis* see Stephen Halliwell, *The Aesthetics of Mimesis* (Princeton, NJ: Princeton University Press, 2002), 1–33. Greek *mimēsis* had to do with the visual, musical, and performance arts, which combined world-disclosiveness (lifelike portrayal) and psychological force (audience identification). It was the artifice of mimetic forms that accounted for the Greek recognition of "falsehood" in poetry (expressed even by poets themselves), yet not in the sense of an "error" but an "apparent truth" (verisimilitude, *convincing* appearances). Such a positive sense of appearance should always be kept in mind when considering Nietzsche's critique of truth, which was never simply a dismantling of knowledge but also an opening for other forms of disclosure disparaged by the tradition. Moreover, Nietzsche's promotion of irreducible artistic imagery helps illuminate a notorious passage from *GS* (P, 4): Nietzsche tells us that artists, like the Greeks, are "adorers of forms, tones, words," as opposed to the impulse to "unveil" a truth hidden beneath the surface of things. The Greeks, because of their delight in beguiling forms and appearances were "superficial (*oberflächlich*) — out of profundity."
17. In an 1868 letter, Nietzsche talked of producing music "which happens to be written with words instead of notes." See *Sämtliche Briefe*, vol. 2, eds. G. Colli and M. Montinari (Munich: Deutscher Taschenbuch Verlag, 1986), 298.
18. Contemporary notebook entries argue for the intrinsic correlation of philosophical concepts and artistic forces such as metaphor and imagery (*KSA* 7, 443ff.).
19. Notice the reference to *Zarathustra* in *Ecce Homo* that highlights music and receptivity: "Perhaps the whole of *Zarathustra* may be reckoned as music; certainly a rebirth of the art of *hearing* was among its preconditions" (*EH* III, Z, 1). For an important article, see Babette E. Babich, "*Mousiké Techné*: The Philosophical Practice of Music in Plato, Nietzsche, and Heidegger," in *Between Philosophy and Poetry*, eds. Massimo Verdicchio and Robert Burch (New York: Continuum, 2002), 171–180. See also three articles in *International Studies in Philosophy* 35/3 (2003): Tracy B. Strong, "The Tragic Ethos and the Spirit of Music"; Kathleen Marie Higgens, "Music and the Mistaken Life"; and Richard Schacht, "Nietzsche, Music, Truth, Value, and Life." Note also Nietzsche's 1881 fragment (*KSA* 7, 359–69), translated by Walter Kaufmann as "On Music and Words," in Carl Dahlhaus, *Between Romanticism and Modernism*, trans. Mary Whittal (Berkeley: University of California Press, 1980).
20. For an insightful discussion of the mythical function of eternal recurrence, see Magnus, *Nietzsche's Existential Imperative*, ch. 6. Magnus, however, sees a mythical sense as contrary to a literal sense (177 ff.), something that I am trying to revise. John Richardson, while stressing the existential version of eternal recurrence, mentions that Nietzsche might have thought that recurrence would have to be taken as a cosmological claim (as a "holy lie") in order to register its existential impact. See *Nietzsche's System* (New York: Oxford University Press, 1996), 283. A rare instance in accord with my approach is John T. Wilcox, "The Birth of Nietzsche out of the Spirit of Lange," *International Studies in Philosophy* 21/2 (1989). Wilcox claims that the existential version of recurrence presupposes its truth, otherwise it can be dismissed as lacking any binding force (87).
21. Maudemarie Clark recognizes something along these lines when she makes room for an "unrealistic" belief in eternal recurrence that "plays the game" in an uncritical manner: *Nietzsche on Truth and Philosophy* (New York: Cambridge University Press, 1990), ch. 8, especially p. 270.
22. On the phenomenon of mimetic identification in reading, see Robert Storey, *Mimesis and the Human Animal* (Evanston, IL: Northwestern University Press, 1996), ch. 4. The alternative to stipulating moments of mimetic identity in language would be a radically reflective posture in perpetuity, which would seem to be an impossible prospect or at least a misrepresentation of the fund of nonreflective practices and receptions of language—witness the program of cognitive redescriptions of natural behaviors (e.g., rational choice theories) or the appeal to unconscious inferences in explaining spontaneous performances that phenomenologically do not exhibit logical schematics. The reflective posture of academic practice itself makes it seem natural to detect reflective structures and problems in natural

speech and reading. But could the revelatory power and appeal of even, say, a text about the irony of texts ever register if a radically ironic stance was taken toward *that* text? What am I saying!—it is obvious that it could be so because this kind of schizoid orientation marks a lot of academic textual practices of reading and writing, especially in "postmodern" circles (some authors feel pressed to apologize for writing in a treatise form or to play with techniques of "decomposition"). Much of this amounts to a self-conscious alienation from language, bypassing direct, revelatory moments in reading (eclipsing the "innocence of reading," if you will). A reflexive posture toward texts is important, of course, but not when eclipsing nonreflective forces in language. When texts are read *as* texts, or when texts are written about "texts," the world-disclosive power of texts can be missed, suppressed, or perhaps conspicuously absent (in academics whose "textual" skills may betray intellectual exhaustion, the lack of *anything to say*).

23. Recalling Nietzsche's association of creation with nuptial union, I also note an early noun form of "make," which, regarding humans, referred to a mate, lover, or spouse.

24. Gary Shapiro argues that eternal recurrence *expands* the self as an openness to the world: *Nietzschean Narratives* (Bloomington: Indiana University Press, 1989), 92ff.

25. There is evidence that the writings of some Presocratic philosophers were memorized and recited by rote. See Charles H. Kahn, "Philosophy and the Written Word: Some Reflections on Heraclitus and the Early Greek Uses of Prose," in *Language and Thought in Early Greek Philosophy*, ed. Kevin Robb (La Salle, IL: The Monist Library of Philosophy, 1983), 110–124.

26. In Greek, *parabolē* means illustration or comparison, but it has an interesting root in *paraballō*: to expose oneself to danger, to hazard what one values to chance, to go by sea, and to cross over.

27. It should be noted that the passage Nietzsche quotes from *Zarathustra* (III, 9) describes parabolic speech as being "upright" (*aufrecht*), "straightforward" (*aufrichtig*), and issuing "straight talk" (*gerade redet*).

28. Pierre Klossowski, *Nietzsche and the Vicious Circle*, trans. Daniel W. Smith (Chicago: University of Chicago Press, 1997), 72–73.

29. And Zarathustra refers to himself as something like a prophet, a *Wahrsager* (*Z* III, 16, 1).

30. It is true that *GS* 341 presents eternal recurrence as a kind of hypothetical exercise ("What if a demon …"). But I do not think this rules out the kind of textual impact I am trying to suggest, which is drawn from a broader consideration of Nietzsche's approach.

31. For an outstanding study that stresses the existential charge of reading the texts, see Allison, *Reading the New Nietzsche*.

32. In this light we can understand the role of "great contempt" in *Zarathustra*, as well as the notion of bad conscience turning against itself toward life-affirming possibilities (*GM* II, 16; III, 27).

33. It should be said that Nietzsche possessed a less reconciled attitude toward his mother and sister, calling them his "most abyssmal thought" and "the most profound objection to eternal recurrence" (*KSA* 6, 268).

34. In fact, Nietzsche makes the case (in *GS* 48) that pessimism does not arise in times of trouble or from experiences of suffering. Rather, such conditions are more likely to arouse life instincts; pessimistic dispositions arise out of sustained conditions of comfort, safety, and success, wherein occasions of pain are experienced more acutely as more of an assault upon life than in previous eras of difficulty: "pain is now hated much more than was the case formerly; one speaks much worse of it; indeed, one considers the existence of the mere *thought* of pain scarcely endurable and turns it into a reproach against the whole of existence."

35. As I will suggest in the next chapter, it is conceivable that Nietzsche saw eternal recurrence as not only a matter of human authenticity, but also in its way the most "objective" expression of the world possible.

36. I am even contrarian toward contraries. All of my books, in fact, have been attempts to reconcile presumably incompatible pairings: myth and philosophy, Nietzsche and democracy, Heidegger and ethics.

Chapter 6

1. See, for example, Nehamas, *Nietzsche: Life as Literature*, 142–43, and Milic Capek's article in *The Encyclopedia of Philosophy*, vol. 3, ed. Paul Edwards (New York: Macmillan, 1967), 63.

2. Ivan Soll, "Reflections on Recurrence," in *Nietzsche: A Collection of Critical Essays*, ed. Robert Solomon (New York: Doubleday, 1973), 339–40.

3. See Kathleen Marie Higgens, *Nietzsche's* Zarathustra (Philadelphia, PA: Temple University Press, 1987), 160ff.
4. Arthur Danto, *Nietzsche as Philosopher* (New York: Columbia University Press, 1980), 205ff.
5. Simmel, *Schopenhauer and Nietzsche*, 172–73.
6. Soll, "Reflections on Recurrence," 327–28. See also Small, *Nietzsche in Context*, 122ff.
7. Müller-Lauter, *Nietzsche: His Philosophy of Contradiction and the Contradictions of His Philosophy.*
8. Karl Löwith, *Nietzsche's Philosophy of the Eternal Recurrence of the Same*, trans. J Harvey Lomax (Berkeley: University of California Press, 1997).
9. Lampert maintains that Nietzsche's scientific experiments should not be called a "failure" or something inconsistent with the "spiritual" aspect of eternal recurrence, but rather an honest attempt to bolster his project with the science of his day: *Nietzsche's Teaching*, 259–260.
10. See Nehamas, *Nietzsche: Life as Literature*, 144ff.
11. Richard Schacht, *Nietzsche* (London: Routledge and Kegan Paul, 1983), 253–266.
12. Richardson, *Nietzsche's System*, 91–72, 138–140, 283.
13. Lampert, *Nietzsche's Teaching*, Part 3; Shapiro, *Nietzschean Narratives*; and Allison, *Reading the New Nietzsche*, 119–128.
14. Tracy B. Strong, *Friedrich Nietzsche and the Politics of Transfiguration*, expanded ed. (Urbana: University of Illinois Press, 2000), 263, 270–71, 283, 287).
15. Higgens, *Nietzsche's* Zarathustra, 159–201.
16. Magnus, *Nietzsche's Existential Imperative*, chs. 5–6, esp. p. 142.
17. Nehamas, *Nietzsche: Life as Literature*, ch. 5. Shapiro questions this approach because he sees eternal recurrence forcing a confrontation with the dissolution of self-identity (*Nietzschean Narratives*, 86ff.). For an overall criticism of "aesthetic" interpretations of Nietzsche, see Bernd Magnus, Stanley Stewart, and Jean-Pierre Mileur, *Nietzsche's Case: Philosophy As/And Literature* (New York: Routledge, 1993).
18. Clark, *Nietzsche on Truth and Philosophy*, ch. 8, esp. p. 257.
19. A classic formulation of this approach is found in Karl Jaspers, *Nietzsche: An Introduction to the Understanding of His Philosophical Activity*, trans. Charles F. Wallraff and Frederick J. Schmitz (Chicago: Henry Regnery Co., 1965), 353ff. See also Löwith, *Nietzsche's Philosophy of the Eternal Recurrence of the Same*, 85; and Simmel, *Schopenhauer and Nietzsche*, 52. Arnold Zuboff, in "Nietzsche and Eternal Recurrence" (in *Nietzsche: A Collection of Critical Essays*), argues that eternal recurrence not only presents an ethical imperative, it also functions in a manner analogous to afterlife doctrines of reward and punishment, by pressing on us the task of creating lives that we will have to live with eternally.
20. For an insightful critical assessment of ethical interpretations, see Magnus, *Nietzsche's Existential Imperative*, ch. 5.
21. *A Nietzschean Defense of Democracy*, 174–185. Lester H. Hunt makes the interesting case that eternal recurrence is not a measure for moral action but a prompt for virtue, for a basic way of living characterized by overcoming revenge: "Eternal Recurrence and Nietzsche's Ethic of Virtue," *International Studies in Philosophy* 25/2 (1993), 3–11.
22. See Paul S. Loeb, "The Moment of Tragic Death in Nietzsche's Dionysian Doctrine of Eternal Recurrence: An Exegesis of Aphorism 341 in the *Gay Science*," *International Studies in Philosophy* 30/3 (1998), 131–143. Loeb helpfully connects this passage with the surrounding sections 340 and 342.
23. See Eric Oger, "The Eternal Return as Crucial Test," *Journal of Nietzsche Studies* 14 (Autumn 1997), 1–18.
24. Gilles Deleuze, *Nietzsche and Philosophy*, trans. Hugh Tomlinson (New York: Columbia University Press, 1983), 71–72. Strong follows Deleuze on this view (*Friedrich Nietzsche and the Politics of Transfiguration*, 270–71).
25. Higgens, in *Nietzsche's* Zarathustra, recognizes the problem of affirming moral atrocities (and Zarathustra's problem with the small man), but identifies its source in misreading eternal recurrence as pertaining to factual cases and all moments as such, rather than as a focal concentration on the *present* moment as an attitude toward the temporal structure of life (198–201). In fact, she prefers to stress the joyful aspects of eternal recurrence over its (admittedly plausible) darker aspects, and even calls Zarathustra's traumatic reactions a form of bad faith (191ff.). Naturally I find this reading problematic. The "dark side" of eternal recurrence is intrinsic to its generation of authentic life affirmation, as Nietzsche sees it.
26. See Lampert, *Nietzsche's Teaching*, 149–50, and Klossowski, *Nietzsche and the Vicious Circle*, 104.

27. Stambaugh, *Nietzsche's Thought of Eternal Return,* 103 ff. Subsequent page cites given in the text.
28. Robert Gooding-Williams, *Zarathustra's Dionysian Modernism* (Stanford, CA: Stanford University Press, 2001), 296–97.
29. Jaspers, *Nietzsche,* 352–367.
30. Deleuze, *Nietzsche and Philosophy,* 71–72.
31. See the following works of Heidegger: *Nietzsche,* vol. 2, *The Eternal Recurrence of the Same,* trans. David F. Krell (New York: Harper and Row, 1984); and *What Is Called Thinking?* trans. Fred D. Wieck and J. Glenn Gray (New York: Harper and Row, 1968).

Chapter 7

1. See Ivan Soll, "Reflections on Recurrence."
2. See also *BGE* 21–22; *TI* 6,8; *WP* 552, 1066.
3. One reason for Nietzsche's opposition to mechanistic determinism is that it obviates meaning (*WP* 617).
4. See, for example, the *Odyssey* 3, 230ff.
5. For *anankē* as compulsion, see *Odyssey* 10, 434; as enslavement, see *Iliad* 6, 458. For *tuchē*, see Hesiod's *Theogony* 360, Sophocles' *Philoctetes* 1326, and Plato's *Republic* 10, 619c. Parmenides joins *anankē* and *moira* as a binding power (fragment 8, lines 30 and 37). And Sophocles' *Ajax* contains the phrase *anankaia tuchē*, "necessary chance" (485, 803). For an interesting discussion of this latter term, see Bernard Williams, *Shame and Necessity* (Berkeley: University of California Press, 1993), 104, 123–24.
6. In the *Timaeus* (47e ff.), *anankē* is an errant, random cause that must be governed by *nous.* In *Metaphysics* 5, 1015a20ff., Aristotle describes one meaning of *anankē* as a painful force that works contrary to choice and reasoning. See also *On the Generation of Animals* 778a30–31 for "necessary causes" that are blind, nontelic sources of natural anomalies. On chance as nontelic movement, see *Physics* II, 4–6.
7. See *Z* III, 13, 2, where the animals, purporting to speak for Zarathustra, say: "I myself belong to the causes of eternal recurrence."
8. See Amy Mullin, "Nietzsche's Free Spirit," *Journal of the History of Philosophy* 38/3 (July 2000), 383–405.
9. See J. Gonda, "Reflections on the Indo-European Medium," *Lingua* 9/4 (1960), 30–67.
10. Oedipus expresses a stark middle voice perspective when he declares both Apollo and himself as the cause of his downfall (*Oedipus the King,* 376, 1329ff.).
11. See Strong, *Friedrich Nietzsche and the Politics of Transfiguration,* 278–281.
12. This is confirmed by Aristotle when he argues that the narrative structure (*muthos*) of the drama takes precedence over individual characters; indeed, *muthos* (and not characterization) is the origin (*arché*) and life (*psuchē*) of a tragedy (*Poetics* 6).
13. For a comparable analysis of what Nietzsche calls "Russian fatalism," see *EH* I, 6.
14. Indeed, advancing determinism as a philosophical project opens up quite a conundrum: If I am a libertarian, then the argument of determinism aims to persuade me to think otherwise. If it were to succeed in getting me to accept a deterministic world, then by these lights it could not be otherwise that I come to think otherwise than my previous conviction—which thought otherwise than that my conviction cannot be otherwise (sorry, it scans).
15. The deployment of physics here must be taken as a rhetorical device against moralism rather than a straightforward grounding of creativity in science.
16. See Mattias Risse, "Nietzsche's Joyous and Trusting Fatalism," *International Studies in Philosophy* 35/3 (2003), 147–162. For insightful discussions of the compatibility of freedom, creation, and fatalism, see two essays by Robert C. Solomon, "Nietzsche as Existentialist and as Fatalist: The Practical Paradoxes of Self-Making," *International Studies in Philosophy* 34/3 (2002), 41–54 and "Nietzsche on Fatalism and 'Free Will,'" *Journal of Nietzsche Studies* 23 (2002), 63–84. See also Brian Leiter, "The Paradox of Fatalism and Self-Creation in Nietzsche," in *Nietzsche,* eds. John Richardson and Brian Leiter (New York: Oxford University Press, 2001), 281–321. Leiter rightly challenges readings of Nietzsche that emphasize self-creation or that try to reconcile the texts with some form of free agency. He faces Nietzsche's fatalism squarely and argues for its compatibility with self-creation if Nietzsche is understood as a "causal essentialist," which is different from both classical fatalism and classical determinism. Causal essentialism fixes one's nature and capacities in terms of circumscribed constraints that allow for specific variations, rather than a lawlike regulation

that predetermines every aspect of activity. My reservations include (1) Leiter's assumption that Nietzsche's naturalism must be couched in terms of scientific causality, and (2) the lack of attention to eternal recurrence and its apparent challenge to a loosened fatalism.

17. See, for example, *TI* 9, 33; *BGE* 29; *WP* 287, 984; and *Z* I, 17. See my discussion in *A Nietzschean Defense of Democracy*, 28–39.

18. See also *WS* 122, 127 for the positive relationship between conventional and poetic language.

19. There is a story about Beethoven performing one of his piano sonatas. Afterward, a woman approached him and asked: "Herr Beethoven, what were you trying to say in that piece?" Without a word, he went to the piano, played the entire piece again, and walked away. In this act, there is an echo of Nietzsche's satisfaction with the nontelic, noncausal, nonexplicable immediacy of events.

20. Bernd Magnus, in "Self-Consuming Concepts," *International Studies in Philosophy* 21/2 (1989), 63–71, offers a telling and elegant reaction. He claims that eternal recurrence entails affirming each moment unconditionally for its own sake, and that only an *Übermensch* or a god could will such a thing. We should be honest and admit that we cannot help but live edited lives, cannot help but imagine a life better than what is or has been the case. Who would not will recurrence *minus* extermination camps? One problem with Magnus's account is the assumption of affirming moments in themselves, apart from their necessary relation to (all) other moments. The latter notion opens space for a Nietzschean response to this important question.

21. It should be noted that Nietzsche in this respect grants the utmost seriousness to morality and its fundamental purpose of finding *meaning* in certain value preferences.

22. Richard A. Smith suggests that there may be no such distinction, that Nietzsche himself may be guilty of resentment in his attacks upon slave morality: "Nietzsche: Philosopher of *Ressentiment*?" *International Studies in Philosophy* 25/2 (1993), 135–143. Yet I have argued that Zarathustra's nausea, as that which must finally be overcome in the task of affirmation, subverts any such charge. See Jonathon Cohen's critical response to Smith in the same volume (145–49).

23. Magnus, "Self-Consuming Concepts," 69.

24. Notice what absolutism and relativism have in common: the former identifies *one* uncontestable truth while the latter simply postulates *many* uncontestable truths (each being equally valid for those who hold them and thus immune from external judgment).

25. This analysis points back to *Homer's Contest* and the distinction between good and bad *Eris* (strife); see also *WP* 361.

26. In Homer, a decidedly different "virtue ethics" is described when a hero defends a certain enthusiasm for war: heroes earn their station and advantage through risking death. If there were no dangers of death, no such honor and glory would be possible. But human life *is* mortal, so heroic risk *is* worthy of pursuit (*Iliad* 12, 310–328).

27. Ethical self-deconstruction matches a previous point about the inconsistency of a historically emergent belief system extolling conditions of stability that would make impossible its own occurrence. Such analyses give Nietzsche's naturalistic critique a powerful weapon. Yet Schopenhauer, once again, can offer a clarifying admission, if his thought can be taken as a code for the Western tradition: Schopenhauer concedes that pessimistic will-denial is a conceptual contradiction, in that the phenomenal self moves to deny and disarm the noumenal will; but the paradox can be sustained because existence itself is absurd and the noumenal will is not subject to the principle of sufficient reason (*The World as Will and Representation*, vol. 1, 402–408). In this way a deconstructive "critique" is derailed by a self-exposing inconsistency that confesses its radically alien posture toward life.

28. See also *GM* II, 12, which declares the equivalence of will to power and action.

29. For all the different characteristics of Western culture challenged by Nietzsche, I think one central common thread can be located in the course of ancient, medieval, and modern thought: the ideal of *self-sufficiency*. In different ways and registers, the notion of unimpeded, unneedful, independent, unencumbered, self-causing agency and power can be found in Plato and Aristotle's conversion of early Greek theology (from poetic narratives of gods engaged with the world toward self-sufficient transcendence), in medieval conceptions of divine omniscience and omnipotence, and in the modern paradigm of the rational subject (which grounds epistemological warrants in the certainty of self-posited methods and principles, and political warrants in the freedom of self-directed agency).

30. Some of what follows is taken from my discussion in *A Nietzschean Defense of Democracy*, ch. 6.

31. For textual sources of these indications, see *BGE* 34; *GM* II, 12; *TI* 6, 5; *WP* 259, 534, 552, 556, 568, 590, 966. An early text disowns the idea, frequently attributed to Nietzsche, that truth is reducible to power: "*Truth requires power.* Truth is not power in and of itself.... Rather, it must draw power over to its side" (*D* 535).

32. On this important point see Daniel W. Conway, "*Wir Erkennenden*: Self-Referentiality in the Preface to *Zur Genealogie der Moral*," *Journal of Nietzsche Studies* 22 (Fall 2001), 116–132.

33. In *BGE* 34, both the object and the subject are called fictions. With less hyperbole, Nietzsche claims that the inner world is no less an interpretation than the outer world (*WP* 477).

34. For a discussion of how Nietzsche's deployment of perspective and interpretation is generalized beyond common, particularly subjective, connotations of these terms, see Christoph Cox, "The 'Subject' of Nietzsche's Perspectivism," *Journal of the History of Philosophy* 35/2 (April 1997), 269–291.

35. See Schrift, *Nietzsche and the Question of Interpretation*, chs. 6 and 7; and Clark, *Nietzsche on Truth and Philosophy*, ch. 5.

36. For Nietzsche's critique of skepticism and its complicity with a weak-willed objectivism, see *BGE* 207–208. My discussion of this matter in the context of ethics can be found in *A Nietzschean Defense of Democracy*, 182–85. If skepticism means an interrogative openness regarding beliefs and an opposition to dogmatism, then it is right to call Nietzsche a skeptic. But there are three reasons why we should be skeptical about attributing to Nietzsche some familiar forms of philosophical skepticism: (1) Antidogmatism need not preclude commitment to one's beliefs and judgments of alternative beliefs; the agonistic structure of will to power permits both a rejoinder to dogmatism and an invitation to take a stand in intellectual competitions. (2) Nietzsche would reject the idea that one should suspend judgment on beliefs that have not been justified by demonstrative proof; such proof is not the ultimate proving ground in philosophy for Nietzsche; anyway, skepticism of this sort is simply the flip side or evil twin of dogmatism. (3) Radical skepticism (regarding knowledge in general, the external world, etc.) would violate Nietzsche's radical naturalism. We can question anything that happens, but the happening itself, or the happening of interrogation itself, cannot be questioned; that would be a recipe for, if not an instance of, nihilism and life-denial. From a performative standpoint, we are always already immersed in life projects of meaning-making in a finite world and in contest with other projects. To seek or stipulate global judgments of the entire field of play (whether this be dogmatism or skepticism) is a disengagement (or retreat to the sidelines) animated by dispositional infirmities.

37. See Jürgen Habermas, "The Entwinement of Myth and Enlightenment: Rereading *Dialectic of Enlightenment*," *New German Critique* 26 (1982). For discussions of the problem of self-reference in Nietzsche, see Schrift, *Nietzsche and the Question of Interpretation*, 184–94; and Clark, *Nietzsche on Truth and Philosophy*, 138–58. See also the panel of essays by Robin Alice Roth, Daniel W. Conway, and Babette E. Babich in *International Studies in Philosophy* 22/2 (1990), 67–109.

38. Consider, for instance, Nietzsche's positive analysis of the Christian life for those who must bear existence in the mode of withdrawal and denial (*A* 34–35, 39–40).

39. For this reason, Deleuze is mistaken when he reads the affirmative innocence of the child in *Thus Spoke Zarathustra* as the dismissal of struggle, war, and competition from Nietzsche's vision (*Nietzsche and Philosophy*, 82).

40. Dan Conway has posed this question to me in a personal communication.

Epilogue

1. For a thorough treatment of this debate, see Paul S. Loeb, "The Conclusion of Nietzsche's *Zarathustra*," *International Studies in Philosophy* 32/3 (2000), 137–152.

2. This is Loeb's argument in "The Conclusion of Nietzsche's *Zarathustra*."

3. Parts of my analysis are drawn from two essays of mine: "Laughter in Nietzsche's Thought: A Philosophical Tragicomedy," *International Studies in Philosophy* 20/2 (1988), 67–79; and "The Satyr: Human-Animality in Nietzsche," in *A Nietzschean Bestiary: Becoming Animal beyond Docile and Brutal*, eds. Christa Davis Acampora and Ralph R. Acampora (Lanham, MD: Rowman & Littlefield, 2004), 211–219.

4. See Xavier Riu, *Dionysism and Comedy* (Lanham, MD: Rowman & Littlefield), 1999, and Winkler and Zeitlin, eds., *Nothing to Do with Dionysos? Athenian Drama in Its Social Context*.

5. See A. W. Pickard-Cambridge, *Dithyramb Tragedy and Comedy*, 2nd ed., revised by T. B. L. Webster (Oxford: Oxford University Press, 1962).

6. Kerenyi, *Dionysos*, 330–348.
7. Sourvinou-Inwood, *Tragedy and Athenian Religion*, 172–77.
8. It is important not to construe comedy's safe zone of "harmless negation" as mere comic relief, as nothing more than psychological solace or ventilation. Greek comedy performed a serious function as well, in its contribution to democratic debate and its revelatory aims in a wide range of social concerns. See Jeffrey Henderson, "The *Demos* and the Comic Competition," in *Nothing to Do with Dionysos?*, 271–313.
9. Mention should be made of the "wisdom of Silenus" as it functions in *BT*. The relation between the satyr and Silenus is unclear, although the former has human legs, the latter equine legs. Originally they seem to have been separate fertility daemons, but in time both came to be associated with Dionysus. It is not clear if they were taken as substantively different or if Silenus was a proper name rather than a generic type. Nietzsche seems to conflate satyr and Silenus, although the latter may be a proper name referring to a kind of pessimistic wisdom (It is better never to have been born; next best to die soon) that Nietzsche wants to bring into the picture (*BT* 3). The problem is that the satyr chorus is an affirmative force that saves the Greeks from nihilism and revulsion against life (*BT* 7). It may be that Silenus represents a danger in Dionysian experience wherein the pain of individuation can prompt an ecstatic denial of individuation in favor of annihilation. It is clear that for Nietzsche, the wisdom of tragedy reflects an overcoming of such pessimism through the "reciprocal necessity" of both Dionysian ecstasy and the beauty of Apollonian individuation (*BT* 4). The satyr effect, especially its relation to comedy (*BT* 7), seems to have a life-affirming quality, so the satyr-Silenus relation would need clarifying on this count. Nietzsche's text, however, does not provide clarification.
10. See M. S. Silk and J. P. Stern, *Nietzsche on Tragedy* (Cambridge: Cambridge University Press, 1981), 142ff.
11. See François Lissarraque, "On the Wildness of the Satyrs," in *Masks of Dionysus*, eds. Thomas H. Carpenter and Christopher A. Faraone (Ithaca, NY: Cornell University Press, 1993), 208ff.
12. Lissarraque, "On the Wildness of the Satyrs," 207.
13. Timothy Ganz, *Early Greek Myth* (Baltimore, MD: Johns Hopkins University Press, 1993), 137.
14. Vernant and Vidal-Naquet, *Myth and Tragedy in Ancient Greece*, 204.
15. Lissarraque, "On the Wildness of the Satyrs," 214ff.
16. Vernant and Vidal-Naquet, *Myth and Tragedy in Ancient Greece*, 183.
17. Burkert, *Greek Religion*, 104, 173.
18. For what follows, see P. E. Easterling, "A Show for Dionysus," in *The Cambridge Companion to Greek Tragedy*, ed. P. E. Easterling (Cambridge: Cambridge University Press, 1997), 37–44.
19. Vernant and Vidal-Naquet, *Myth and Tragedy in Ancient Greece*, 152.
20. *Briefwechsel: Kritische Gesamtausgabe*, eds. G. Colli and M. Montinari (Berlin: Walter de Gruyter, 1967ff.) III 5, 516–17.
21. A precedent for Loeb's account is Shapiro's chapter in *Nietzschean Narratives*, "Festival, Carnival, and Parody (Zarathustra IV)." Shapiro argues that parody in Part 4 is a gesture against the "authority" of the text, in a manner consistent with the radical immanence of eternal recurrence, which disallows any universal spectator, author, or omniscient narrator (122). See also Kathleen M. Higgins, "Nietzsche and the Mystery of the Ass," in *A Nietzschean Bestiary* (100–118), and Walter Brogan, "Zarathustra: The Tragic Figure of the Last Philosopher," in *Philosophy and Tragedy*, eds. Miguel de Beistegui and Simon Sparks (London: Routledge, 2000), 152–166.
22. Cited by Walter Kaufmann, *Basic Writings*, 422.
23. For an important study, see Kathleen M. Higgins, *Comic Relief* (Oxford: Oxford University Press, 2000). Higgins argues that comedy and tragedy are both responses to the threat of meaninglessness, and that for Nietzsche, comedy is the more profound orientation, since it combines self-limitation with delight and an affirmation of life's value despite the absence of teleological justification.
24. See Paul Loeb, "Zarathustra's Laughing Lions," in *A Nietzschean Bestiary*, 121–139.
25. Thus I do not want to follow Brogan's suggestion that eternal recurrence might be "the ultimate philosophical joke" ("Zarathustra: The Tragic Figure of the Last Philosopher," 164).
26. Translation by Peter Meineck in *Aristophanes I* (Indianapolis, IN: Hackett Publishing Co., 1998), 233.

References

Acampora, Christa Davis and Ralph R. Acampora, eds. *A Nietzschean Bestiary: Becoming Animal beyond Docile and Brutal.* Lanham, MD: Rowman & Littlefield, 2004.

Allison, David B. *Reading the New Nietzsche.* Lanham, MD: Rowman & Littlefield, 2001.

Aristophanes. *Aristophanes I,* Trans. Peter Meineck. Indianapolis, IN: Hackett Publishing Co., 1998.

Augustine. *The City of God.* Trans. Marcus Dods. New York: Random House, 1950.

———. *The Confessions.* Trans. F. J. Sheed. New York: Sheed and Ward, 1943.

Burkert, Walter. *Greek Religion.* Trans. John Raffan. Cambridge, MA: Harvard University Press, 1985.

Carpenter, Thomas H. and Christopher A. Faraone, eds. *Masks of Dionysus.* Ithaca, NY: Cornell University Press, 1993.

Clark, Maudemarie. *Nietzsche on Truth and Philosophy.* New York: Cambridge University Press, 1990.

Cox, Christoph. *Nietzsche: Naturalism and Interpretation.* Berkeley: University of California Press, 1999.

Dahlhaus, Carl. *Between Romanticism and Modernism.* Trans. Mary Whittal. Berkeley: University of California Press, 1980.

Danto, Arthur. *Nietzsche as Philosopher.* New York: Columbia University Press, 1980.

de Beistegui, Miguel and Simon Sparks, eds. *Philosophy and Tragedy.* London: Routledge, 2000.

Deleuze, Gilles. *Nietzsche and Philosophy.* Trans. Hugh Tomlinson. New York: Columbia University Press, 1983.

Derrida, Jacques. *Margins of Philosophy.* Trans. Alan Bass. Chicago: University of Chicago Press, 1982.

Dissanayake, Ellen. *What Is Art For?* Seattle: University of Washington Press, 1988.

Dodds, E. R. *The Greeks and the Irrational.* Berkeley: University of California Press, 1968.

Easterling, P. E., ed. *The Cambridge Companion to Greek Tragedy.* Cambridge: Cambridge University Press, 1997.

Frazer, J. G. *The Golden Bough.* New York: Macmillan, 1963.

Freeman, Kathleen. *Ancilla to the Presocratic Philosophers.* Cambridge, MA: Harvard University Press, 1966.

Ganz, Timothy. *Early Greek Myth.* Baltimore, MD: Johns Hopkins University Press, 1993.

Gooding-Williams, Robert. *Zarathustra's Dionysian Modernism.* Stanford, CA: Stanford University Press, 2001.

Grene, David and Richmond Lattimore, eds. *The Complete Greek Tragedies.* Chicago: University of Chicago Press, 1959.

Guthrie, W. K. C. *The Greeks and Their Gods.* Boston: Beacon Press, 1950.

Habermas, Jürgen. *The Philosophical Discourse of Modernity.* Trans. Frederick G. Lawrence. Cambridge, MA: MIT Press, 1987.

Halliwell, Stephen. *Aristotle's Poetics.* Chicago: University of Chicago Press, 1998.

———. *The Aesthetics of Mimesis.* Princeton, NJ: Princeton University Press, 2002.

Hatab, Lawrence J. *Myth and Philosophy: A Contest of Truths.* Chicago: Open Court, 1990.

———. *A Nietzschean Defense of Democracy: An Experiment in Postmodern Politics.* Chicago: Open Court, 1995.

Havelock, Eric A. *Preface to Plato.* Cambridge, MA: Harvard University Press, 1963.

———. *The Muse Learns to Write.* New Haven, CT: Yale University Press, 1986.

Heidegger, Martin. *Nietzsche.* Vol. 2: *The Eternal Recurrence of the Same.* Trans. David F. Krell. New York: Harper and Row, 1984.

———. *What Is Called Thinking?* Trans. Fred D. Wieck and J. Glenn Gray. New York: Harper and Row, 1968.

Higgens, Kathleen Marie. *Nietzsche's Zarathustra*. Philadelphia, PA: Temple University Press, 1987.
———. *Comic Relief*. Oxford: Oxford University Press, 2000.
Honig, Bonnie. *Political Theory and the Displacement of Politics*. Ithaca, NY: Cornell University Press, 1993.
Jaspers, Karl. *Nietzsche: An Introduction to the Understanding of His Philosophical Activity*. Trans. Charles F. Wallraff and Frederick J. Schmitz. Chicago: Henry Regnery Co., 1965.
Kaufmann, Walter. *Nietzsche: Philosopher, Psychologist, Antichrist*. Princeton, NJ: Princeton University Press, 1974.
Kerenyi, Carl. *Dionysos*. Trans. Ralph Manheim. Princeton, NJ: Princeton University Press, 1976.
Kirk, G. S., J. E. Raven, and M. Schofoeld. *The Presocratic Philosophers*. 2nd ed. New York: Cambridge University Press, 1983.
Klein, Wayne. *Nietzsche and the Promise of Philosophy*. Albany, NY: SUNY Press, 1997.
Klossowski, Pierre. *Nietzsche and the Vicious Circle*. Trans. Daniel W. Smith. Chicago: University of Chicago Press, 1997.
Kofman, Sarah. *Nietzsche and Metaphor*. Trans. Duncan Large. Stanford, CA: Stanford University Press, 1993.
Lampert, Laurence. *Nietzsche's Teaching: An Interpretation of* Thus Spoke Zarathustra. New Haven, CT: Yale University Press, 1986.
Long, A. A. and D. N. Sedley, eds. *The Hellenistic Philosophers*. Vol. 2. Cambridge: Cambridge University Press, 1987.
Löwith, Karl. *Nietzsche's Philosophy of the Eternal Recurrence of the Same*. Trans. J. Harvey Lomax. Berkeley: University of California Press, 1997.
Magnus, Bernd. *Nietzsche's Existential Imperative*. Bloomington: Indiana University Press, 1978.
Magnus, Bernd, Stanley Stewart, and Jean-Pierre Mileur. *Nietzsche's Case: Philosophy As/And Literature*. New York: Routledge, 1993.
May, Simon. *Nietzsche's Ethics and his War on Morality*. Oxford: Clarendon Press, 1999.
Müller-Lauter, Wolfgang. *Nietzsche: His Philosophy of Contradictions and the Contradictions of His Philosophy*. Trans. David J. Parent. Urbana: University of Illinois Press, 1999.
Nehamas, Alexander. *Nietzsche: Life as Literature*. Cambridge, MA: Harvard University Press, 1985.
Neiman, Susan. *Evil in Modern Thought: An Alternative History of Philosophy*. Princeton, NJ: Princeton University Press, 2002.
Ong, Walter J. *Orality and Literacy*. New York: Routledge, 2002.
Otto, Walter F. *Dionysus: Myth and Cult*. Trans. Robert B. Palmer. Bloomington: Indiana University Press, 1965.
Parkes, Graham, ed. *Nietzsche and Asian Thought*. Chicago: University of Chicago Press, 1991.
Pickard-Cambridge, A. W. *Dithyramb Tragedy and Comedy*. 2nd ed., revised by T. B. L. Webster. Oxford: Oxford University Press, 1962.
Prier, Raymond A. *Thauma Idesthai*. Gainesville: Florida State University Press, 1989.
Richardson, John. *Nietzsche's System*. New York: Oxford University Press, 1996.
Richardson, John and Brian Leiter, eds. *Nietzsche*. New York: Oxford University Press, 2001.
Riu, Xavier. *Dionysism and Comedy*. Lanham, MD: Rowman & Littlefield, 1999.
Robb, Kevin. *Literacy and Paideia in Ancient Greece*. New York: Oxford University Press, 1994.
____, ed. *Language and Thought in Early Greek Philosophy*. La Salle, IL: The Monist Library of Philosophy, 1983.
Sallis, John. *Crossings: Nietzsche and the Space of Tragedy*. Chicago: University of Chicago Press, 1991.
Sandbothe, Mike. *The Temporalization of Time*. Trans. Andrew Inkpin. Lanham, MD: Rowman & Littlefield, 2001.
Santaniello, Weaver, ed. *Nietzsche and the Gods*. Albany, NY: SUNY Press, 2001.
Schacht, Richard. *Nietzsche*. London: Routledge and Kegan Paul, 1983.
Schopenhauer, Arthur. *The World as Will and Representation*. Vol. I, trans. E. F. J. Payne. New York: Dover, 1969.
Schrift, Alan D. *Nietzsche and the Question of Interpretation: Between Hermeneutics and Deconstruction*. New York: Routledge, 1990.
Shapiro, Gary. *Nietzschean Narratives*. Bloomington: Indiana University Press, 1989.
Sherover, Charles M. *The Human Experience of Time: The Development of its Philosophical Meaning*. New York: New York University Press, 1975.
Silk, M. S. and J. P. Stern. *Nietzsche on Tragedy*. Cambridge: Cambridge University Press, 1981.
Simmel, Georg. *Schopenhauer and Nietzsche*. Trans. H. Loiskandle, D. Weinstein, and M. Weinstein. Amherst: University of Massachusetts Press, 1986.

Small, Robin. *Nietzsche in Context*. Burlington, VT: Ashgate, 2001.

Solomon, Robert, ed. *Nietzsche: A Collection of Critical Essays*. Garden City, NY: Anchor Books, 1973.

Sourvinou-Inwood, Christiane. *Tragedy and Athenian Religion*. Lanham, MD: Lexington Books, 2003.

Stambaugh, Joan. *Nietzsche's Thought of Eternal Return*. Baltimore, MD: Johns Hopkins University Press, 1972.

Storey, Robert. *Mimesis and the Human Animal*. Evanston, IL: Northwestern University Press, 1996.

Storm, William. *After Dionysus: A Theory of the Tragic*. Ithaca, NY: Cornell University Press, 1998.

Strong, Tracy B. *Friedrich Nietzsche and the Politics of Transfiguration*. Expanded ed. Urbana: University of Illinois Press, 2000.

Verdicchio, Massimo and Robert Burch, eds. *Between Philosophy and Poetry*. New York: Continuum, 2002.

Vernant, Jean-Pierre and Pierre Vidal-Naquet. *Myth and Tragedy in Ancient Greece*. Trans. Janet Lloyd. Atlantic Highlands, NJ: Humanities Press, 1981.

Warren, Mark. *Nietzsche and Political Thought*. Cambridge, MA: MIT Press, 1988.

White, Richard. *Nietzsche and the Problem of Sovereignty*. Urbana: University of Illinois Press, 1997.

Williams, Bernard. *Shame and Necessity*. Berkeley: University of California Press, 1993.

Winkler, John J. and Froma I. Zeitlin, eds. *Nothing to Do with Dionysos? Athenian Drama in Its Social Context*. Princeton, NJ: Princeton University Press, 1990.

Index

A

Acampora, Christa Davis, 169n. 7, 171n. 18, 172n. 18
Agonistics, 10, 16–17, 33
    different from destruction, 63
    and ethics, 138–143
    and freedom, 130–131
    and life-affirmation, 46–47, 63, 108–110, 138–142
    in philosophy, 36–37
    and selfhood, 47
Allison, David, 118, 176n. 31
Amor fati, 49, 128–129, 132, 140
Ansell-Pearson, Keith, 172n. 17
Apollo/the Apollonian, 25–27, 30–32, 95–98
    and poetic language, 96
Appearance, 31–32, 35, 145–146, 170n. 9
Aristophanes, 166
Aristotle, 2–3, 58–59, 101, 141–142
Art, 25–29, 147
Asceticism/the ascetic ideal, 8, 43–44, 46, 109–110
Augustine, 59–60

B

Babich, Babette, 169n. 4, 175n. 19, 180n. 37
Becoming, 21, 25
    and being, 13–14, 62–63, 74–75, 85, 136–137, 146
    innocence of, 62, 132
Brobjer, Thomas H, 170n. 9
Brogan, Walter, 181n. 21, 25
Buddhism, 174n. 31
Burkert, Walter, 170n. 3, 171n. 17, 181n. 17

C

Causality, 128–130
Chance, 129–130
Christianity, 3, 20, 59–60
    and invention of history, 59
    as life-enhancing, 47

Clark, Maudemarie, 119, 175n. 21, 180n. 37
Cohen, Jonathan, 179n. 22
Comedy/the comic, 156–158
    and the *komos*, 157
    links with tragedy, 157–163
    and truth, 161–165
Consciousness, 50–52
    and knowledge, 31–33
Conway, Daniel W., 180n. 32, 37, 40
Cox, Christoph, 169n. 4, 180n. 34
Creativity, 53–54, 56, 62, 74–76, 87–88, 102, 133–137
Culture, 33, 75
    and nature, 24–29, 158–163

D

Dance, 165–166
Danto, Arthur, 116
Death of god, 6, 14–15, 105–106
Deleuze, Gilles, 122, 124, 177n. 24, 180n. 39
Derrida, Jacques, 92
Descartes, René, 174n. 34
Determinism, 127–133
Dionysus/the Dionysian, 24–29, 30–32, 95–98, 134, 156–161
    and eternal recurrence, 104–105, 109–110
    and music, 96
Dissanayake, Ellen, 175n. 14
Divinity, in Nietzsche and the Greeks, 28–29
Drama, 132
    Greek, 24–28, 95–98, 157–161
Dutton, Blake D., 174n. 34

E

Easterling, P.E., 181n. 18
Ecce Homo, 107–109
Eternal recurrence
    central to Nietzsche's philosophy, 4–6, 57–58, 64
    and circular time, 70–73